Global Media and Communication Policy

Also by Petros Iosifidis

EUROPEAN TELEVISION INDUSTRIES (*with J. Steemers and M. Wheeler*)

PUBLIC TELEVISION IN THE DIGITAL ERA: Technological Challenges and New Strategies for Europe

REINVENTING PUBLIC SERVICE COMMUNICATION: European Broadcasters and Beyond (*edited*)

Global Media and Communication Policy

Petros Iosifidis

First published 2011 by
PALGRAVE MACMILLAN

Palgrave Macmillan in the UK is an imprint of Macmillan Publishers Limited, registered in England, company number 785998, of Houndmills, Basingstoke, Hampshire RG21 6XS.

Palgrave Macmillan in the US is a division of St Martin's Press LLC, 175 Fifth Avenue, New York, NY 10010.

Palgrave Macmillan is the global academic imprint of the above companies and has companies and representatives throughout the world.

Palgrave® and Macmillan® are registered trademarks in the United States, the United Kingdom, Europe and other countries.

ISBN: 978–0–230–21879–6 hardback

This book is printed on paper suitable for recycling and made from fully managed and sustained forest sources. Logging, pulping and manufacturing processes are expected to conform to the environmental regulations of the country of origin.

A catalogue record for this book is available from the British Library.

Library of Congress Cataloging-in-Publication Data

Iosifidis, Petros.
    Global media and communication policy / Petros Iosifidis.
        p. cm.
    Includes bibliographical references and index.
    ISBN 978–0–230–21879–6 (hardback)
    1. Mass media policy. 2. Communication policy. 3. Globalization.
    I. Title.
P95.8.I67 2011
302.23—dc23
                                                                    2011021103

Printed and bound in the United States of America

My deepest thanks as ever to my wife Stavroula for her love and support, without which this book would not have been written

Contents

Tables

Figures

Acknowledgements

This volume would not have been written without the generous sabbatical scheme of the Department of Sociology, City University London, which allowed me to take research time. I would like to express my gratitude to the anonymous reviewers of the book proposal for their welcome comments and suggestions at the beginning of this effort. I am indebted to Cees Hamelink for providing the Guest Foreword and to Robert Picard, Marc Raboy, Philip Napoli and Terry Flew for writing the blurbs for the back cover. I am also very grateful to Peter Humphreys, Steven Barnett, Jeanette Steemers and Mark Wheeler, who commented on earlier incarnations of this volume. Thanks are due to two institutions that hosted me during periods of working on this book: the Central European University of Budapest and the Technological University of Cyprus. Thanks also to the Media, Communications and Cultural Studies Association policy network, from which I derived useful information and inspiration. Catherine Mitchell at Palgrave Macmillan has provided helpful advice throughout this project and I am grateful for her enthusiasm and support. Responsibility for any remaining errors, omissions and confusions is, of course, entirely mine. Every effort has been made to trace all copyright holders, but if any have been inadvertently overlooked, the publisher will be pleased to make the necessary arrangements at the first opportunity.

Preface

This book addresses what I perceive to be an increasingly prominent subject in the field of media and communications, and one that has attracted increased attention in areas such as sociology, economics, political science and law: global media policy and regulation. Specifically, the book considers the wider social, political, economic and technological changes arising from the globalization of the communications industries and assesses their impact on matters of regulation and policy. It focuses on the convergence of the communication and media industries and makes reference to the paradigmatic shift from a system based on the tradition of public service in broadcasting and telecommunications delivery to one that is demarcated by commercialization, privatization and competition.

The book tackles a key question in the field: to what extent do new media developments require changes in regulatory philosophy and objectives? Within the current complex and rapidly changing environment, there is a need to comprehend the interactions between broadcasting, telecommunications, the press and the Internet in order to assess whether technological and industry convergence can result in international regulatory convergence. Therefore, policy researchers should look beyond national communications policies and acknowledge the international dimension of political and regulatory decision-making. In exploring the different regulatory modes and the interplay between the local and the global in policymaking, this book proposes various possible meanings of the 'public interest' concept.

The book aims to enhance the reader's knowledge and understanding of policy and regulatory issues, particularly at global level. Thus it assesses the impact of the technological, market, political and regulatory changes that affect the communications industries and discusses how media policymakers have reacted to these challenges mainly in the USA, the UK and the European Union. The unique features of this book are, first, the effort to integrate policy relating to print media, broadcasting, telecommunications networks and the Internet, and second, the reflection of the international scope of regulatory philosophy and objectives. The book incorporates and synthesizes the wide-ranging relevant academic literature in the field and there is an extended discussion on existing methodologies concerning the internationalizing of policy and regulation and the role of national delivery of policy. The book is grounded in theory and research related to the meaning of the 'public interest' concept in media policymaking, which is considered to be the most appropriate analytical framework for a book of this type. The book's other principal original feature is an empirical survey that outlines new industrial changes and policy/regulatory responses. Through its strong theoretical and empirical grounding this publication is intended primarily as a detailed monograph. However, it can also serve as an advanced text for graduate students in the field of media and communications, especially through its thorough incorporation of the relevant literature. Scholars, industrialists and policymakers could benefit from the book's rigorous examination of the policy implications of increasing media globalization and the ongoing processes of technological convergence.

Guest Foreword

My personal interest in the topic that Petros Iosifidis addresses so ably and lucidly in this book dates from the 1970s. This was the decade of international debates about a re-ordering of global communication and information structures.

The aspirations of the, often heated, exchanges at these 'Cold War'-type diplomatic gatherings, and of their promising resolutions, were the creation of new international realities that would reflect greater fairness and balance in global communication and information dissemination.

One of the instruments that became prominent in the realization of these ambitions was the design and implementation of national communication and cultural policies. Such policies attempted to develop guidelines and institutional mechanisms for the promotion and protection of autonomous communication systems. A crucial part of this exercise (largely supported by the UN agency UNESCO) was rule-setting, with the concomitant development of institutions and best practices.

It was a time of great excitement and hopeful expectation, both of which nevertheless eventually petered out and never developed into real societal changes. The grand ideal of communicative democracies was hardly anywhere realized.

Having been actively involved in policy/planning missions for UN agencies and in the organization of training courses on communication policy and planning, I was intrigued by the renewed interest in regulatory reform. Obviously, crucial technological innovations stimulated the formulation of new traffic rules for the communication and information domain in the late 1990s and the early twenty-first century. However, the intriguing question was: had anything changed since the 1970s? Clearly, an important change was reflected by the prominence of the concept of 'multistakeholderism', and particularly by the increasingly active role of representatives of civil society and the convergence of once separated technological domains into a common digital playing field.

Yet, although these changes were undoubtedly significant, the key issues remained! The problem of failing global governance (across politics, economy and culture) kept coming back as a result of the lack of legitimacy of governing institutions. By and large, around the globe, electorates did not feel that the supranational institutions really represented their interests or were even willing to listen to them.

Also the problem persisted of how to take the 'public interest' (however one defines this) seriously in political situations where democracy is absent or where the political system has only a weak, representative character. In many 'nominal' democracies the defence of the public interest is outsourced to collective and individual representatives that are inclined to pursue their own political agendas.

Another challenge to which no solution was found is how to conceive policymaking as a reiterative process that recurrently addresses such key challenges as inclusiveness, participation, universal access and freedom.

The governance of communication systems and institutions remained a somewhat quixotic enterprise, akin to regulating a tropical rain forest.

To help us come to terms with this complex domain we need the kind of intellectual analysis that Petros Iosifidis offers us. He does that through a comprehensive, analytical account that is supported by solid documentary evidence and transparent argumentation. Despite all this laudable and scholarly work he leaves us with an essential problem – for which he is not to be blamed: in making policies, defining rules and setting up governance mechanisms we have to assume that we have knowledge of future realities that will be shaped by our regulatory efforts.

We do not! We plan for a future we do not know and that may not even happen. The perplexing issue of our deep ignorance about the future stays with us. It would be unfair to expect Iosifidis to have resolved this for us – he has given us a study that inspires further thought and we should be very grateful for that.

Cees J. Hamelink
Professor Emeritus International Communication
University of Amsterdam

Introduction

Global media and communication Policy

This book concerns global media policy and regulation – it attempts to examine the sociocultural, political, economic and legal issues that are used to regulate the media, telecommunications and the Internet in contemporary society. It aims to analyze the policy process, consider policy issues and shape policy debates, which are increasingly taking place at a supranational level. The bulk of the relevant academic literature up to now has mainly conceived media policy as the process of state-initiated and -implemented mechanisms for structuring media and communication systems. Although the role and power of national governments in the media policy process remain important – this volume argues that today the nation-state[1] indeed remains the decisive player in media policy formation – the book acknowledges that the exercise of policy is not confined to the state, for other actors, such as supranational corporations, multilateral clubs, the industry and the global civil society, have an increasingly significant presence in media policymaking. The shaping of policy has become more complex and increasingly competitive. In a global world, policy and regulation at national level is no longer sufficient.

There is a growing body of literature on global media policy and regulation, showing that there is increased interest in the field (see, for example, Castells, 1996; Castells and Cardoso, 2006; Chakravarthy and Sarikakis, 2006; Hamelink, 1994, 2000; Marsden, 2000; Ó Siochrú, Girard and Mahan, 2002; Raboy, 2002; Silverstone, 2007). Yet, 'this field of study appears to be under-theorized, not well-defined in its boundaries and open to controversial interpretations regarding the main processes and actors involved as well as the approaches and methods through which research is being conducted' (Raboy and Padovani, 2010: 4). The above article by Raboy and Padovani presents an overview of the conceptual framework through which a global media policy (GMP) mapping project has been initiated within the context of the International Association for Media and Communication Research

1

(IAMCR). The project confirms GMP as an emerging field of study and its ultimate goal is to build capacity for policy intervention.

This volume acknowledges the absence of a disciplinary and methodological home for GMP studies. It contributes to the understanding of the issues, practices and actors involved in global media policymaking by covering a lot of ground, theoretically as well as empirically. It also suggests a plurality of approaches and perspectives on the relevant phenomena. The core argument is that technology, economics, politics, culture and the legal framework are all important in the development of global media and communication policy and in the dynamics of media systems. Borrowing from the GMP mapping project it attempts to elaborate on the key terms 'global', 'media and communications' and 'policy and regulation'. For this purpose, the 'global' is considered as a multilayered and transnational space in which different communication systems operate and different models of policy and regulation are adopted. The book synthesizes the classic works on the debate on globalization for a better understanding of 'the global' and to shed light on the relationship between the local/national and global/supranational in the context of communication policy. Does globalization lead to the elimination of state regulation or does it result in new forms of global governance?

The concept of 'media and communications' is not uniform, for there are different types of media and different media systems across the world. Braman (2009: 2) reminds us that the word 'media' was coined in the 1920s to refer to the growing number of entries in this category and that only in the 1930s were separate regulatory systems developed to deal with then-new, and then-distinct, electronic broadcasting and telecommunications media. The types of media include newspapers (local and national, dailies and Sunday, quality and popular) and magazines, recorded music and film, radio and television (with local or national coverage, transmitted via terrestrial channels, satellite or cable, analogue or digital), video and computers, telecommunications and new digital, on-demand and online media. In today's 'mediated' world, alongside traditional 'mass media', one can observe newer communication technologies such as mobile and handheld devices, digital media and the Internet.

This book will show that the development of the Internet, the globalization trend and the process of technological and industrial convergence blur the boundaries between media and communication platforms and challenge traditional regulatory models. The substantive areas that characterize the communication policymaking domain are 'content' and 'structure', the former referring to policies that impact on the nature of the content offered by the media outlets and the latter signifying the structural elements of the media markets, such as ownership patterns and competitive conditions. Whereas the press has been largely a regulation-free sphere, there has been a long tradition of content regulation in broadcasting focusing both on imposing 'affirmative' requirements, related to educational programming and localism, and 'protective' policies on matters like indecent language, the protection of minors and the portraying of violence. Broadcasting has also been subject to structural policy requirements focused on ensuring diversity of ownership and restricting foreign ownership, both aimed at enhancing media pluralism.[2] But globalization, new technologies and convergence have introduced new forms of content into the media and offered new mechanisms for the delivery of content, effectively blurring the distinction between communications markets.

'Policy and regulation' (or 'global governance', a fashionable mantra denoting structural changes in policymaking) has clearly been affected by globalization. Media policies have so far been mainly national, nation-states being the main actor initiating and implementing policy within specific territorial boundaries. New forms of policy/governance need to be developed to result in a fresh dynamic between the state, the market, the citizen and the media. An array of actors and processes are involved in contemporary policymaking, shaking the relatively stable traditional pattern of policymaking that served the 'public interest'. Although there are contradictory versions of the meaning of the public interest in media and communications, this volume uses 'public interest' to refer to the collective cultural, political, social and informational benefits to the society which serve both the democratic processes of participation of all citizens to society and politics, and the cultural, social and economic well-being of people (see below and Chapter 1).

But it is not only globalization and convergence that affect media policymaking; other structural changes have had an impact. These can be summarized as privatization (the situation where state-operated media enterprises turn private), commercialization (the introduction of market forces to the communications industry), industry consolidation (see Table 0.1 for a selective record of merger activity in the USA) and reregulation, referring to the relaxation of strict rules for broadcasting and telecommunications and the introduction of 'light touch' regulatory frameworks.[3]

Meanwhile, technological advances and the accompanying proliferation of channels of communication and modes of content delivery have challenged the rationale of imposing strict regulation. In the UK, for example, multichannel development (see Table 0.2) provided the rationale for the government to implement 'light touch' regulation in broadcasting with the passing of the 2003 Communications Act.

The public interest

The question arises as to how these developments are reflected in media policies, which traditionally have been sector-specific and directed at mass media (mainly broadcasting). The meaningful boundary lines of

Table 0.1 Global growth and consolidation patterns in the USA

1985 – Murdoch's News Corporation buys Twentieth Century Fox
1986 – Matsushita acquires RCA for $6.4 billion (then the largest non-oil acquisition in history)
1989 – Sony acquires Columbia Pictures (and Tristar) (Japanese electronics hardware company buying entertainment software companies)
1990 – Time and Warner merge
1991 – Matsushita acquires MCA (the acquisition lasted only four years)
1994 – Viacom acquires Paramount ($8 billion) and Blockbuster ($8.5 billion)
1995 – Westinghouse acquires broadcasting network CBS ($5.4 billion)
1995 – Disney acquires ABC/Capital Cities ($19 billion) (vertical integration)
1995 – Seagram acquires Universal Studios
1996 – Time Warner acquires Turner Broadcasting ($7.4 billion)
1998 – AT&T acquires TCI (inc. Liberty) (telecom/media convergence)
1999 – Viacom and Columbia Broadcasting System (CBS) merge ($80 billion)
2000 – Vivendi (French firm) acquires Seagram/Universal ($35 billion)
2000 – America on Line (AOL) acquires Time Warner ($220 billion) (biggest acquisition in history between an Internet service provider and a media conglomerate) (but AOL departed in 2009)
2003 – News Corporation buys a controlling interest in Hugh Electronics (DirecTV) ($6.6 billion) (US satellite/global satellite TV)
2003 – General Electric (owner of broadcasting network NBC) buys Vivendi Universal ($5.2 billion) to create the NBC-Universal
2004 – Sony and Bertelsmann (German conglomerate) merge music units into Sony BMG ($5 billion)
2005 – News Corporation acquires social network MySpace ($580 million) (the first acquisition between a traditional media outlet and a new medium)
2006 – Disney acquires Pixar ($7.4 billion)
2006 – Google, acquires online video site YouTube ($1.65 billion)
2008 – Liberty Media acquires DirecTV ($16.2 billion)
2009 - Global financial data and news empire Bloomberg LP acquires BusinessWeek from McGraw-Hill ($2 million)
2010 – Cable and broadband company Comcast buys NBC-Universal from general Electric ($13.8 billion)
2011 – America on line (AOL) buys Huffington Post ($315 million)

Source: Hardy, 2010: 12 (including author's updates).

communication policy do not any longer revolve around particular communication technologies (Napoli, 2001). In line with McQuail (1992a) this book argues that it might be more appropriate to define the communication policy field in terms of its emphasis on particular substantive communication objectives. McQuail clearly noted in the early 1990s that policy is grounded in the political and cultural dimensions of communication processes. This perspective is reflected in more recent works, such as Braman's (2004, 2009). Braman argued that media policy is co-extant with the field of information policy that deal with the sociocultural issues of freedom of expression and participatory decision-making. Media and regulatory

Table 0.2 Multichannel development in the UK, 1993–2009 (number of homes in '000s)

Year	Satellite	Cable	DTT	Total
1993	2,387	625		3,012
1995	3,060	973	–	4,033
1997	3,804	1,845	–	5,649
1999	4,184	2,942	–	7,126
2001	4,991	3,490	529	9,010
2003	6,409	3,440	873	10,600
2005	7,277	3,363	4,216	14,327
2007	8,437	3,301	8,831	18,637
2009	9,440	3,585	14,008	22,471

Note: DTT = digital terrestrial television
Source: http://www.barb.co.uk.

activity could then be justified with reference to broad normative goals or, as Feintuck and Varney (2006) put it, 'to a claim of the public interest'.

This book proposes to refer to the various possible meanings of the concept of the public interest in exploring the different regulatory modes and the interplay between the local and the global in policymaking. This is because the public interest idea provides a comprehensive mechanism via which policymakers and researchers can pass judgements upon the performance of media systems. Despite its long and contentious history in communications policymaking, the public interest notion serves as the benchmark against which most media policies are assessed (see Napoli, 2001). It certainly refers to economic and competitive factors related to revenues and efficiencies, but most importantly requires that attention be paid to the broader normative criteria of pluralism and diversity, freedom, access and objectivity (McQuail, 1992a). The concept of the public interest reflects a broader awareness of policy outcomes that would benefit 'the public', rather than the interests of individuals.

Media systems

In the simplest terms, the types of media systems are the Western media system, which is characterized by a mix of publicly and privately supported media, the free flow of ideas and diversity of views; and the communist and/ or authoritarian media system, where the main media are owned and controlled by the state and 'news' is typically what is important to state interests. The main question, though, is why the media serve different purposes and appear in different forms in different societies. A few analysts have come up with empirically grounded models. In an early attempt to classify the world's media system into a small number of simple, discrete models, Siebert, Peterson and Schramm (1963) presented four major theories behind the functioning of the world's media: the Authoritarian theory, which was based on the idea that truth is the product of a few wise men; the Libertarian theory, which asserted that the search for truth is one of man's natural impulses; the Social Responsibility theory, stating that newspapers should face up to their social responsibility, especially in one-paper cities, or that electronic media should provide equal time for political candidates; and the Soviet Communist theory, an expanded and more positive version of the Authoritarian theory.

In a more recent study based on a survey of 18 countries, Hallin and Mancini (2004) replaced the above four theories with a new set of models: the Liberal model (prevailing across North America, Britain and Ireland); the Democratic Corporatist model (observed in northern continental Europe); and the Polarized Pluralist model (existing in the Mediterranean countries of southern Europe). The Liberal model is characterized by a dominance of market mechanisms and of commercial media; the Democratic Corporatist model is characterized by the coexistence of commercial media and media tied to organized social and political groups, although the state still plays an active role; and the Polarized Pluralist model is characterized by the integration of the media into party politics, the weaker presence of commercial media and a more central role of the state. It can be seen that in contrast to Siebert, Peterson and Schramm, who covered a wide range of media systems, the nearly half-a-century later Hallin and Mancini's work was confined to the developed capitalist democracies of North America and Western Europe. Still, the authors admit, in their introduction, that many variations emerge once one begins to adapt these models to individual countries.

Despite the trend towards globalization and the regulatory integration processes taking place at global level, or global governance (issues that will be examined in the course of this book), national variations in media systems still apply and are important to the understanding of media policies. To take just one example, the American and British media systems that Hallin and Mancini discuss as examples of the Liberal model differ markedly when it comes to broadcasting. Unlike the UK, where broadcasting began in the 1920s under the control of state-owned and -operated enterprises, the USA chose to grant local broadcast licences to nongovernment entities – primarily to commercial firms to provide advertising-supported programming, but also to colleges, universities and churches. In contrast, the UK created a hybrid model in which a nongovernment organization (the British Broadcasting Corporation, BBC), supported by public funds, became the broadcasting monopoly.

True, both the USA and the UK can be dubbed liberal political systems securing political neutrality in broadcasting, but the British model of governance protects the BBC from political control by having professionals run the corporation instead of politicians exercising management control (Hallin and Mancini, 2004: 31), whereas in the USA a nonprofit, nongovernment Corporation for Public Broadcasting (CPB) to provide financial support to local public television and radio stations was established without the sustained funding or authority to build a strong national network (Baer, 2010). While successive British governments have encouraged the BBC to remain a strong public service provider and adopt an expansive digital strategy, public broadcasting in the USA largely missed out on the opportunity to enter the era of multichannel television (Noam and Waltermann, 1998: 7).

Defining media and communication policy

It is not an easy task to define the broad field of media and communication policy, for the focus can be on media systems, or on politics, or on law and regulation. However, it can be said that communication policy refers to the regulation of different mass media (radio, television, the press) and telecommunication, which in the era of digital convergence embraces new digital and online media, computers and the Internet. It is a field of media research that began to emerge in a substantial way in the early and mid-1980s as the reregulation policies of the Reagan presidency spread to Britain and the rest of Europe (Tumber, 2000: 3–4). According to McQuail (2007: 10), media policy acquired relative stability and recognition in the final quarter of the twentieth century to deal with the issues of public accountability and control of the dominant medium of television. The incentives were on the one hand the wish to check television output for political reasons and on the other to ensure that the public interest was maintained and promoted.

Policy institutions are tasked with regulating the structure, production and distribution of media. Put simply, media policy today can be understood as a set of laws and regulations that typically tackle issues such as (Flew, 2007: 17):

- Promotion of indigenous content that reflects the national culture and identity.
- Promotion of content that caters for the needs of both the majority and minorities.
- Control over market entry in order to ensure the efficient functioning of the media industry.
- Limits on the concentration of media ownership in order to preserve pluralism and diversity.
- Prevention of the distribution of material that is deemed harmful to the community.
- Setting of programme standards that ensure fair and accurate coverage of public interest issues.

However, media policy has always been controversial since it assumes state intervention, which limits freedom of expression and the right to communication. The freedom to communicate has been constrained by general civic and criminal law, as well as by laws and regulations specific to the media. Media firms are also subject to a series of technical, marketplace and conduct regulations governing elements of ownership, content and performance (ibid.: 171). Many media policies can simultaneously impinge upon the speech rights of particular individuals or groups. For example,

Napoli (2001) notes that the same policies to diversify media ownership in the name of enhancing free speech can be viewed as impinging on the individual speech rights of those owners of media enterprises seeking to expand into other areas and reaching new markets. The state has thus been portrayed as a threat to media freedom, and regulation has been attacked as an obstacle to consumer satisfaction (Curran and Seaton, 2010: 357). State interference in the field of media and communications might be justified according to public interest criteria on behalf of a national citizenry, but as will be shown in the first three chapters of this book there are various public interest paradigms: for instance, the broadcast model ensures that the public has access to quality content, while the telecommunications model refers to public's access to infrastructure.

The problem is further complicated by the fact that the formerly separate worlds of broadcasting, telecommunications and print are coming together as a consequence of technological convergence, which necessitates a common regulatory approach for all communications. Communication policy consistency has been evident in the USA with the long presence of the Federal Communications Commission (FCC), the agency responsible for regulating both telecommunications and broadcasting. This coherent vision for setting up a single regulator for the communications industry as a whole was also pursued in the UK under successive Conservative administrations during the 1980s and New Labour, in power for over a decade after 1997. The unifying theme of an integrated communication policy advanced by the then New Labour government was best reflected with the establishment of a super regulator, the Office of Communications (Ofcom), in 2003 to replace a number of formerly sectoral regulatory bodies.[4] This book will argue that, like its US counterpart, the UK regulatory agency has adopted primarily an economic imperative and has largely neglected sociocultural objectives.

Indeed, the main driving force shaping media and communication policy since the 1980s has been free market ideas, which have encouraged competitiveness and the adoption of reregulatory policies. Media policies are sought to create the conditions of independence from government, of wide range of choice, and of open competition, thus enabling the consumer to exercise sovereign control. The prevailing ideology of neoliberalism asserts that reliance on market mechanisms both empowers the consumer and fosters freedom, and creates the conditions for market efficiency. Broadly speaking, neoliberalism can be perceived as the stage of capitalism defined by four indicators: privatization, deregulation, liberalization and globalization. It was initially adopted by various rich countries such as the USA and the UK as a policy response to the 1970s global economic crisis and since the early 1980s it has evolved internationally 'to make market functioning (and the openness of national economies to global market forces) the *overwhelming* priority for social organization' (Couldry, 2010: 4). The 1970s crisis was seen as a consequence of the failure of Keynesianism (the preceding economic policy regime), and neoliberalism opened the way for a new approach to politics and economics in which market competition is common practice and the state may no longer have an interventionist role (see Harvey, 2005; Peet, 2007: 77, cited in Coundry, 2010: 4).

Reinforced by technological change (the advent of cable and satellite together with digitalization and the emergence of the Internet, which have undermined the 'spectrum scarcity'[5] rationale for regulating broadcasting) and social shifts (greater individualization and fragmentation in society), reregulation (or 'light touch' regulation) in broadcasting and telecommunications has gained momentum, while the press has remained intact since it is shaped along free market lines.

This pro-market movement away from the onerous regulation of electronic media in favor of setting general objectives and co- and/or self-regulation[6] has found support and has been implemented quite straightforward in the telecommunications sector, which has traditionally been subject to infrastructural (but not content) regulation. However, it contrasts sharply with the continuing commitment to public control of broadcasting in order to maintain content quality, plurality of voices, impartial and accurate news, all of which are desirable goals that the market at present cannot be relied upon to deliver. The social market approach, which believes in principle in the free market while giving rise to public interventions intended to sustain media diversity, plurality of ownership and programming quality, was incorporated during the late 1990s and early 2000s in New Labour's broadcasting policy in the UK. According to Curran and Seaton (2010: 377), UK broadcasting policy 'can be viewed as an attempt to square a circle: a fervent belief in the market, combined with a highly developed sense of its limitations. This is a standard social market position that justifies – and indeed elevates – the regulator as champion of the public interest'.[7]

It is striking how current debates in the field of broadcasting are focused more than ever on the publicly funded BBC and its expanding online and digital activities at a time when competitive terrestrial TV channels are facing deep economic difficulties as well as on British Sky Broadcasting (BSkyB)'s persistent campaign to shrink the scope of public broadcasters. Not bound by the BBC's tradition of impartiality, Murdoch-controlled BSkyB is already larger than the BBC, with a turnover of £5.9 billion in 2010 compared with the BBC's turnover of £4.8 billion (Sabbagh, 2010). However, with the BBC's licence fee income frozen by the current Conservative–Liberal Democrat coalition government as well as the suggestion to cut BBC Online's budget by 25 per cent,[8] BSkyB may increase its financial and political power in the UK media market, especially if the UK competition authorities approve parent company News Corporation's bid to buy the 60 per cent of BSkyB that it does not already own.[9] Meanwhile, any cut to the BBC licence fee raises a fundamental question about the BBC's independence from government (Barnett and Seaton, 2010a, 2010b).

Media policy and cultural policy

Media policymaking is premised upon the special role that media play in the processes of culture, politics and the market. It is therefore articulated within the society, polity and economy. But the boundaries separating these areas are not always clear and are actually being broken down as digitalization, convergence and globalization blur traditional technological and regulatory distinctions. It should therefore be recognized that the boundaries between media policy and cultural policy (and even information policy) are becoming less distinct. In fact, Hesmondhalgh (2005: 95) makes a case that media policy could be considered together with cultural policy as these two areas of policy have tended to be analyzed as separate domains, at least in the Anglophone world. Cultural policy has typically been associated with the subsidized arts sector. Schlesinger (2009a) makes reference to the so-called 'creative industries' idea of the New Labour government when it first took office in the UK in 1997, an arbitrary grouping of diverse cultural, communicative and technological practices: advertising, architecture, art and the antiques market, crafts, design, designer fashion, film, interactive leisure software, music, the performing arts, publishing, software, and television and radio.

Referring to the UK cultural policy in the 1950s–1960s, Lury (1994) wrote that this consisted of a series of preventative steps to preserve high art forms, like opera, theatre, dance, the visual arts and literature. A more integrated conception of cultural policy emerged in Europe and particularly France, where national cultural policy has been tasked with the preservation and promotion of heritage, creation and democratization. In contrast, media and communication policy has been considered in terms of economics and politics. While recognizing the important differences between the two domains, Hesmondhalgh (2005) believes that media policy and cultural policy need to be considered in relation to each other and in relation to public policy more generally. This is because both areas of policy concern the relationship between symbolic representation and a government's *cultural policy* and also issues of national and civic identity.

Williams (1984: 3) identified a function of cultural policy as 'display' which means that policies doing most to preserve or inflect cultural attitudes may not be those nominally attributed to 'culture'. McGuigan (2004: 61–91) developed Williams' thought by drawing up a distinction between 'cultural policy as display' and 'cultural policy proper'. Whereas the former is characterized by various kinds of public panoply and the instrumentalization of cultural resources for political and economic purposes, the latter attends to the 'proper' object of cultural policy (defined by McGuigan as aiding the 'democratic practices of art, culture and the media'). Following Williams' distinction between cultural policy as display (national aggrandizement and economic reductionism) and cultural policy proper (public patronage of the arts, media regulation and the construction of a national identity), McGuigan (2004: 65) argued that cultural policymaking between the member states of the European Union (EU) falls within the latter category.[10] Other thoughtful commentators have suggested that there is a need to assess the broader political debates leading to the formation of media policy. Horwitz (1989) and Streeter (1996) argued that media policy could be equated to media politics. Recent work by Chakravarthy and Sarikakis (2006: 4–5) asserts that a separation of politics from policy is an artificial and ideologically loaded position that falsely claims neutrality. Also this separation may not be desirable for the purpose of critical analysis of and reflection upon the contexts that determine the availability of communication channels and conditions for personal and cultural, social and political expression. The scholars point out that removing politics from the policymaking process in broadcasting, telecommunication and digital media content has been a great success in the USA in that it has shifted the discourse of policy.

Academic research

According to Schlesinger (2009a), cultural policy is formed where culture and politics interact: it creates a relationship between diverse ways of life and the institutionalized form of the state. But while acknowledging the academics' obligations to disseminate their research widely and the requirement for intellectual openness and interdisciplinary research, Schlesinger rightly argues that there is a need for resources to conduct research in the fields of cultural and communication policies. Here, national research councils, foundations, government departments, public bodies, charities and the European Commission all have their own agendas. How they articulate their 'strategic priorities' will always have effects on what academics do and where they focus. So too do universities' own research strategies. Undeniably, it is becoming increasingly hard to be heard in the world of media and cultural policy formation and harder still to be influential. Influencing the terms of debate is difficult because the shaping of policy has become both more competitive and more complex. Academics today have to compete to make their views known with management consultancies, government advisers, business journalists and research teams within communications regulators (ibid.).

Political agendas and partisanship notwithstanding, academic researchers have the required skills and qualifications to contribute to rational media and cultural policymaking. After all, regulatory agencies like the FCC and Ofcom have to, by law, combine their in-house expertise with an objective and transparent collection of evidence when initiating rules and policies. However, as regulatory bodies increasingly display an inherent bias toward results-driven decision-making, academic researchers rarely achieve the same status as that of economists and consultants. Frieden (2008) noted that, with increasing regularity, the FCC generates and seeks empirical data from market consultants and policy advisers that supports preferred or pre-ordained policies. In effect, academics' efforts have little influence on the FCC and also generate limited recognition. Chapter 3 will show that similar trends are evident on the other side of the ocean, particularly in the case of Ofcom in the UK.

Media policy and regulation

Media policy looks at the ways in which policies are initiated and implemented and examines their impact on the communications industry. Media policy has traditionally referred to actions of government and public administration that have specific objectives alongside specific means for achieving them. Here, Freedman (2008: 13) makes a distinction between policy and regulation: 'if media policy suggests the broader field where a variety of ideas and assumptions about desirable structure and behaviour circulate, then regulation points to the specific institutional mechanisms for realising these aims'. In this sense, media regulation follows media policy: where policy refers to the development of objectives to shape the structure and behavior of media systems, regulation points to the means and mechanisms for achieving these objectives. In other words, regulation implies the application of rules developed through the policy process. Along these lines, Abramson (2001: 301–2) observes that media regulation flows from media policy: 'where policy sets out the state's role in bringing its preferred mediascape into being, regulation is the instrument through which the state supervises, controls, or curtails the activities of nonstate actors in accordance with policy'.

Media and communication policy paradigms

Recent research on the concept of media policy typically begins by referring to communication and media policy paradigms. Van Guilenburg and McQuail (2003) distinguish three paradigmatic phases in the historical development of media policy: emerging communications industry policy, from the mid-nineteenth century until the Second World War. The ultimate objective of media policy during this period was efficiency – pursued in the public interest, which was defined as efficient public service under state control. A principal characteristic was the separation of regimes, with particular reference to the means of distribution: print media were governed by guarantees of freedom of expression; common carriers (telegraphy and telephony) were regulated in terms of infrastructure and ownership but not of content; strong regulation of access and content applied to broadcasting.

The second phase of media policy, which extended from the Second World War until about the 1980, was driven by democracy – normative and political considerations, rather than technology – and by the search for national cohesion and stability. In both the USA and Europe there was a tendency to break national monopolies and to privatize the media, although in Europe there was more political debate on the issue and a greater attempt to develop new media potential through public investment and protectionism than in the USA, where what prevailed was frenetic deregulation of media and telecommunications. Since the 1990s there has been a new policy paradigm, driven by the convergence of communication infrastructures and services. Van Guilenburg and McQuail (2003) single out that the third phase promotes the ideals of freedom of communication, access, and accountability/control (this dualistic concept is defined as control over access coupled with answerability for the use made of that access).

Media governance

A contemporary trend that reflects the shifting of power from national towards supranational or global levels is that of media governance. Freedman (2008: 14) observes that media governance is a broader term than regulation, both spatially and instrumentally. Borrowing from McQuail (2005: 234), he writes that media governance refers to the formal and informal, national and supranational, centralized and dispersed mechanisms that aim to organize media systems. Braman (2009: 3) makes a case that governance is part of what she calls the 'information policy' field, which includes the following: 'government' (formal institutions of the law); 'governance' (decision-making with constitutive [structural] effect, whether it takes place within the public or private sectors and whether formally or informally); and 'governmentality' (cultural predispositions and practices that produce and reproduce the conditions that make particular forms of governance and government possible).

McQuail (2003: 98) explores various types of media governance by adopting formal/informal and internal/external distinctions. This results in the following typology (see Table 0.3):

The complexity of media governance can be attributed to the fact that the media are located in civil society but operate in the marketplace, and meanwhile are linked to state institutions. What is more, the media as societal systems function simultaneously in economic, political and cultural terrains.

Table 0.3 Types of media governance

	Formal	Informal
Internal	Management and financial control; Self-regulation	Professionalism; Organizational culture; Norms and ethics
External	Law and regulation	Market forces and relations; Pressures and lobbies; Public opinion review and criticism

Source: McQuail, 2003: 98.

Table 0.4 Interaction between culture and commerce

Culture represents:	Commerce represents:
Citizenship[11]	Consumership
Human rights	Property rights
Politics	Markets
Public sphere	Privatization
Spirituality	Materialism
Trust	Contract

Source: Hamelink and Nordenstreng, 2007: 232.

Given the complexities of modern society it might be difficult – or even impossible – to create a clear distinction between culture and commerce. What is more, media governance is caught between culture and commerce, which represent different realms. In an attempt to unravel the issue of media governance, Hamelink and Nordenstreng (2007: 232) analyze the interaction between culture (as symbolic production) and commerce as follows (see Table 0.4):

A policy question here might be: how can one promote free trade applied equally to cultural commodities? This is an important, albeit difficult, question to answer in the modern global world. In the end, any policy decisions could be pursued through compromises that take into consideration the various contradictions inherent in regulation to achieve protection and openness, competition and social cohesion, and so on.

Main questions and book structure

The increasing power of free market ideology, media market reregulation, privatization and liberalization, combined with the globalization of the media and communication markets, has resulted in a new, international, communication discourse. Alongside technological convergence these trends have rocked the foundations of media policy and regulation. The traditional national, sovereign communication policymaking scene is now challenged by global flows and transnational systems of governance. While the overarching issues remain the same (for example, normative standards such as freedom, pluralism/diversity and inclusiveness/participation still apply in the new era), the formerly static policy field has become fast-moving, much wider and more diffuse, and it is constantly shifting. As Braman (2009: 1) notes, there are fields in which traditional policy ideals require reinterpretation in order to be applied in a qualitatively changed environment. Traditional issues such as inclusiveness, diversity and privacy appear in new forms as new technologies emerge and Internet penetration increases. Besides, policymaking today needs to follow the logic of both sociocultural and economic/consumerist values: the wider society, the marketplace, the wishes of consumers and citizens, should all form priorities for policymakers.

Hamelink and Nordenstreng (2007: 228) note that 'at all times communication policy has been driven by the idea of public interest with a distinct national approach'. But this tendency has been challenged by the processes of globalization, privatization and liberalization. How is the public interest defined in the electronic environment, where multiple actors initiate and implement policy alongside the state? How are new policy subjects, such as the Internet, challenging traditional views about media policy and regulation? What are the powers of the nation-state in shaping media policy in the new global, borderless era? These are but a few of the questions to be addressed in this volume. An expanded (but not exhaustive) list of the main questions posed is:

- To what extent and why is the traditional paradigm for regulating the media and telecommunications under challenge?
- To what extent and why has there been in increase in global policy issues and associated policymaking bodies? What is the role of the nation-state?
- To what extent and how should the media and telecommunications sectors be regulated in the multimedia, digital era where the boundaries between different media sectors are blurred?
- What should be the balance between the traditional media policy objectives of ensuring pluralism and diversity, and the increasingly transnational economic priorities of media companies?
- Should sector-specific horizontal regulation be withdrawn and replaced by general competition rules that can apply equally to all media?
- Should 'public interest' regulation still apply and why?
- Should there be special treatment for public service broadcasting or is there scope for alternative forms of public provision in a digital environment?

These questions are approached in the four parts of the book. More specifically:

Part I consists of three chapters that elaborate on the theoretical foundations of an understanding of the ongoing developments in communication policy and regulation by providing definitions of the concept 'public interest'. There has been a great amount of literature dealing with the main challenges that modern media policy faces, namely the problem of regulating the private media sector, the issue of whether to offer a comprehensive or restricted public broadcasting service, and the problem of how to make the media accountable to the populace. This part tries to contribute to this scholarly work and account for some of the prominent themes in public interest research in the media field with the aim of identifying what counts as being in the public interest in the light of new developments.

Chapter 1 starts by providing a definition of the term 'public interest' and continues with a discussion on the concept of the 'public sphere' and the 'citizen versus consumer' dichotomy. The chapter takes a critical stance in relation to those who celebrate the digital media and the Internet as tools that inevitably result in democratization and 'pluralization' of the public sphere. It is often argued that the new media and the Internet can shift control over communication towards individual users, but instead of a liberating effect new communication technologies may bring about new forms of exclusion and hierarchy. **Chapter 2** consists of an in-depth debate on media regulation on public interest grounds and an assessment of the impact of media market liberalization on telecommunications, broadcasting, and the print and Internet sectors. It analyzes some of the structural changes in the media sectors and considers whether the public service aspect of the public interest has been narrowed in the neoliberal world characterized by free market competition, commercialization and globalization. **Chapter 3** closes this part by making several observations, among them that there is no universally acceptable definition of the concept of the public interest, that the term can change over time and that it applies, with different interpretations, to different media sectors and fields of study. It is proposed that the public interest could be best investigated in relation to the field of study or discipline concerned with normative principles as common denominators. To sum up, Chapter 3 sets the stage for the chapters that follow.

Part II comprises two chapters, which examine the theoretical dimension of media policy and regulation by defining the relevant terms that allows the reader to consider the conflict between the local and the supranational when referring to policy and regulation. The chapters in this part engage in the debate on globalization within the media and communications sectors, and center on the question of the impact of the forces of globalization and new media technologies on the nature and dynamics of national policymaking.

More specifically, **Chapter 4** provides a historical account of the various global communication paradigms that have dominated the field in the past half-century or so: modernization theory; cultural or media imperialism; critical political economy and cultural studies; and media globalization. This key chapter distinguishes the book from other work in this area by paying detailed attention to contextualizing media within the larger body of relevant social theory. **Chapter 5** offers another review of the relevant body of literature by discussing timely and important issues of new forms of governance in the media and communications sector, relevant for both policy researchers and students. In particular, it discusses the contemporary role and power of the state in initiating and implementing media policy in the light of the fundamental technological and sociocultural changes brought about by the transition to an informational, multicultural and increasingly global society. It assesses the impact of globalization on national media policymaking and, after critically exploring the view that globalization leads to reduced national government power and ability to regulate, it presumes that the nation-state retains a significant role in the terrain of global policy.

Each of the chapters in the first two parts serves as a theoretical introduction and a contextual element in order to enable the reader to consider trends in the development of media policy and regulation and their effects on different societies. The following part provides the empirical dimension in terms of communication policy and regulation by focusing on the approaches to the regulation of the electronic and print media adopted to date, by international organizations, the USA and the EU. In particular, the two chapters in **Part III** focus on supranational bodies that have transformed the rules of global communication governance. These supranational organizations can result in a loss of national autonomy and the reorganization of the state's functions. **Chapter 6** attempts to shed light on the role of these largely un-scrutinized and poorly understood bodies in processing global media policy. The key bodies in the field of trade liberalization include the World Trade Organization (WTO) and the General Agreement on Trade in Services (GATS), while the International Telecommunications Union (ITU) and World Intellectual Property Organization (WIPO) are key organizations which pursue multilateral cooperation in the areas of technical standards and intellectual property rights respectively. The Internet Corporation for Assigned Names and Numbers (ICANN) is examined as the dominant institution involved in global Internet governance, whereas the United Nations Education, Scientific and Cultural Organization (UNESCO) and nongovernmental are presented as key players in the protection and promotion of cultural diversity and freedom of expression. Special attention is paid to the role of the World Summit on the Information Society (WSIS) in the process of global decision-making and in promoting political and sociocultural processes.

Chapter 7 focuses on the approaches to the regulation of the electronic and print media adopted to date by the EU. The EU is viewed as one of the most powerful international/regional bodies that can influence policy in the field of media and communications. The chapter looks at the processes through which the EU has progressively become a main player in national communication policy and regulation. It focuses on the principal European institutions – the European Commission (EC), the European Parliament (EP), the European Court of Justice (ECJ) and the Council of Europe (CoE) – and investigates their influence in shaping and directing national communications practice mainly in the areas of media ownership, pluralism and public service broadcasting. Although these institutions have different objectives and varying degrees of influence, the discussion reveals that there is a pattern of policy convergence emerging within the EU aiming at the following:

completion and efficient functioning of the internal market; pursuing reregulation and soft governance initiatives. This goes hand in hand with the 'new paradigm' of media policy prioritizing economic goals over social and political welfare (Van Guilenburg and McQuail, 2003). It also reflects the broad political and ideological endorsement of market-based solutions or, as succinctly put by some commentators (Wheeler, 2004; Michalis, 2007), the EU has sought to encourage the expansion of media services through the principles of liberalization and harmonization.

While recognizing the enormity of ongoing technological, political, economic and sociocultural changes, the **Fourth and Final part** of the book deals with the convergence phenomenon in media and communications and asks whether technological, industry and market convergence necessarily results in regulatory convergence. Convergence is a vital topic from a policy standpoint, even if it has rather lost its lustre in the discourse on media industry strategy. **Chapter 8** intends to provide a framework for understanding convergence issues. It identifies the different types of convergence as *technological* (convergence between the information technology, telecommunications and media sectors), *industrial or corporate* and *market convergence* (the situation where the same corporations are active in the technology sector, the content services sector and the Internet), and *convergence at the level of services and markets*. The work argues that technological, corporate and market convergence occur at the same time as *publisher–user* or *producer–consumer convergence*, referring to the blurring of boundaries between media companies and their audiences, itself triggered by the interactivity potential and the rise of the Internet. In sum the chapter explicates the nature of convergence and prepares the reader for the in-depth discussion on the policy implications of the phenomenon of convergence to be conducted in Chapters 9 and 10.

In particular, **Chapter 9** links the conceptual to the concrete. It aims at providing an overview of the emergent governance pattern in communications and describing its main characteristics. It also discusses the policy and regulatory implications resulting from convergence. In this context, there is a discussion over 'institutional convergence' in the UK and the USA (the cases of Ofcom and **the** FCC) and an analysis of the EU policy for regulatory convergence. The chapter scrutinizes the argument that technological change and globalization must inevitably lead to reregulation of the media industry. Following from this, **Chapter 10** offers guidelines for regulatory reform and makes an assessment as to whether it is sector-specific or economic regulation that provides an adequate regulatory response to the concerns expressed in the previous chapters. The work then moves on to assessing the need for a new, common regulatory framework for the converged information and communications sectors and the extent to which traditional communications regulation models are applicable to new services.

The last chapter also tackles privacy, copyright law and freedom of expression, as these are fundamental ideals in need of reformation and protection in the globalized network society. Network neutrality is also analyzed as it has been a hot issue on both sides of the Atlantic. Next, the work explores the balance between competition law and sector-specific regulation, such as content and media ownership regulation, before it examines the cases for self- and co-regulation, which have gained momentum in recent years. There is a critical stance on self- and co-regulation, which are increasingly being promoted as instruments of regulation in the Internet era and are often associated with the 'better regulation' agenda pursued by various Western governments.

The **Concluding part** summarizes the key issues that emerge in the content of new media policies in light of the emergent spaces for global media policy governance. The work here is brief given the substantive contributions of Chapter 10.

Limitations

This book analyzes policy and regulation at international level. The book draws evidence primarily from the USA, the EU (and the UK in particular). This is not just because most of the media production – particularly film and television output – that circulates globally takes place in these territories, but also because the USA and the EU cases have value to other political systems in that many of their institutional models and regulatory approaches have been adopted in developed or emerging markets. The trends in the development of communications laws and regulations have been 'exported' to other countries and the consequences of these trends can be seen around the world. For example, the organization of the independent US regulatory agency, the FCC, has been adopted in Canada and various Latin American countries as well as South Korea, while the UK communications regulator Ofcom serves as a model for similar independent bodies in other European nations. Similarly, the rhetoric and operations of media market liberalization and reregulation, which began in the USA, the UK and other large EU countries, have been exported to the rest of the world. Most countries have for some time now been importing American and UK programme formats and shows like *Pop Idol* and *The Apprentice*. Meanwhile, the BBC provides a model for public service broadcasting across the globe. The notion of new superpowers, such as China, being exporters of culture may seem far-fetched, but this may change; it was once hard to imagine India churning out Bollywood movies.

However, the reader should be made aware of the limitations of the Anglo-Saxon angle taken in this volume, the 'Western' preferences and the limited focus on continents and countries beyond the trio of USA/UK/EU. By evolving around an Anglo-American paradigm the book is primarily Western and it is preoccupied with the values and processes that characterize the large and dominant media and communications systems spawned within the above trio. Only sporadic attempts are made to link communication policy and regulation to emerging nations and potential new superpowers such as China and India, or to East Asian, Latin American and African regions. A comprehensive survey of the media and communication policies of non-Western countries is beyond the scope of this volume. However, the basic assumption is that in a global world there are no countries or regions that function completely independently in media policy, and although policy developments in individual nations are not exclusively determined by external influences, most societies in the world are following the USA, UK and EU in moving towards media liberalization and reregulation. As a striking example, China's television business has developed largely in isolation from the rest of the world, but in an unusually forward-looking move the authorities have recently allowed Western media enterprises to operate.[12]

Part I

A Trilogy on the Public Interest in Media

1
Media Policy in the Public Interest

Introduction

Media and communications policy is framed by various theoretical constructs, which provide the basis for the formulation of criteria for assessing the performance of media systems and designing policies that might enhance such performance (McQuail, 1992a). These criteria may vary across different national contexts, but there are some core principles that underpin effective media policies. Serving the public interest is a normative principle that presents the standard that most media policymakers are expected to adhere to in their decision-making process. The concept of the public interest is embedded within normative criteria ranging from pluralism and diversity, to freedom and access, to objectivity and competition (ibid.). Although the specific criteria vary across nations and over time according to regulatory philosophies and structural/technological circumstances, the idea of the public interest has traditionally served as a 'normative guidepost' for media policymakers (Napoli, 2001). It is a direct mechanism through which regulators examine the performance of media systems and propose policy changes in the light of new technological, sociopolitical and market developments. These developments reflect a broad tension that has characterized media policymaking – the tension between sociocultural objectives such as ensuring political pluralism and a diversity of viewpoints, and fostering economic goals like competition and market efficiency.

A thorny issue for media and communications is whether regulatory intervention in a free market can be justified on public interest grounds. In the media politics of Western societies during the past four decades or so, debates about the public interest in the mass media have focused on the central issue of whether they should be based on the functioning of the free market. Many analysts have looked at the performance and policy of the mass media system from a variety of perspectives. McLuhan (1964), McLuhan and Powers (1993), Enzensberger (1970) and Forester (1985) advanced the technological determinist argument, while Owen et al. (1974), Noam (1985), Hendon et al.

(1986), Collins, Garnham and Locksley (1988) and Garnham and Locksley (1991) examined media market economics. Ideology as a decisive influence on mass media performance was examined by Negrine (1988). Dyson and Humphreys (1990), Freedman (2008) and Couldry (2010) looked at the politics of pluralism and neoliberalism, whereas Murdock (1990) examined the influence of private ownership patterns from the point of view of neo-Marxism. The political and cultural influence of the media was tackled by Seymour-Ure (1991) and the sociology of media industry organization by Tunstall (1970, 1972, 1991).

Blumler (1992), Tracey (1998) and Iosifidis (2007, 2010a) identified the social values at stake as far as the organization of broadcasting is concerned, while Hutchison's work (1999) covered broadcasting, the press and the cinema. McQuail (1992a) carried out an assessment of mass media performance in economic, social, aesthetic and moral terms, whereas McQuail (1992b) focused on the principles of freedom and diversity. Feintuck and Varney (2006) examined media regulation specifically in relation to the public interest. In her study of telecommunications policy in America, Aufderheide (1999) identified several dimensions of the public interest in US policy, ranging from economic prosperity and peace to the ideal of universal service and social welfare, and finally to competition and the free market (especially after the 1996 US Telecommunications Act). Napoli (2001) also focused on communications policy in the USA and identified several media policy principles: localism, free market, universal service, competition and diversity. Most of the aforementioned works dealt with the main challenges that modern media policy faces, namely the problem of regulating the private media sector, the issue of whether to offer a comprehensive or restricted public broadcasting service, and the problem of how to make the media accountable to the populace.

This part of the book, consisting of three chapters, tries to contribute to the scholarly work and account for some of the prominent themes in public interest research in the media field with the aim of finding out what counts as being in the public interest in the light of new developments. The current chapter starts by providing a definition of the term 'public interest', followed by a discussion on the concept of the 'public sphere' and the 'citizen versus consumer' dichotomy as thinking about this dichotomy provides a valuable tool for assessing the way media services cater for their audiences. The chapter also explores the issue as to whether the Internet allows the creation of an inclusive and a global sphere (a 'networked public sphere') by enabling people to fulfill the promise of greater interchange between media institutions and citizens. Chapter 2 provides a debate on media regulation on public interest grounds and an assessment of the impact of media market liberalization on telecommunications, broadcasting and the print and Internet sectors. Chapter 3 closes this section by making several observations, among them that there is no universally acceptable definition of the concept of the public interest, that the term can change over time and that it applies with different interpretations to different media sectors and fields of study.

Defining the public interest

The term 'public interest' is broad, vague and loosely constructed. It changes over time and when considered from different perspectives; therefore, defining it is notoriously difficult. Sills (1968), in the *International Encyclopaedia of the Social Sciences*, states that the term is 'elastic and relative [... and ...] has no a priori content waiting to be revealed [... It] serves to remind parties immediately concerned that there are considerations extending beyond their goals [...]' (cited in McQuail, 1992a: 20). Moreover, 'it assumes the existence of a common interest, although specific manifestations cannot be agreed upon'. Even if it presupposes the existence of a common interest, there is no consensus on what is in the common interest and on the particular policies that are required to achieve it. This is because governments, intergovernmental bodies, commercial groups and civil society 'each relate to media in different ways, seeing opportunities and threats to their own objectives' (Buckley et al., 2008: 6). Furthermore, the precise content and meaning given to the public interest notion and the means proposed for achieving it vary widely within different contexts (countries) and time segments. The concept is not static but evolves, as society and media themselves change because of political, economic and technological developments.

There are contradictory versions of the meaning of the 'public interest'. Downs (1962) mentioned three main schools of thought as to how the public interest can be identified. The first originates from 'the will of the people': the public interest is what the majority wants. Such a definition of the public interest was adopted in the USA in the 1980s by the regulatory agency Federal Communications Commission (FCC), which, through its then Chairman Mark Fowler, argued in 1982 that the public interest was the collection of private choices. According to this point of view, 'the public's interest defines the public interest' (Fowler, 1982). This echoes the classic 1960 statement of Canadian Broadcasting Corporation executive Frank Stanton: 'A program in which a large part of the audience is interested is by that very fact [...] in the public interest (cited in Buckley et al., 2008: 7). The equation of the 'public interest' with 'popular interests' has been criticized on several grounds. The weakness of this theory, according to Held (1970), is that there is a conflict between a particular means of identifying the public interest (for example, a majority vote or mass consumer demand) and the broader notion that public interest means something more than the sum of individual preferences.

Majoritarian perspectives aggregate individual preferences, but as Dewey (1983 [1927]) argued on this point, the public and its interest is not necessarily synonymous with the consumers and their interests, nor is it the sum total of individual opinions on the events of the day. The public is that field of activity that shares the consequences of private and state action and performs effectively in its own interest. For instance, when citizens of a municipality suffer the consequences of polluted water and act to cope with the problem (perhaps through an environmental or parents' coalition) they function as the public. On the contrary, when they cannot group together to solve their common problem, they do not function as the public (Aufderheide, 1992: 53). In the case of media and communications, the majoritarian approach would best be represented by allocating more freedom to individuals so they can maximize their personal welfare even at the expense of others. Along these lines, broadcasting or print media systems should be governed by market mechanisms, which will eventually identify winners and losers.

The second school of thought described by Downs states that the public interest is decided according to some absolute standard of value regardless of what citizens want. In this case the interests of the public override the interests of individuals in order to establish a common value. McQuail (1992a: 3) pointed out that this system could be applied to public service broadcasting (PSB), for it is referred to in terms of the benefits that it is supposed to bring to the public – universality; minority provision; preservation of national culture and identity; provision of educational and informational services. However, McQuail also noted that the defect of this theory is twofold: first, it may be insensitive to popular wants; second, the theory's frequently authoritarian, paternalistic or ideologically contestable character makes it problematic.

The third, 'realist' or 'pragmatic', class of theory asserts that the public interest is what political institutions arrive at by their decision-making. Here, the common interest is not the summing up of individual preferences or opinions, but it is an interest that is shared and agreed upon by the society as a whole. Very few would dispute, for example, that all people should have access to clean water, be able to breathe fresh air, be allowed to access public services at minimal cost, and so on. This 'common good' approach presupposes that the society benefits in the long-run by adapting principles that are accepted by the entire citizenship, even though immediate benefits are not visible. In the media and communications field, this approach would apply to the notion of an all-inclusive information society and the requirement of an informed and participating public in order for it to benefit from the fruits of the network era.

A similar classification was suggested by Held (1970), who also identified three main variants of public interest theory: 'preponderance' theories, 'unitary' theories and 'common interest' theories (see also Feintuck and Varney, 2006: 108). These correspond with Downs' versions of the public interest described above. McQuail (1992a, 2003), in an attempt to define a public interest in public communication, advocated Held's 'common interest' variant (similar to Downs' 'realist' theory). He ruled out those versions that depend heavily on the voice of the people as expressed in opinion polls or market research because, in his view, one cannot rely on majority votes to settle complex issues when public communication has to serve many and divergent purposes. He also challenged those versions which rely on some absolute value commitment on the grounds that there is no longer a unitary value system to which one can appeal in order to settle broad issues.

McQuail focused on the third type of theory (the 'middle way' as he called it) because in that context specific objectives and mechanisms of achievement can be named and deployed in argument. For McQuail (1992a: 3) the public interest can be defined as 'informational, cultural and social benefits to the wider society which go beyond the immediate, particular and individual interests'. The principle of freedom of speech and publication, for example, may itself have to be supported on grounds of long-term benefits to society that are not immediately apparent or clear to many individuals.

Various theories of public interest have thus been advanced. Their very existence testifies to the elastic, dynamic and abstract nature of the principle. Borrowing from McQuail (and since the concept assumes the development of common interests), I use the idea of public interest to refer to the collective cultural, political, social and informational benefits to society, which serve both the democratic processes of political participation and cultural, social and economic well-being. It follows that individual claims are not included in the concept.

Public interest, public communication and the public sphere

In the media the term public interest was first mentioned with reference to radio broadcasting in the early twentieth century. Originally contained in US public utility law, the 'public interest, convenience and necessity' provision was incorporated into the Radio Act of 1927 to become the operational standard for broadcast licensees. The Communications Act of 1934 expanded upon the Radio Act to include the telephone and telegraph industries, while later versions of the Act accommodated telecommunications, cable technologies and television (The Museum of Broadcast Communications, no date). The obligation to serve the public interest was in this context integral to the 'trusteeship' model of broadcasting – the trusteeship paradigm was used to justify government regulation of broadcasting in order to safeguard the public from the possible selfish motives of broadcasters. Because the electromagnetic spectrum is a limited resource belonging to the public, only those most capable of serving the public interest are entrusted with a broadcast license (ibid.). However, interpretation of the 'public interest, convenience and necessity' has always been a source of controversy and, as will be shown below, after the deregulatory fervor of the 1980s the 'trusteeship model' was replaced by the 'marketplace model'.

In relation to the media one might initially argue that something counts as being in the public interest only if it serves the aims of all those who participate in public communication and not just those of a minority. Public communication is central to the democratic process. As Garnham (1990: 104) argued, 'citizens require [...] equal access to sources of information and equal opportunities to participate in the debates from which political decisions rightly flow'. A definition of the term 'public communication', with reference to the mass media, has been suggested by Ferguson (1986: ix) as 'those processes of information and cultural exchange between media institutions, products and publics which are socially shared, widely available and communal in character'. The context in which these transactions take place is the so-called 'public sphere' – that is, as articulated in particular by the political theorist Habermas (1989 [1962]), a space for rational and universalistic politics distinct from both the state and the economy, a scene of activity in which people are addressed as citizens, as rational political beings, and not merely as consumers.

The citizen–consumer dichotomy

Before examining in some detail the concept of the public sphere, it is worth defining the terms 'citizen' and 'consumer', as thinking about the distinction between them will provide a useful tool for assessing the way media services cater for their audiences (Iosifidis, 2011a; Livingstone, Lunt and Miller, 2007; Lunt and Livingston, 2007). The 'consumer versus citizens' dichotomy linked to the media can be traced back to the early days of broadcasting, as social forces and groups struggled over how to define and control the potential that new technology offered. Elites in the industrialized countries already recognized, in the 1920s, that the influx of increasingly market forces in newspapers, magazines, film and popular music had resulted in an upsurge of popular – or 'mass' – culture, which engendered values that intellectuals and leaders on both the left and the right found disturbing.

In the UK, the experience of the already highly commercialized radio environment in the USA led to the setting-up of a public service broadcasting system, the BBC, in which 'public service' was defined in noncommercial terms: not competitive, and opposed to marketplace (popular or mass) ideas (Hilmes, 2004). Until the 1980s, 'public' intervention was considered necessary, in Europe in particular, to link broadcasting to the interests of the nation-state. However, since the opening up of the media and communication markets during the USA's and Europe's 1980s transition phase – characterized by an ideological shift to the right and the admission of competition – there has been an overtly terminological debate on these matters in the context of wider concerns about the 'public interest'.

It can be argued that the European experience in particular reveals some ambiguous evidence with regard to whether the arrival of a competitive market in broadcasting brings identifiable benefits. Though the modern multichannel era, with its apparently wider range of choice on offer, may seem attractive from a consumerist perspective, it may also seem to pose substantial challenges to the citizenship-oriented values of the previously dominant public service tradition (Feintuck and Varney, 2006: 40–1). Left-wing scholars have argued that in a purely market-driven system more media outlets do not necessarily mean more public argumentation and rational discourse; it simply means more ways to address people as consumers (Garnham, 1986: 31).

In this respect, there is some reason to believe that media commercialization and the increase in the number of media outlets brought about by new technologies do not upgrade or strengthen the space for political and social discussion (the Habermasian public sphere). In the course of time, consumption (conceptualized as an individual activity) has begun to be conceived as opposed to citizenship (citizens' means of expression is enhanced and can address every aspect of cultural, social and economic life in the so-called public sphere). The citizen model (European, not American) has been empowered by the comparison, since to be a 'citizen' is clearly preferable to being a 'consumer' (Hilmes, 2004).

But are citizens and consumers such opposite and contradictory identities? According to Hilmes (2004), this is not the case, as they are always and inevitably entwined in a capitalist society. Raboy, Proulx and Dahlgren (2003: 325) note that communication policy positions the individual simultaneously as citizen and consumer and argue that 'in order to be relevant to policy, research must address both the broader structures that constitute the media environment and the multiple ways in which individuals negotiate those structures'. With regards to political citizenship, Van Zoonen (2005) attempts to link up popular culture (and its elements of pleasure and dramatization) with the concept of citizenship by arguing that popular culture helps to convey political messages and in the process makes politics more accessible and widespread.

By distributing opinions, values and knowledge, popular culture can thus serve as a form of citizen participation in politics. It follows that it is not only experts but all people who are engaged in rational critical debate about matters of public concern. In the same vein Dahlgren (2005, 2008) sought to answer the question of where the political resides and how it is positioned against that which is considered nonpolitical. With reference to television, he argued that the medium contributes to political communication by conveying current affairs information alongside entertainment. In this sense the boundaries of political and nonpolitical (entertainment or popular) spaces become blurred. So does the traditional distinction of *citizens'* involvement with politics and *consumers'* attachment to popular culture.

More recently, the semantic terrain of terms has been enriched to incorporate 'customers', 'users' and 'end-users' of telecommunications, computing and online services, which reflects the difficulty in addressing people's collective relation to digital media. So what is meant by 'public interest' or 'citizen interests' today? Can the interest of the public be furthered by the development of new communication technologies and market competition, such as that represented by new technologies like digital television and the Internet? Livingstone, Lunt and Miller (2007: 614) offer a close reading of the use of terms that define 'the public' in policy documents in order to comprehend the ideological and practical dilemmas that beset media policy and regulation. To structure their analysis the authors follow the narrative of the passing of the Communications Act 2003 in the UK, focusing on the clause that sets out the general duties of the new powerful and converged media regulator, the Office of Communications (Ofcom), and argue that the convergence–diversity agenda was encapsulated in the moves to place the 'citizen-consumer' at the heart of a new regulatory regime.

In fact, the Communications Act of 2003 stated, in Clause 3.1, that the principal duties of Ofcom should be to further the interests of both citizens and consumers in relation to communication matters. Ofcom recognizes that 'these interests are often different', which means that it may be necessary to 'resolve tensions between them' and that 'protecting these interests may involve distinct regulatory approaches'. Over the years it has become clear that one of the regulator's main concerns is 'serving the citizen-consumer in the digital era', thereby conflating the identities of citizen and consumer. In its Second Public Service Broadcasting Review, titled 'Putting Viewers First', Ofcom (2009) showed signs of a commitment to expansive notions of the public interest and public service, but as in its first stage of consultation (see Hesmondhalgh, 2005) it argued for further marketization of media and communications. The Digital Britain 2009 report confirmed the introduction of market principles into public service broadcasting, which echoed the then-Labour government's policies more generally (DCMS/DBERR, 2009; see also Iosifidis, 2010b).

Whether they are conceived as citizens or consumers, audiences or users, customers or communities, there is growing momentum behind the argument that ordinary people are being – and must be – repositioned, by technology, the market, society and, hence, the regulator. Livingstone, Lunt and Miller (2007: 616) argue that it is a struggle to resolve the notions of 'the public' into 'citizen' and 'consumer' as ambiguities reemerge and boundary disputes problematize proposed regulation. The study suggests that this has been achieved, controversially, by combining the terms to produce the 'citizen-consumer'. However, as they demonstrate, this elision of terms matters, for it may bring a new balance of market relations and civic interest, or it may be part of a broader agenda of implementing centralized regulation. Lunt and Livingston (2007: 153) note that Ofcom has become 'a significant site [...] for consumer representation and deliberation among stakeholders' and that the regulatory agenda is shaped by the dominance of consumer and competitive considerations.

However, as new technologies open up possibilities beyond broadcasting (see Tambini and Cowling, 2004; Lowe and Bardoel, 2007; Moe, 2008; Iosifidis, 2010a; Jakubowicz, 2010), audiences may embrace new modes of engagement with audiovisual products, many of them seamlessly shifting from the role of consumer to that of producer. Meikle and Young (2008) have noted that new modes of distribution and consumption are emerging and new media technologies empower users in unexpected ways and increasingly recast TV as something that audiences create as well as watch (see also Napoli, 2009). The emerging new media environment gives users control over the flow of the media; *consuming media* increasingly includes *producing media*; and people's media behavior seems to involve some kind of participation, co-creation and collaboration, depending on the degree of openness of the media involved (Deuze, 2010: 454–5). In this regard, content, distribution channels, business models, cultural habits and indeed regulatory approaches are changing in ways that suggest that a fixed dichotomy between 'consumer' and 'citizen' may be unhelpful.

The public sphere

Let me now return to the core concept of the public sphere, which remains a central analytical tool to help us to make sense of the relationship between the media and democracy (civic engagement). In his *Structural Transformation of the Public Sphere*, written in 1962, the German philosopher and sociologist Habermas[1] explained that in the late eighteenth century a new political class (the bourgeoisie) came to the fore in Britain in particular and formed a public body that – in sharp contrast to the old authorities, notably the state and the church – provided the conditions for reason-based, public opinion. The creation of a network of institutions by the bourgeoisie within civil society, and more specifically the launch of a number of newspapers, provided the means through which private thoughts could become public. Libraries and universities became the places for public debate, while publishing enterprises became the means by which government was criticized. That new public sphere was in principle open to all and protected from the power of both the church and the state.

However, Habermas pointed out that this space for rational and universalistic politics created by the capitalist market was historically damaged by both the extension of the state and the evolution of monopoly capitalism. The formation of large private institutions (advertising and public relations agencies) and the deals they made with each other and with the state while excluding the public, led to the replacement of rational public discourse by power politics. The role of the media was central to the replacement of the ideal speech situation by conditions of 'distorted communication'. Whereas the independent press at the turn of the nineteenth century had led to the formation of rational public debate and public decision-making on political and judicial matters, it later functioned as a manipulative agency controlling public opinion. The media's role in the public debate shifted from the dissemination of unbiased and independent information to the formation of public opinion. Following the changing communications environment, the public sphere is discovered as a platform for advertising and public relations.

Habermas's theory merits consideration because he accurately conceptualized the nature of the public sphere, viewing it as an achievement of the new bourgeois (or capitalist) class in Europe, and an outcome of its successful struggle against feudalism and church or state oppression. The shift from *opinion* to *public opinion* is documented with regard to the public sphere's preeminent institutions, the mass media (Boeder, 2005). However, Habermas's thesis has been questioned on historical grounds. Many have argued that he idealized the early period of history he referred to and particularly the notion of the 'independent' eighteenth-century press (Mortensen, 1977; Hohendahl, 1979; Curran, 1991a, 1991b). Koss (1981, 1984), in his analysis of the British political press, pointed out that political control by proprietary interests was exercised in a large part of the press as early as the eighteenth century. Koss's analysis showed that the early British press was not independent to the degree that Habermas described and therefore, one would argue, did not contribute to rational discourse to the degree Habermas claimed.

The German scholar has also been criticized for his rationality argument. Curran (1991a) mentioned that 'the newspapers celebrated by Habermas were engines of propaganda for the bourgeoisie rather than the embodiment of disinterested rationality'. Dutton (2007) found the notion of the public sphere inspired but 'too closely tied to a romantic view of the past' and 'not able to capture the rise of an entirely new sphere of influence'. In today's global, multicultural society, criticisms of Habermas's ideal public sphere could include its universalizing angle and the apparent neglect of 'difference', its emphasis on the national rather than global space, and its normative concept of a unified national space signified and constituted by the media. According to Fraser (2007), nowadays there is little consensus on a common good and universal values, which are increasingly determined through exchanges between various local, national and transnational actors, including states, corporations, civil society actors, citizens and consumers, between mainstream and marginalized groups.

Although the historical accuracy of Habermas's theory may be questionable, he was nevertheless a pioneer in pointing out that the public sphere – a conceptual rather than physical space – and democracy – expressed through engagement in rational discussion – are closely connected. Habermas's thinking, through the contributions and limitations of his thesis, provides valuable theoretical resources to advance important issues relating to democratic society in the contemporary era. He offered a starting point for understanding the media's role in public communication. The question about whether and how the media conceive the public sphere impacts greatly on people's understanding of social and political issues, practices and identities. Garnham (1986), for example, although questioning Habermas's historical assumptions, adopted his central analysis and, by connecting the notion of the public sphere to that of public service, used it as a justification for public service broadcasting.

Along these lines, the media should facilitate the process of rational argumentation by providing a context of public discourse, which is essential for the formation of free and reason-based public opinion. The media should maximize debate over political ideas and contribute to public information and argumentation, which are essential to the maintenance of democracy. Public information is essential both for expressing the common interest and for taking part in the debate about that common interest. But the nature of people's participation in the public sphere has shifted. In his *Theories of the Information Society*, Webster (2006) acknowledges that the public sphere has been damaged as a result of the intrusion of public relations, which jeopardizes the criteria of rationality that once shaped public discourse. Schlesinger (2009b) notes that the public sphere has been reshaped because of the multiplication of cultural and communication management consultancies, the proliferation of 'special advisers' in government, the growth of research teams within communications regulators, and the development of specialist media and communications business journalism. The presence of all these actors has important implications for the nature of people's engagement in an increasingly complex public sphere.

However, the public interest arguments are not just political arguments. Habermas's theory is limited to the political context, but there are countless interpretations of 'public interest' in the context of society as a whole. There are arguments about the preservation of cultural heritage and the environment, public health and universal education, to mention but a few. Over the course of time, these desirable objectives have been interpreted and characterized as 'public good'.[2] One version of the public interest argument has found its fulfillment in the provision of universal education in most Western European countries since the nineteenth century (Smith, 1989). Another has valued the right to authentic cultural expression and the right to participate in defining the historical development of a given culture (White, 1994). Provision for the arts, in particular, has often remained a state responsibility both because cultural heritage was regarded as a service that needs to be preserved for future generations and to ensure that all social classes had access to the arts. The notion of public interest has thus been spread to include important public services at zero or low cost for the interests concerned.

The Internet and the use of Web 2.0 media

The debates surrounding the idea of the public sphere have acquired renewed interest since the emergence of the Internet and other new online media and social networks[3] that provide new communication spaces where debate can be conducted. Since Habermas's work, published well before the digital revolution, computer-mediated communication has taken the place of coffeehouse discourse (Boeder, 2005). It is often argued that the Internet creates new public spheres for political intervention, thus expanding the realm of democratic participation. The diffusion of the Internet, first deployed in 1969, but also mobile communication, digital media and the wide range of social software tools have prompted the development of interactive communication (Castells, 2007: 246). As was previously the case with radio, television and other media, the Internet terrain has produced new spaces for information, debate and participation – as well as new possibilities for manipulation and social control (Kellner, no date). As will be shown below, the Internet is a contested terrain capable both of enlightening individuals and of manipulating them.

The new media terminology is already characterized by terms such as 'global village', 'cyber democracy', 'virtual democracy', 'virtual community', 'electronic agora', or even more recent terms, which have not yet entered the dictionary: 'net-sphere', digi-sphere', 'info-sphere', 'blogosphere', 'twitter-sphere'. These online forums or social spaces of the Web 2.0[4] differ substantially from the traditional media such as that of public service broadcasting in a number of ways: first, they attract many more people than traditional media. Latest statistics indicate that by March 2011 Facebook added 150 million users, and over one fifth of them were in the US, which remains the largest-represented country on the site (see http://www.allfacebook.com/facebook-surges-toward-650-million-users-2011-01, accessed 17 June 2011). This is out of reach for traditional media such as radio and television stations. In fact, if Facebook were a country it would now be the third most populous on earth after China and India. Other social networks are also becoming popular. For example, in mid-2011 the registered users of Twitter were 200 million (see http://socialtimes.com/200-million-twitter-accounts-but-how-many-are-active_b36952, accessed 17 June 2011). But it is not only numbers/scale that matters, for social networks allow more interactivity and many-to-many communication, rather than one-to-many as is the case with traditional broadcast media.

At the same time, these new digital spheres where people come together have some interesting similarities to Habermas's concept of the public sphere, namely: Twitter and other net spheres are public places that are outside state control; they allow individuals to exchange views and knowledge as well as critical points of view; and they are spaces where public-minded rational consensus can be developed (Stumpel, 2009). However, there are important differences from Habermas's concept of the public sphere, especially relating to issues of access to information and interactivity. As Murru (2009: 143) put it, 'in online contexts anyone can potentially take the role of speaker with practically no cost, thus multiplying the source of news and freeing the flux of communication and information from any sort of system control (economic or political)'.

So can the Net act as a public sphere where critical discourse can emerge and influence political action? Can the twitter-sphere recreate the conditions that made ideal speech and public interest a possibility during the era of the Habermasian public sphere? Like the development of all previous new technologies, the appearance of the Internet prompted a discussion about its democratizing and mobilizing power. In the period that Habermas referred to (the eighteenth century), the bourgeoisie were informed and mobilized by newspaper articles; later the telegraph enabled people to communicate at long distance; the invention of radio in 1895 enabled people to broadcast unauthorized messages (from 'pirate' radio stations) until authorities were set up to control the airwaves; passive television viewing dominated the second half of the twentieth century. The Internet, of course, is not confined to physical constraints such as frequency bandwidth – at least in developed nations –, but instead can expand to infinite length, allowing everyone to be a 'publisher' or 'producer'. In theory, this open, free and decentralized space could create the conditions for ideal speech and enhance the ability to voice one's opinion and organize collective action (the very notion of democracy).

The Internet's contribution to politics

In campaigns and elections, many still view the Internet as largely irrelevant or marginal, though others argue that it is likely to undermine democratic institutions and erode traditional institutions of representative, deliberative democracy by providing the means for citizens to participate directly in public policymaking. According to Dutton (2007), these fears raise important issues but tend to conflate two very different institutional arenas. One is an effort to use the Internet to enhance existing democratic institutions and processes, such as voting or parliamentary consultations with citizens. This sees e-democracy as being focused primarily on supporting a more efficient and equitably 'managed democracy' based on traditional representative processes. The other arena prioritizes the networking of individuals to enable the public to hold all institutions of government and politics more accountable. This provides a novel means of holding politicians and mainstream institutions accountable through the online interaction between ever-changing networks of individuals. Dutton provides the dramatic example of the use of texting after the 11 March 2004 Madrid train bombings to alert people to anti-government rallies, which challenged the government's claims and contributed to unseating José María Aznar's Partido Popular (PP) administration (ibid.).

The Internet's contribution to politics is evidenced by the fact that since the mid-1990s most political parties in democratic countries have had official websites, whilst the main political parties across the globe are trying to improve their online activities. More recently, the Internet played a big part in Barack Obama's rise from 'upstart' senator to President. Obama and his team used new media and the Internet to obtain support, raise money and communicate with voters. According to *The Economist* (2010c: 33), the Internet's main function was to help Obama's campaign to do old-fashioned things, for much of the money he raised online was spent on television advertisements, and supporters recruited via websites were deployed to canvas voters face to face. But one should not underestimate the power of traditional media like television to influence public opinion, for Britain's first television debate on 15 April 2010 between the leaders of the Labour, Conservative and Liberal Democrat parties, which was shown on commercial channel ITV and watched by 9.4 million Britons, was followed by a ten-point swing to the Liberal Democrats. This verifies that even in the Internet era traditional media like television can still be highly effective at delivering political messages.

The democratization and globalization of the public sphere

The Internet's democratizing potential has been highlighted in such works as Rheingold (1993) and Kellner (1997), whose central thesis is that cyberspace provides an ideal basis for transnational exchanges. Another optimistic view is that the Internet tends to democratize access to information and undermine hierarchies. For example, De Sola Pool (1983) viewed computer-based communication networks like the Internet as inherently democratic 'technologies of freedom'. In response to this freedom-versus-control debate, Dadashzadeh (2002) noted that the Internet can support and reinforce many different forms of network. These connect in the traditional one-to-many pattern of the mass media but also one to one, many to one, many to many, and so on. Therefore, the Internet can be shaped by developers, users and regulators to support the 'communicative power' of both institutions and individuals in many ways.

In a more recent work, Dutton (2007) went a step further to argue that the growing use of the Internet and related information and communication technologies (ICTs) allow a new form of social accountability to emerge in what he called the 'Fifth Estate'. Dutton's conceptualization of the Fifth Estate builds on the depiction by Manuel Castells (2007) of the Internet as creating a *space of flows*, rather than a *space of places*. Essentially, the Internet enables people to network with other individuals and with a vast range of information, services and technical resources. This is being achieved in ways that can lead to greater accountability not only in government and politics, but also in other sectors. Dutton notes that this could be as important – if not more so – to the twenty-first century as the Fourth Estate has been since the eighteenth century. Equally important is the Internet's role in reconfiguring access to people, information, services and other resources with its potential to create new local and global networks. As Dutton (2007) writes:

> the Internet can reconfigure access in two fundamental ways. First, it can change the way we do things, such as how we get information, how we communicate with people and how we obtain services and access technologies. Second, the use of the Internet can alter the outcomes of these activities. It changes what we know, whom we know and whom we keep in close touch with. We are also using the Net to change what services we obtain, what technologies we use – and what know-how we require to use them.

The Internet can facilitate the spread of debate and deliberation across many parts of the population that may be spatially dispersed. In this sense, the democratic potential of the Internet can be realized through the much larger (and ever increasing) quantity of rational critical debate that can take place than through the traditional media, which are confined within national borders. Viewed this way, the emergence of the Internet (and other new online and international media) leads to a globalization of the public sphere and public opinion. Public discourse and the formation of public opinion increasingly take place in a transnational context. The new technologies have allowed the formation of a transnational or global public sphere as a forum for political discussion. While the traditional media in the form of the printed press and public television played an integral part in the creation of a national public sphere, there is a widespread assumption that new spheres of communication networks can provide the basis for shared concerns, common tastes, and political and cultural objectives at global level.

But there have been voices that take a critical stance on the global nature of the public sphere. With regard to news, Hjarvard (2007) has argued that it is *national* media that continue to play the most important role in public political discourse, with transnational dialogue merely involving 'cosmopolitan elites'. In response to this national-versus-transnational debate, Corcoran's (2010) work on the public sphere raised serious concerns about the effects of transnational mergers between advertising, marketing, public relations and lobbying firms on the global public sphere. The above thinkers share the view that the Internet and other transnational media may not often include debate or dialogue involving all sections of the society.

Theoretical perspectives: the social capital and social exchange paradigms

In an attempt to understand what factors are conducive to citizen engagement and contribution within the public sphere, scholars like Coleman

(1988) and Putnam (1993) consider the theory of social capital as a governance mechanism that provides 'closeness' and 'trustworthiness' among people, while O'Keefe, Kernaghan and Rubenstein (1975) have used the terms 'cohesiveness' or 'embeddedness'. Coleman (1988: 96) defined social capital according to its function. It is not a single entity but a variety of entities, with two elements in common: they all consist of some aspect of social structure, and they facilitate certain actions by actors (individuals or corporate) within that structure. A similar definition has been provided by Bourdieu and Wacquant (1992: 119), who said that social capital is 'the sum of the resources, actual or virtual, that accrue to an individual or a group by virtue of possessing a durable network of more or less institutionalised relationships of mutual acquaintance and recognition'. Social capital then is composed of a network or cluster of norms, values and expectations that are shared by members of a group (Halpern, 2005).

Putnam's (1993) study of social capital in a particular nation (Italy) directly relates social capital to civic engagement between citizens, the larger community and government. Putnam investigated the relationship between social capital in the northern and southern Italian regions and found that while the northern region comprised vibrant communities where social ties were dense and social trust was high, social capital in the southern region was influenced by the hierarchical structure of the Catholic church, which was not conducive to social trust and community-building. Halpern (2005) observed a similar association between (weak) social capital and poorly performing government institutions within various African nations and post-Soviet territories. Therefore, government's encouragement of citizens' participation in and contribution to the public sphere is an important enabling mechanism. Thanks to current technological advances like the use of Web 2.0 media, online social network platforms could promote civic engagement that allows the bridging of social capital across geographical, organizational, hierarchical, temporal and spatial barriers (Shing and Chung, 2011).

But while social capital theories emphasize the crucial role of social structures in governing certain desirable actions by various actors, the social exchange paradigm holds that the value of social exchange is not the same for all participants in social exchange networks. The social relation exerts governance over the content and form of the exchange and therefore influences the value of that exchange. Social exchange theory and network analysis are two core approaches to the study of social structure in domains such as sociology and microeconomics (ibid.). Social exchange theory, as articulated by Emerson (1976), looks at social structure explicitly as a configuration of social relations and positions. So both social exchange theory and network analysis consider social structure as the central concept in explaining how a set of individual actors are diversely linked into social networks (Shing and Chung, 2011).

The Internet and the public sphere: myths and realities of online participation

Much has been written about the democratizing and empowering influence of the Internet and the new social media, and much of it can be dubbed as idealistic and representative of technological determinism (see Nieminen, 2009: 40). Not surprisingly, the attempt to ground theoretically and empirically the 'ideal speech situation' (at least as formulated by Habermas) on the Web has been met with skepticism. Coleman (1999) suggests that much online discussion can be characterized as bad-tempered, perhaps as a result of the decline in public debate in physical spaces such as meeting houses and street corners, where people first learnt to argue effectively. Wilhelm (1999) also refers to the dangers of poor dialogue and a skewed distribution of contributors in cyberspace. As Boeder (2005) argues, it is often the case that major decisions and actions concerning transnational matters occur without intense public attention.

In fact, the view that electronic networks can recreate the public sphere may be flawed for a number of reasons (see Iosifidis, 2011b). First, the open participation facilitated by the Internet can turn chaotic, as there are no rules of behavior, thereby preventing structured conversation. Written and oral contributions could result in anarchic, rather than democratic, forms of participation. A relevant point is that blogging sites are typically dominated by white male voices and characterized by polarized opinions. Furthermore, most blogs are of a personal character. According to the Pew Internet and American Life Project, 52 per cent of bloggers say that they blog mostly for themselves, while 32 per cent blog for their audience. Perhaps more interestingly, the study found that only 11 per cent of new blogs have political ends/aims (cited in Castells, 2007: 247). But it is also the very notion of the Internet's openness that might be at stake, for, as the current FCC Chairman has said, there is limited competition among internet service providers, while there is an explosion of traffic on the Internet (Genachowski, 2009).

Second, there is a problem of inclusiveness. Despite the apparent openness of this new technology compared with traditional media, not all sections of society use it either because they cannot afford to or because they lack the skills to do so. Presumably, some simply have no interest in doing so, or lack the time. As Murdock (2004) argued, access to the Internet through personal computers remains highly stratified by income, age and education, with substantial numbers of poorer households, elderly people and educational dropouts facing the prospect of permanent exclusion. According to Dutton (2007), socioeconomic status does not explain all patterns of adoption and use, for the making of what can be termed 'digital choices' about whether or not to use the Internet also comes into play. For instance, many people choose not to use it, even when they are not excluded (for example, on the basis of their economic wherewithal or disabilities that would prevent them from being able to gain access). This is perhaps most evident for older people (the 'age divide'). Many countries in North America and Europe, especially Scandinavia, have the majority of their population online, but many more countries have a minority, such as those across the global south (the 'geographical divide'). But even if more people achieve basic connectivity, the 'always on/always there' high-speed broadband links needed to access the full range of Internet facilities will remain out of reach for large sections of the population.

Third, censorship might be an issue since in certain countries, including China, North Korea and Cuba, the government restricts its citizens' Internet access by blocking specific websites. Facebook, Twitter and YouTube are all explicitly blocked in China, whilst in March 2010 Google withdrew from China owing to repeated attempts to hack its email system and ever stronger censorship of its searches. Domestic Chinese equivalents of these sites have been launched: Baidu, Taobao, Renren and QQ, the last being the most popular instant-messaging service, with 567 million users in 2009 (*The Economist*, 2010e). The '9/11' terrorist attacks prompted privacy and freedom concerns even in countries with a strong democratic tradition, as evidenced by the passing of the 2001 Patriot Act in the USA, which expanded law enforcement's surveillance and investigative powers. In fact, a Privacy and Human Rights Report (PHR, 2004) found that in the aftermath of 11 September 2001 many democratic governments across the globe used the pretext of a terrorist threat to set up laws permitting spying and surveillance that affect privacy and civil liberties. As highlighted in *The Economist* (2010b), in some cases there is a new social contract: '[D]o what you like online, as long as you steer clear of politics'. For instance, government-controlled Internet-access providers in Belarus provide servers full of pirated material to keep their customers happy.

Fourth, the Internet has become a major arena for corporate activity, as have other branches of the cultural industry. The individualization of consumption has been accompanied by the consolidation of media ownership, producing global multimedia corporations intent on redeveloping cyberspace as retail real estate (Murdock, 2004). As will be shown as this book progresses, a large number of corporate giants, such as News Corporation, have moved into the terrain of the Internet.

Fifth, using the Internet can cause harm by intent (spammers, fraudsters, pornographers, bullies, terrorists and other groups) or accident. Extremist groups, for example, can establish an Internet presence as a resource for recruiting, funding and magnifying their images, just as 'positive' environmental or political movements can exploit the medium (Dutton, 2007).

Sixth, extensive dialogue and critical discussion (the very essence of the public sphere) is often absent on the Net. In the case of Twitter, for example, dialogue is limited by the fact that it allows only the exchange of short messages. This means that there might be an increase in the number of participants in social networks (as shown above), albeit such increase does not necessarily translate into a space for substantial and political dialogue involving groups and individuals. Undeniably, the democratic merit of Net spheres such as Twitter and Facebook is apparent when it comes to the overturn of suppression and censorship of mass media and public opinion by authoritarian regimes. Splichal (2009: 392) provides the recent case of the 'Twitter revolution' in the former Soviet Republic of Moldova. Aided by social networking website tools like Twitter, LiveJournal and Facebook, demonstrators in Moldova organized mass protests against the (allegedly forged) April 2009 parliamentary election results.

Computer-mediated communication also contributed to the June 2009 struggles against the authoritarian Iranian government. When thousands of young Iranians took to the streets to protest against the apparent rigging of the presidential election, it was the protesters' use of Twitter that supplied much of the coverage in the Western media. The fact that the Internet is fomenting revolution and promoting democracy in Iran is but one example of the belief that the Internet is pro-democratic. Groups in Facebook can choose to support the liberalization of Tibet. Facebook and Twitter enabled Barack Obama's campaign to recruit supporters. Staying on the issue of politics, social networks can help to stimulate discussion and marshal action. The importance of social networks in this context is evidenced by a 2010 meeting between Britain's new prime minister, David Cameron, and Mark Zuckerberg, founder and head of Facebook, to swap ideas about ways in which networks can help governments to tackle issues like cutting public spending (*The Economist*, 2010f). Twitter often has real-time updates on events such as the 2009 Mumbai terrorist attacks. Social networks like Meedan can host articles dedicated to the discussion of Middle East news, in either English or Arabic, thus contributing to the availability of a wide range of views in the region. These examples highlight the informative and mobilizing power of the Internet, but they are mainly confined to opposition to authoritarian regimes. However, a recent book (Morozov, 2010) suggests that authoritarian governments often understand the political uses of the Internet better than Western governments and offers various cases where the Web is used to support the government line – the plethora of Chinese pro-government bloggers; the spread of propaganda by Hugo Chávez via Twitter; the 'Net Delusion' of the Russian government's Internet advisers.

Seventh, it has been argued that most of the Internet's content is highly partisan (see Humphreys, 2008). Take, for example, political blogs and their user-created content, which make blogs that claim to be politically independent suspect. Unlike websites, which are mostly static, weblogs are often dynamic and interactive. But despite having an almost unlimited array of content at their fingertips, the users of the Internet and the Web typically choose to access only a narrow spectrum related to what most interests them (Sunstein, 2007). The Web has empowered many individuals to function both as citizen-journalists and political commentators, but according to Hindman (2008) it does not democratize politics, for the extreme 'openness' of the Internet has fuelled the creation of new political elites. As Hindman puts it, 'online speech follows winners-take-all patterns'.

Dahlberg (2007) has found that the online debate is polarized and there is generally a lack of listening. He pointed out that the Internet fails to adequately consider the asymmetries of power through which deliberation and consensus are achieved, the subjective basis of meaning, the centrality of respect for difference in democracy, and the democratic role of 'like-minded' deliberative groups. What is often absent in online deliberations is a majority-opinion-based, justified and rational decision. Moreover, many of the people who produce online content are not professional journalists but amateurism who are spewing misinformation or trivial noninformation while marginalizing high-quality journalistic coverage (Keen, 2007).

Last, despite its increasing prominence as a place where people can access news and advertisers spend money, the Internet remains a distribution medium, not a source of original news content. Although Internet companies invest in this medium, the investment has tended to be in technology and not in journalism. Internet sites unaffiliated with traditional media typically collect stories from various newspapers and wire services, or comment on the news, but undertake little original local news coverage or investigative reporting. For example, according to a study conducted in 2007, three of the five most popular news sites on the Web generate no more than 2 per cent of their own news reporting: both Yahoo and AOL relied on wire services and other news outlets for 99 per cent and 98 per cent, respectively, of their lead news services. Google relied exclusively on news wires or other news outlets (see The State of the News Media: An Annual Report on American Journalism, 2008, at http://www.stateofthemedia.org/2008/index.php, accessed 8 December 2010).

Can the Internet create a healthy public sphere?

So, is it just a myth that the Internet has the ability to create a healthier public sphere? Is the creation of new social and political units by social media a cyber-fantasy? Not quite. If traditional media like newspapers helped to set up public spaces where people initiated forms of communication within nation-states, new social media can do likewise in the international space in which citizens increasingly invest their time to communicate with each other and create content such as text and personal videos. Lessig (2006) predicted that online communities would transcend the boundaries of conventional states and this is true if one thinks of Facebook with its 500 million users. *The Economist* (2010f) writes that Facebook is unprecedented not only in its scale but also in its ability to blur boundaries between the real world and virtual worlds. From the users' viewpoint, the social network can be seen as a liberal polity: a space in which people may air opinions, rally support and right wrongs (ibid.). Viewed this way, Facebook can make the world more open and connected, more like the 'global village' forecasted in the 1960s by futurologist McLuhan.

I would argue that, in the end, it all depends on how one uses the Internet. Like all new media technologies, the Internet may be a useful *tool* for the creation of a public sphere, the *basis* of a public sphere, but it cannot itself create such a space. To use Kellner's words (no date) the Internet – like all new media technologies – can be used as an instrument of empowerment or of domination. Communications technology in general, and the Internet in particular, is not inherently pro-democratic; it can be just as effective in sustaining propaganda and authoritarian regimes. New forms of citizenship and public life are simultaneously enabled by new technology and restricted by market power and surveillance (Boeder, 2005). Castells (2007: 242) observes that the media constitute by and large the space where power is decided, but they are not the holders of power. What is certain is that the media are not the place where the public sphere resides, nor the public sphere per se, but a *vehicle* through which such a space may be created.

Another relevant point is that the Internet can certainly facilitate 'public spaces' where people might get a hearing. Although these spaces are now common, they do not constitute public spheres in any rigorous sense, for they allow the public merely to feel involved rather than to advance actual participation in civic life. Public intellectuals and social movements in civil society are considered 'outsiders' compared with 'mainstream' think tanks, policy advisers and industry figures, who have dominant influence in shaping 'the news' and economic and cultural agendas and who are increasingly engaged as experts in the public sphere in a so-called 'knowledge economy' (see Chapter 3). It appears that the vision of the electronic agora made possible by new technologies and implemented through decentralized networks is utopian. As Dahlgren (1995) noted, the public sphere is not just an 'information exchange depot' but a means for generating and disseminating culture. The free expression of culture, values and the will of the people might be hard to achieve in a marketplace of ideas where the balance between large media companies, the state and civil society tips decidedly in favor of the first two.

Conclusion

This chapter started by providing a definition of the broad, vague and loosely constructed term of 'public interest' in media and communications and by exploring the various theories of public interest that have been advanced. It has been argued that something counts as being in the public interest only if it serves the aims of all those who participate in public communication and not just those of a minority. The context in which public communication takes place is the so-called 'public sphere' and this chapter provided an in-depth discussion on the concept of the public sphere. At the same time, the 'citizen versus consumer' dichotomy was investigated, as thinking about this distinction provides a useful tool for assessing the way media services cater for their audiences. A large amount of space was devoted to examining whether new media technologies such as the Internet and Web 2.0 enable the creation of a more participatory public sphere or even a global sphere. In this context, a number of concepts and theories were sketched – social capital paradigm; social exchange theory; Castells' network society; Dutton's 'Fifth Estate' – to explore whether the Internet and social media allow a new form of public engagement and social accountability to emerge. Having analyzed several limitations of the Internet and its 'open participation', the chapter concluded that the new media, including the Internet, are not the place where the public sphere resides, nor the public sphere per se, but a vehicle through which such a space may be created. It all depends how one uses the Internet – it can be used as an instrument of empowerment or of domination.

2
Media Regulation in the Public Interest

Introduction

The growth of a complex system of regulation of various industries, including the mass media, on grounds of a supposed public interest, has been evident since the early twentieth century. As indicated in the previous chapter, historically societies have extended the concept of public interest to cover free or inexpensive public services such as universal education, the preservation of public amenities, environmental protection, state- or municipality-run transportation, to name but a few. Melody's (1990) account of the public interest in the emerging information society refers to the historical notion of certain industries being recognized in law and custom as 'business affected with a public interest'. These were often connected with transport and other public utilities, in which monopoly conditions were likely to arise and where needs for service were likely to be pressing. In these circumstances, public regulation was often applied in order to ensure equity, efficiency, and fair and adequate provision to all at reasonable prices. In certain countries and regions, for example, there has long been a public interest argument in favor of municipality-run buses: in order to ensure that people at all levels of income enjoy cheap and reliable transport (Smith, 1989).

This chapter examines how the public interest concept has been incorporated into the regulatory systems of telecommunications, broadcasting, print media and the Internet. A large amount of space is devoted to analyzing the media and cross-media ownership rules in the UK and the USA as mechanisms for protecting public interest ideals such as pluralism and diversity and the rationale for relaxing them on both sides of the Atlantic. But while media policy in relation to telecommunications, broadcasting and the print media has been evident, albeit in various forms and degrees, media policy in relation to the Internet is largely nonexistent, for there is reliance on self-government of the Web. However, the Internet has brought about a new area of study, 'Internet governance', which, contrary to the conventional policies for other media with a national focus, extends beyond the domain of governments to embrace a broad range of social institu-tions, including private and civic sectors. After touching upon the theme of Internet governance (although the term 'governance' will be investigated in greater depth in Chapter 5), the chapter moves on to considering whether the public service aspect of the public interest has been narrowed in the neoliberal world characterized by free market competition, commodifica-tion and globalization.

Telecommunications

Telecommunications in the USA: the early days

Historically, certain types of industry appear to have been instituted with a public function or 'affected with a public interest' and have been regulated to serve that purpose. Horwitz (1989) pointed out that the industries con-sidered to be imbued with a public function are *transportation, telecommuni-cations, energy utilities* and the *system of currency exchange*. He labelled them infrastructures, for they are the channels for trade and discourse that bind together a community, society or nation. They are central to the circulation of capital and both constitute the foundation of and limit the economic functioning of a society. The telecommunications sector, more specifically, adopted the so-called 'common carrier' model, which called for the regula-tion of infrastructure. The main principle of common carrier law was that a carrier must allow nondiscriminatory (fair and equitable) access to its serv-ice at reasonable prices (ibid.: 13).

In the telecommunications domain, universal telephone service was adopted as a policy objective in both the USA and Europe to encourage economic and social interaction within the country as a way of promoting national unity (Melody, 1990). State support, together with the imposition of regulatory controls, helped the establishment and successful operation of the American telecommunications system. The telegraph industry received in its infancy federal and state subsidies, while telephony was established as a 'natural monopoly' and regulated in order to facilitate the expansion of the nationwide telephone network (Horwitz, 1989; Smith, 1989; Melody, 1990; Aufderheide, 1999; Napoli, 2001). The telephone system was united by the giant American Telephone and Telegraph Company (AT&T).

The regulatory body Federal Communications Commission, set up in 1934, was given the role of supervising telecommunications and of protect-ing the existing structures and corporate interests involved. But it was not only a commerce-based public interest that underlay the US system of tele-communications regulation. At the same time, the FCC had the mandate to secure broader public interest goals such as universality, fairness and equity. Telephone and telegraph enterprises were legally obliged to provide service to all citizens at fair and reasonable rates. In part due to such obligations, according to Horwitz (1989), the US telephone network was universal and efficient and the service was inexpensive for the customer.

Telecommunications in Europe: the early days

In Europe, telecommunications networks were run by nationally based, mainly publicly owned, postal and telecommunications authorities (dubbed public, telephone and telegraph systems, PTTs). Each national PTT held a monopoly over the whole network – transmission, switching and equipment – and was itself in charge of the introduction of new services, acting as both supplier and regulator (Hills and Papathanassopoulos, 1991). As in the USA, systems were regarded as natural monopolies and as 'public goods' (see Chapter 1 for a definition of the term). Governments emphasized the importance of the penetration of the systems in assuring access to all citizens at low costs. The difference from the United States was that the European PTTs were state-run, whereas at the other side of the Atlantic AT&T was a privately owned network operator controlled through an independent agency – the FCC. The European telecommunications sector was mostly subject to competition law for the control of the infrastructure, the guarantee of open access.

Broadcasting

Broadcasting in the USA: the early days

Despite the fact that it was based on different structural models, the technology of broadcasting in both the USA and Europe was regulated by the state in terms of access and content. The broadcasting model involved content regulation, as opposed to the 'common carrier' telecommunications model, which called for the regulation of infrastructure but not of content. But as was the case in telecommunications, broadcasting was regarded as a 'public good' on both continents. Private broadcasters in the USA were given licences to monopolize a given radio frequency but those licences were not regarded as a property right. Broadcast regulation was founded upon the public domain argument that the airwaves were a natural resource held in common, and consequently the state acted to protect that resource.

The public domain rationale or, to put it another way, the rationale for regulation was based on the concept of 'spectrum scarcity' – the limited nature of the electromagnetic resource. The FCC allocated access to limited airwaves and obliged successful operators to fulfil certain aims. In return for the grant of a licence to operate, broadcasters were placed in the position of public *trustees*; that is, they had the duty to serve the public interest by fulfilling the tastes, needs and desires of everyone within the service area (Rutkus, 1982). The 1934 Communications Act clearly mandated that 'broadcasting be treated as a public good that serves goals of benefit to the public and therefore be subject to government regulation' (Kellner, 1990: 185).

The FCC's 1946 statement on the 'Public Service Responsibility of Broadcast Licensees', popularly known as the Blue Book,[1] emphasized the public nature of broadcasting and attempted to give a concrete meaning to the term 'public interest'. It identified four public interest issues in terms of programming policy: the 'carrying of sustaining programmes', the 'carrying of local live programmes', the 'carrying of programmes devoted to public discussion', and the 'elimination of commercial advertising excesses' (Hoynes, 1994). Krugman and Reid (1980), in their own assessment of the public interest criteria used by the FCC when considering broadcast licence applications, identified the criteria of 'balance', 'heterogeneity', 'dynamism', 'localism' and 'diversity'.

These criteria were supplemented by other principles, such as the 'Fairness Doctrine'. At the heart of the 'public trusteeship' model of broadcasting, the Fairness Doctrine (deriving from the 1934 Communications Act) obliged broadcasters to cover issues of public importance or controversy and to provide a reasonable opportunity for the presentation of contrasting viewpoints on such issues (Brennan, 1989; Horwitz, 1991). However, in 1987 the FCC decided to abandon the Fairness Doctrine on grounds that it was no longer necessary, both because it was inefficient and because of changes in the media environment.[2]

An evaluation

The Fairness Doctrine, the Blue Book and licensing requirements represent good examples of regulations implemented early on by the regulatory agency to safeguard the public interest. The FCC may not always have acted in accordance with its own rhetoric on the importance of the public interest. Some voices put it that it simply served the interests of those it was supposed to regulate (Kahn, 1978) and others emphasized the inherent weakness of the FCC as a regulatory body (Baughman, 1985). The claim that the FCC has not always acted in the public interest can be demonstrated by its 2003 decision to further liberalize media ownership rules (among other media ownership restrictions) by raising the national television cap (audience reach) from 35 per cent to 45 per cent, obviously to please corporate parties who had been lobbying hard for the relaxation or even removal of ownership rules.

History has proven that the effectiveness and accountability of the FCC is subject to prevailing political forces, which have the final word on its leadership. For example, its opposition to strict media ownership rules was increased in 2001under the chairmanship of Michael Powell, son of former Secretary of State Colin Powell, just after the election of George W. Bush in 2000. Similarly, the FCC did not fulfil its role to guarantee free speech and the free flow of information at the time when George W. Bush launched systematic attempts to influence news content in his 'War on Terror' in the aftermath of '9/11'.[3] This does not deny that overall the regulatory agency's policy agenda has contributed positively to the understanding of broadcasting (and telecommunications) as a kind of public utility. But it does imply that the FCC's policy has been subjected to the prevailing political ideology. During his presidential campaign, the current President of the United States, Barack Obama, published a detailed agenda for media and communications that represented a fundamental shift towards communications policy in the public interest in that it would pursue the following objectives: create a more democratic media system; promote universal access to communications technologies, including access to high-speed Internet networks; foster increased diversity of media ownership; and reinvigorate and transform public media (Freepress Action Fund, 2008). These principles have been fully endorsed by the current Chairman of the FCC, Julius Genachowski, who in a 2009 speech (see Chapter 3) highlighted the issue of Internet openness.

Broadcasting in Europe: the early days

In Europe, most countries similarly imposed public service obligations on their broadcast media, but unlike the USA's, where local broadcast licences were granted to nongovernment entities – primarily to commercial firms to provide advertising-supported programming – the continental European broadcasting model developed outside the market. The European broadcasting system, the so-called public service broadcasting (PSB) model, in its typical form consisted of a national public monopoly that could best serve the public interest by its commitment to quality in return for a basic payment, usually in the form of an annual licence fee.[4] There is indeed an overlap between the idea of the public interest in communication and PSB, since the latter is defined by Garnham (1983: 13–14) as 'a means of providing all citizens, whatever their wealth or geographical location, equal access to a wide range of high-quality entertainment, information and education, and as a means of ensuring that the aim of the programme producer is the satisfaction of a range of audience tastes rather than only those tastes that show the largest profit'.

Therefore, PSB is often defined in terms of the benefits it is supposed to deliver to society: 'universal provision and wide-ranging appeal'; 'services to regions and minorities'; 'attention to national interest, identity and culture'; the 'provision of informational and educational services beyond what the market would require'. More recently, PSB has been tasked to 'reflect different opinions in multi-cultural society' and transform itself into 'public service media', that is to provide public service content on various platforms (see Tambini and Cowling, 2004; Lowe and Bardoel, 2007; Iosifidis, 2010a; Jakubowicz, 2010).

In short, both the broadcasting and telecommunications industries were regarded as public goods – goods held in common, accessible by all, and benefiting everyone. The dominant idea in both Europe and the United States was that the above industries should be treated like air, water and other elements that belong to everyone, or like parks and highways that can be used by everyone (Hills and Papathanassopoulos, 1991: 3). It was recognized that these sectors could not be treated like commercial enterprises. The prevailing idea was that some aspects of public communication were of wide concern to society and should be looked after by the government or by public agencies. For instance, as regards broadcasting in the USA, Johnson (1987: 31) stated: 'reference to the public interest at least contemplates a public purpose, public ownership, public impact of consequence, and a declaration of public policy that, whatever else it may be, broadcasting is not just any other business'.

Likewise, EU member states perceived broadcasting as too important to be left to the profit-seeking mechanisms of the free market due to its significance for democracy. Of course, there are large variations among the national broadcasting systems, which stem from the different traditions, political cultures and regulatory systems that exist across Europe. This makes it difficult to identify a single PSB model and accurately define PSB. In general terms, however, there are some common obligations bestowed upon PSB by society that define the remit of its activities. These obligations can be summarized as follows:

- Universality of content and access.
- Provision of programmes that contribute to social cohesion and democratic process.
- Setting of high quality[5] standards in the areas of entertainment, education and information.
- Contribution to political pluralism and cultural diversity.
- Enrichment of the lives of individuals through education in history, the arts and science.
- Preservation and promotion of national culture and heritage.
- Editorial independence and accountability.
- Serving of the needs of an increasingly multicultural society (new obligation).

An evaluation

In the UK, the Peacock Report, although attacking the broadcasting status quo on the grounds both that it did not enhance consumer choice and that it did not enable programme makers to offer alternative products, nevertheless endorsed the importance of PSB in securing the public interest: 'The fulfilment of this goal, so far from being incompatible with public service activities positively requires them in a sense of "public service"' (The

Peacock Report, 1986: para. 547). At EU level, despite tension between the European Commission and the European Parliament, the former regarding PSB from a deterministically economic perspective and the latter highlighting its sociocultural dimension (see Lowe and Bardoel, 2007: 12), the 1997 Amsterdam Protocol stressed the pivotal role of PSB in European democracies and enabled them to receive public subsidies (licence fees, direct government grants, ad hoc payments, and so on) as long as these did not distort national media markets.[6] However, in more recent years the EU's employment of neoliberal principles has conflicted with normative objectives to deliver public communications services (Wheeler, 2010: 51). In this context, the Competition Directorate has hardened its stance in relation to the application of state aid rules to PSB (see Chapter 7).

A summary

Broadcasting has been subject to both content and structural regulation, the former concerning requirements or limitations as to what can be communicated and the latter referring to ownership rules, which typically set limits on ownership in relevant geographical and product markets.[7] The structural regulation of broadcasting ownership has been designed via systems of licensing, the rules for which are established through acts of parliament. Broadcasting legislation has set rules on who may own and provide broadcasting services, limits on mono-media ownership and cross-media ownership, especially between newspaper publishers and broadcast licensees (Gibbons, 1998; Hardy, 2010: 161). As will be shown below, in both the USA and the UK there has been a tendency to remove restrictions on broadcasting ownership, although in the UK pro-market reregulation was balanced by a social-market policy of keeping some cross-media rules and preserving PSB (Curran and Seaton, 2010).

Print media

In contrast to the electronic media, particularly broadcasting, which has traditionally been subject to extensive statutory regulation, the print media were protected from any governmental interference. As soon as the battles of the emerging middle class against the church and the state were won, freedom of the press became established either in constitutions (in the United States) or in press laws (in most parts of Western Europe). In the USA, the press freedom model applied to the print media and constitutionally forbade regulatory intervention: the print model was not subject to licensing, a fairness doctrine or access requirements. The First Amendment to the Constitution of the USA (1791) states that 'Congress shall make no law [...] abridging freedom of speech, or press' (cited in McQuail, 1992a: 36).

In Europe, the authorities in the member states of the European Union (EU) have been very restrained concerning the regulation of access and content in the written press market, for both historical and political reasons. Throughout Europe, 'press laws are usually formulated tersely and are limited to an ordering framework which accepts the market as the mechanism to control content diversity [... They] are normally limited to the creation of a legal framework of unrestricted press organisations' (Hoffmann-Riem, 1992: 148). In most liberal societies the press is expected to reflect the prevailing diversity of viewpoints and for this reason proponents of liberalization have argued that newspapers and magazines should be in private hands to counterbalance state power. Freedom of the press presupposes private ownership and minimal or no government interference.

In the USA, arguably the most liberal country, which puts its faith in the operation of market forces, the press is subject only to general public interest and anti-monopoly regulation. The newspaper industry in the USA is characterized by localism and there are only a few national titles (*USA Today, The Wall Street Journal, The New York Times* and *The Washington Post*). However, responding to financial difficulties caused by decreasing circulation and advertising revenues, the local newspaper markets have consolidated substantially – to the point that one could refer to locally based monopolies. The availability across the country of these better-resourced 'national' newspapers has only added to the difficulties facing the local press.

Concentration in the US print media

The US print media landscape is dominated by big conglomerates, which, through a long history of mergers and acquisitions, have concentrated their control on what Americans read. Although in 2007 there were 1456 daily newspapers in the USA (almost one fourth of the 6580 daily newspapers existing in the world, see http://www.nieworld.com/cc/NewspaperADailyMiracle. pdf, accessed 8 October 2010), these are under the control of just a few companies.

Table 2.1 provides information about the largest owners of print media in the USA. As can be seen, these firms have diversified to other media, although their main activities concentrate on print.

In the USA concerns about the formation of newspaper chains (and cross-ownership between newspaper companies and radio stations) date back to the 1920s, when they were both economic (for example, potential or actual anticompetitive practices) and political (potential or actual dominance of public discourse by media monopolists). Responding to the trend towards press monopolies, press policy was designed to safeguard diversity and access, limit excessive newspaper concentration and guarantee the viability of the press. As already mentioned, the First Amendment to the US Constitution prevents units of government from regulating the content of print media, so concerns about the concentration of newspaper ownership focused on economic issues (Pritchard, no date). But generally policy has been resisted and denigrated by the press itself due to concerns

Table 2.1   Largest owners of print media in the USA

Ownership chart in the USA: Print
- **News Corporation** (owned by the Murdoch family) (book publisher HarperCollins, print publications including the *Wall Street Journal*, the *New York Post* and *TV Guide*; the magazines *Barron's* and *SmartMoney*). Other holdings include the Fox Broadcasting Company; TV and cable networks such as Fox, Fox Business Channel, National Geographic and FX; film production companies 20th Century Fox, Fox Searchlight Pictures and Blue Sky Studios; numerous websites including Marketwatch.com; and non-media holdings like the National Rugby League. *[2009 revenues: $30.4 billion]*
- **Time Warner** (150 magazines including *Time, Sports Illustrated, Fortune, Marie Claire* and *People*). Other holdings include CNN, the CW (a joint venture with CBS), HBO, Cinemax, Cartoon Network, TBS, TNT, MapQuest, Moviefone, Warner Bros. Pictures, Castle Rock and New Line Cinema. Until 2009 Time Warner owned the Internet portal AOL. *[2009 revenues: $25.8 billion]*
- **Bertelsmann AG** (book publisher Random House). Other holdings include RTL Group and media firm Gruner+Jahr. *[2009 revenues: $20.5 billion]*
- **Cox Enterprises** (43 newspapers and several publishing firms). Other holdings include Cox Cable, Cox Television and Cox Radio, through which it controls 80 radio and 15 TV stations. It also offers broadband Internet access and digital phone service. *[2009 revenues: $14.7 billion]*
- **Advance/Newhouse** (25 daily newspapers in nine states and magazine publisher Conde Nast). Other holdings include Bright House Networks cable operations, online holdings such as CondeNet, concierge.com, epicurious.com and style.com. *[2008 revenues: $7.6 billion]*
- **Gannett** (massive portfolio of print publications with titles such as *USA Today*). Other holdings include 23 TV stations and numerous related operations. *[2009 revenues: $5.6 billion]*
- **Tribune** (26 newspapers, 10 magazines and several publishing companies). Other holdings include 23 TV stations and one radio station. *[2008 revenues: $5 billion]*
- **The Hearst Corporation** (vast interests in newspapers and magazines). Other holdings include digital media, business media and television. *[2008 revenues: $4.8 billion]*
- **The Washington Post** (*The Washington Post, Newsweek* and numerous magazines). Other holdings include six TV stations, Cable One and the educational company Kaplan, Inc. *[2009 revenues: $4.6 billion]*
- **The New York Times Company** (20 newspapers, including the *New York Times*, the *Boston Globe* and the *International Herald Tribune*). Other holdings include numerous online services. *[2009 revenues: $2.4 billion]*
- **The McClatchy Company** (30 newspapers in 29 markets and other print publications). *[2009 revenues: $1.5 billion]*
- **Media News Group** (50 daily newspapers in 11 states). Other holdings include one TV station and four radio stations. *[2007 revenues: $1.6 billion]*
- **E.W. Scripps Company** (14 newspapers). Other holdings include 10 TV stations. *[2009 revenues: $802 million]*
- **Media General** (23 metropolitan and community newspapers, and more than 100 periodicals). Other holdings include 18 TV stations and Blockdot, Inc., an 'advergaming' and game development firm. *[2009 revenues: $657 million]*

Source: Ownership Chart: Print. Available at: http://www.freepress.net/ownership/chart/print (accessed 29 September 2010).

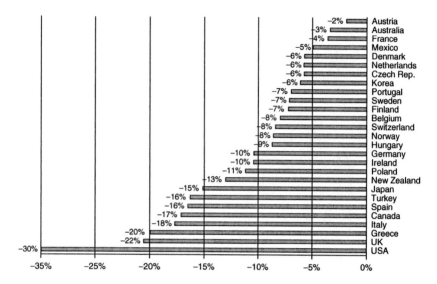

Figure 2.1 Estimated newspaper publishing market decline in OECD countries, 2007–2009 (in %)

Source: OECD (2010a) *News in the Internet Age: New Trends in News Publishing,* OECD Publishing, at http://dx.doi.org/10.1787/9789264088702-en (accessed 8 January 2011).

about hidden motives and unforeseen consequences for press independence (McQuail, 2007: 14–15).

Today the press in the USA is still a regulation-free area, subject only to general antitrust rules. Also in recent years this field of media law and policy has been fairly dormant because of the general weakening of the newspaper industry. The number of daily newspapers is dropping slowly, daily circulation is declining rapidly, and advertising revenue is increasingly moving elsewhere, most notably to the Internet. The worldwide recession of 2008–2009, combined with the rapid growth of Web-based alternatives, caused a serious decline in advertising and circulation, as many newspapers closed or retrenched operations. A 2010 report by the Organization for Economic Cooperation and Development (OECD) revealed that about 20 of the 30 OECD countries face declining newspaper readership, with significant decreases in the USA (30 per cent since 2007) and the UK (22 per cent) (see Figure 2.1).

On the revenue side, the OECD report found that the global newspaper publishing market derives about 57 per cent of its revenue from advertising, rather than copy sales. The reliance on advertising is extremely high in the USA (87 per cent) and moderate in the UK (50 per cent). The online revenues of newspapers are miniscule compared with total revenues (see Figure 2.2). On the cost side, the report notes that expenses unrelated to editorial work,

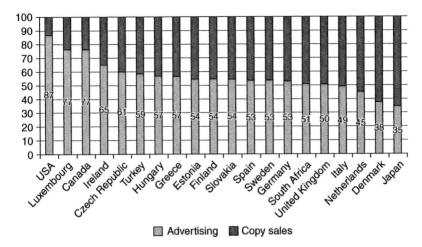

Figure 2.2 Contribution of advertising and copy sales to paid-for daily newspaper revenues (in %), 2008 or latest year available

Source: OECD (2010a) *News in the Internet Age: New Trends in News Publishing,* OECD Publishing, at http://dx.doi.org/10.1787/9789264088702-en (accessed 8 January 2011).

such as production, maintenance, administration, promotion, advertising and distribution, dominate newspaper costs. These large fixed costs make newspaper companies more vulnerable to economic downturns and less agile in reacting to the online news environment.

Market pressure on newspaper owners to merge

To summarize so far, traditional business models, including that for print media, are being eroded and audiences are fragmenting across a constantly increasing number of platforms (Pritchard, no date). Indeed, the traditional newspaper business model has rested on the sale of two things: advertising (selling readers to advertisers) and copy (selling content to readers). But developments in the last few decades have brought about a rise in alternative news sources (radio, TV, Internet), which have resulted in declining readerships and a reduction in newspapers' market share of advertising. The obvious response has been to colonize the new territory and export the business model online, but there are difficulties in creating online content that people will pay for (see the above OECD report, stating that online revenues of newspapers are negligible compared with total revenues). This scenario has put additional pressure on newspaper owners to merge businesses or diversify into other fields, resulting in rising levels of cross-media ownership. Recent literature notes that consolidation can have a dramatic impact on how the media are organized and run, on journalistic practices, and on democracy in general (Levy and Nielsen, 2010).

Table 2.2   Largest owners of print media in the UK

Who owns what in UK media – *Mostly having newspaper interests*
- **News Corporation** (owned by the Murdoch family) (*The Sun, The Times, The Sunday Times, News of the World*, of BSkyB).
- **Telegraph Media Group** (Sir Frederick and Sir David Barclay acquired the business in 2004 for £665 million) (*Daily Telegraph, Sunday Telegraph*, weekly magazine *Spectator, The Scotsman* quality daily newspaper, *Scotland on Sunday* quality Sunday title, and the *Edinburgh Evening News*).
- **Daily Mail and General Trust** (*The Daily Mail, Mail on Sunday, Ireland on Sunday, Mail Today* tabloid, *Metro* urban national newspaper, *Loot* classified directory, *London Lite* free sheet. Until January 2009 the group also owned the dominant paid-for London-area local newspaper *Evening Standard*, which was then sold to Russian billionaire Alexander Lebedev).
- **Guardian Media Group** (wholly owned by limited company Scott Trust) (*The Guardian, The Observer, Manchester Evening News* regional newspaper, Channel M regional TV station, numerous regional radio stations across the UK under the Real Radio, Smooth Radio and Rock Radio brands, EMAP leading international business-to-business publishing, events and information company, jointly owned with Apax Partners).
- **Independent News and Media** (The O'Reilly family had a controlling interest of over 29.5% at July 2008 and Irish entrepreneur Dennis O'Brien had a shareholding of over 27% at May 2008) (*The Independent, Independent on Sunday*. The company also owns the Belfast Telegraph Group, which publishes the *Belfast Telegraph, Ireland's Saturday Night, Sunday Life* and *Ads for Free*).
- **Northern & Shell Network** (owned by Richard Desmond) (*Daily Express, Sunday Express, Daily Star* and magazines *New!* and *Star*).
- **Trinity Mirror plc** (the result of the takeover of Mirror Group Newspapers by Trinity plc in September 1999) (*Daily Mirror, Sunday Mirror, The People, Daily Record, Sunday Mail* and about 120 regional daily and weekly newspapers).
- **Pearson plc** (*The Financial Times, The Economist*).
- **Gannett UK Ltd** (extensive local newspaper holdings).

Source: Author's analysis.

Note: The data in this table do not take into account the closure of *News of the World*. The 168-year-old best-selling Sunday tabloid was accused of hacking into the mobile phones of crime victims, celebrities and politicians and on 10 July 2011 the parent company News International decided to close it down.

Concentration in the UK print media

The trend towards concentration of ownership in the print industry, evident for some time in the USA, is also observable on the other side of the Atlantic. Table 2.2 provides information on who owns what in the UK media, focusing primarily on companies with newspaper and magazine holdings. It can be seen that a few groups own the main print outlets and in some cases, most notably in the case of News Corporation, companies are active in various communications sectors and in several countries.

Press self-regulatory policy: the UK press complaints commission

In terms of policy and regulation, the print media in most European countries are in general not subject to any specific statutory controls on their content and activities. Jeremy Tunstall's view, cited in McQuail (2000: 19), is that 'the press [in the UK] is a non-policy area'. In fact, in the UK (as in most European countries) the press regulates itself, through the Press Complaints Commission (PCC), a non-statutory body that is responsible for maintaining the Editorial Code of Practice and investigating complaints into alleged breaches of the Code. The PCC Code was introduced in 1991 and has been revised several times since, most recently in 2009. The Code prescribes general principles governing accuracy, including the avoidance of 'inaccurate, misleading or distorted material'. It also states that 'newspapers, while free to be partisan, must distinguish clearly between comment, conjecture and fact'. In addition, the Code includes specific restrictions on financial journalism, affecting how financial information is imported and used (Hardy, 2010: 165).

However, the PCC Code does not include any provisions regarding commercial influence on editorial matter. Funded as it is by the newspaper industry, the PCC has been criticized for being incapable of effectively regulating the press; following the coverage of the death of Princess Diana in 1997 the Commission came under intense pressure to reform. Subsequently, its Code was revised to protect privacy more effectively, and also to take account of both the Youth Justice and Criminal Evidence Act 1999.[8] The PCC Code is complemented by the National Union of Journalists' Code, which, contrary to the PCC Code, prohibits the acceptance by journalists of bribes or other inducements and states that 'a journalist shall not lend himself/herself to the distortion or suppression of the truth because of advertising or other considerations' (ibid.).

One of the most common complaints about the PCC is its lack of power to impose penalties. As a self-regulatory body its powers are limited to demanding that an offending publication print an apology. Putting it into a broader context, press self-regulation has brought about two problems. First, the increasing concentration of ownership has led to a situation where the press in most countries is controlled by a few large conglomerates whose interests often spread to other media and non-media concerns. Second, there is a tendency for newspapers to lean towards a right-wing, pro-business point of view, and in some territories to engage in political propaganda. In situations where there is a high degree of press concentration or cross-media concentration the result might be reduced political pluralism and cultural diversity and in such cases governments have imposed either positive (support measures) or negative regulation (typically ownership rules) (Hutchison, 1999: 170). The ongoing hacking scandal opened up a number of issues related to the efficacy of the PCC, journalistic ethics, relations between the press and politicians. The very idea of press self-regulation was challenged on 8 July 2011 by the Prime Minister David Cameron in his address to Parliament. As the details of phone hacking continue to unravel, there is a political consensus that the press has been irresponsible and the PCC was not equipped to address the above issues. But as Tambini succinctly put it, 'when the Prime Minister starts designing self-regulation he ends self-regulation'. Tambini went on to say that the worst thing that could come out of this scandal would be regulation by politicians (see http://blogs.lse.ac.uk/mediapolicyproject/2011/07/08/thoughts-on-phone-hacking-yes-we-need-urgency-but-also-caution-and-clear-principles/, accessed 20 July 2011). The challenge now is how to maintain press independence and safeguard plurality and standards whilst ensuring press accountability and ethical oversight. But these are matters that require thorough discussion which cannot be conducted while the hacking scandal is not over yet.

Media ownership rules in the USA

In the USA, there are six main media ownership rules, five adopted by the FCC and one enacted by Congress (and thus not subject to revision by the FCC). Two rules limit the ownership of TV stations and networks nationwide. The National Television Ownership Limit, enacted by Congress in 2004, places no limit on the number of TV stations a physical or legal person can own, provided a single owner's stations do not exceed 39 per cent of the national TV audience. The FCC's Dual Network Ban permits common ownership of multiple broadcast networks but prohibits mergers between the 'top four' networks, ABC, CBS, Fox and NBC. Two further FCC rules limit the number of broadcast stations an entity can own in a single media market. The Local Television Ownership Limit allows a single entity to own two TV stations in the same local market provided that (a) the signals (the so-called 'Grade B' contours) of the stations do not overlap; (b) at least one of the stations in the combination is not ranked among the top four stations in terms of audience share; and (c) at least eight independently owned and operating commercial or noncommercial full-power broadcast TV stations remain in the market after the combination.

The other rule that limits the number of broadcast stations an entity can own in a single media market is the Local Radio Ownership Limit. This rule incorporates the numerical caps set by Congress in 1996. The caps are based on a sliding scale that increases with the size of the local market. In general terms, one entity may own (a) up to five commercial radio stations, not more than three of which are in the same service (AM or FM), in a market with 14 or fewer radio stations; (b) up to six commercial radio stations, not more than four of which are in the same service, in a market with between 15 and 29 radio stations; (c) up to seven commercial radio stations, not more than four of which are in the same service, in a market with between 30 and 44 radio stations; (d) up to eight commercial radio stations, not more than five of which are in the same service, in a market with 45 or more radio stations.

Two additional rules are intended to limit local cross-media ownership. The Radio/Television Cross-Ownership Limit provides that in a single market one company may own (a) one TV station (two TV stations if permitted by the local TV ownership rule) and one radio station regardless of total market size; (b) up to two TV stations and up to four radio stations if at least 10 independent media voices (for example, broadcast facilities owned by different entities) remain after the merger; (c) up to two TV stations and up to six radio stations or one TV station and up to seven radio stations if at least 20 independently owned media voices would remain post-merger. Parties must also comply with the local radio ownership rule and the local TV ownership rule.

The most controversial media ownership rule, the Newspaper/Broadcast Cross-Ownership Rule, has recently been changed. More specifically, the FCC has modestly relaxed its newspaper/broadcast cross-ownership prohibition as follows:

- The new rule adopts a presumption that a waiver of the cross-ownership rule is not inconsistent with the public interest (i.e. it may be permissible) in the following circumstances: when a daily newspaper seeks to combine with a radio station in a top 20 Designated Market Area (DMA), or when a daily newspaper seeks to combine with a TV station in a top 20 DMA and (a) the TV station is not ranked among the top four stations in the DMA and (b) at least eight independent 'major media voices' remain in the DMA. 'Major media voices' include full-power commercial and noncommercial TV stations and major newspapers. The FCC concluded that such media are generally the most important and relevant outlets for news and information in local markets.
- For markets outside the top 20 DMAs, the FCC has adopted the presumption that it is inconsistent with the public interest for an entity to own newspaper/broadcast combinations and does not approve such transactions. The FCC will reverse the negative presumption in two limited circumstances: when the proposed combination involves a failed or failing station or newspaper, and when the combination results in a new source of a significant amount of local news in a market. The FCC will require any applicant attempting to overcome the negative presumption to demonstrate by clear and convincing evidence that the merged entity will increase the diversity of independent news outlets and increase competition among independent news sources in the relevant market.
- No matter which presumption applies, the FCC's analysis of the following four factors will inform its review of a proposed combination: (a) the extent to which cross-ownership will serve to increase the amount of local news disseminated through the affected media outlets in the combination; (b) whether each affected media outlet in the combination will exercise its own independent news judgment; (c) the level of concentration in the DMA; and (d) the financial condition of the newspaper or broadcast station

and, if the newspaper or broadcast station is in financial distress, the owner's commitment to invest significantly in newsroom operations (see http://www.fcc.gov/ownership/rules.html, accessed 29 September 2010).

Media ownership rules in the UK

In common with other modern democracies, the UK has for some time regulated the communications industry. Media ownership rules have applied because market forces alone, even regulated by competition law, will not necessarily provide the marketplace of ideas that enables democracy to prosper. Media ownership regulation in the UK is enacted by the provisions of the Communications Act 2003 (mostly applying to electronic media) and the Enterprise Act 2002 (most relevant to newspapers), and it is administered by the Office of Communications (Ofcom), the super-regulatory agency set up in 2003 to replace the then existing five regulatory bodies (Independent Television Commission, Radio Authority, Office of Telecommunications, Broadcasting Standards Commission and Radiocommunications Agency). As in the USA and other countries, the main objective for establishing media ownership rules for newspapers, radio and television was to protect the plurality[9] of viewpoints and provide citizens with access to a wide range of sources of news and information.

The UK regulatory regime for *communications law and policy* is influenced by EU stipulations. Examples include the liberalization of UK media and communications law and policy (see below), a process strongly influenced by EU provisions, which increasingly foreground competition law as a means of promoting media pluralism.

A summary of the media ownership rules in the UK is given in Table 2.3.

The public interest test

The *media public interest test*, introduced in 2006, allows the Secretary of State (for Business, Innovation and Skills) to intervene in newspaper, broadcasting and cross-media mergers if they raise public interest concerns. Technological advancements and the desire to promote a more competitive communications industry that will attract greater investment have accelerated the deregulation of the industry. As mentioned, the Communications Act 2003 relaxed certain ownership rules that had applied to broadcast media and to cross-media ownership. This relaxation notwithstanding, the media and cross-media public interest regime provides a safeguard, preventing media mergers from bringing about concentrations of ownership that may operate against the public interest. It enables the Secretary of State to intervene in certain mergers involving media enterprises so as to ensure a sufficient plurality of media ownership, to ensure the availability of a wide range of high-quality broadcasting and to ensure that those with control of media enterprises have a

Table 2.3 Summary of the media ownership rules in the UK

Type	Principle	Geographic application	Media
Local radio ownership rules	Detailed rules about the number of analogue and digital radio broadcast licences one entity can own in a specified area	Local	Radio
Local cross-media ownership rules	Rules that prevent one entity from owning different types of local media over specified market share levels.	Local	Radio, television (Channel 3) and national newspapers
National cross-media ownership rules	Rules that prevent one entity from owning both a Channel 3 licence and one or more national newspapers with an aggregate market share of 20% or more.	National	Television (Channel 3) and national newspapers
National radio multiplex ownership rule	A rule that one entity cannot own more than one national radio multiplex.	National	Radio
Restrictions on holding broadcast licences	Rules that prevent or limit control of TV and radio by owners whose influence might cause concern (political parties/religious bodies). There are also a number of qualified restrictions (Channel 4 and S4C may not hold Channel 3 or Channel 5 licences).	Both local and national (depending on specific rule)	Radio and television
Appointed news provider rules	Rules for the provision of news to Channel 3 by an independent news source unconnected with the BBC, not under the control of religious bodies and well funded.	National	Television (Channel 3)
Media public interest test	Rules allowing the Secretary of State to intervene in proposed media mergers on 'public interest grounds', including plurality. Ofcom's role is to provide advice.	Both local and national	Radio, television and newspapers

Source: Ofcom, 2009.

genuine commitment to the broadcasting standards objectives set out in the Communications Act 2003.

Under the public interest or plurality test, public interest considerations relating to newspaper mergers include:

- The requirement for the accurate representation of news in newspapers.
- The requirement for free expression of readers' opinion in the newspapers involved in the merger.
- The requirement for a sufficient plurality of views expressed in newspapers in each market for newspapers in the UK or its regions.

Liberalization of media ownership under the Communications Act 2003

The Communications Act 2003 freed up the communications industry far more than was expected by media analysts, removing most of the ownership regulations that characterized British broadcasting, as it was thought that these denied companies access to the economies of scale and scope required to expand into foreign markets. The Act provided for the removal of rules preventing

- Joint ownership of television and radio stations.
- Large newspaper groups (for example Murdoch's News Corporation) from acquiring the minor commercial terrestrial broadcaster Five.
- Non-European ownership of broadcasting assets, effectively clearing the field for takeovers by the world's corporate media giants.
- Single ownership of the main commercial terrestrial broadcaster ITV, opening the way for the creation of a single ITV company, which allowed Carlton and Granada to merge and form ITV plc.

Two clauses were particularly controversial:

- The decision to permit the acquisition of Five by a newspaper group.
- The decision to lift the ban on foreign ownership.

These provisions proved New Labour's pro-market credentials and certainly won support from influential media owners (see Freedman, 2008: 119–20). This 'substantial liberalization' and 'reduction of cross-media ownership rules' was accompanied by an increased dependence on 'competition law' as well as the extension of 'self-regulation' wherever possible. Meanwhile, the government introduced a so-called 'public interest plurality test' (Communications Act 2003) for major media mergers (see also Chapter 3).

The merger regime

The UK's sector-specific media ownership rules are separate from the *merger regime*, which applies to all sectors including the media and has a different

Table 2.4   Ofcom's recommendations concerning the media ownership rules in the UK

Geographical coverage	Rules	Recommendations
Local	Local radio ownership rules	Removal
Local	Local cross-media ownership rules	Liberalization so that the only restriction would be on all three of: a) local ownership (with 50% plus share) b) ownership of a local radio station c) ownership of a regional Channel 3 licence
National	National radio multiplex ownership rule	Removal
National	National cross-media ownership rules	No change
Both local and national	Appointed news provider rules	No change
Both local and national	Restrictions on holding broadcast licences	No change
Both local and national	Media public interest test	No change

Source: Ofcom, 2009.

purpose from the media ownership rules. Over the past twenty years or so, merger control in the UK has evolved considerably and through this mechanism the Office of Fair Trading aims at retaining a suitable merger regime in a rapidly changing world. The primary purpose of the merger regime is to prevent consolidation that could result in reduced competition in particular markets. However, the merger regime may indirectly protect plurality by preventing excessive consolidation in a particular market on competition grounds.

Further changes in the media ownership regime – Ofcom's recommendations

In July 2009, Ofcom submitted a number of recommendations to the Secretary of State concerning media ownership rules. These were subject to a consultation process ending in September 2009 but were subsequently adopted without changes. A summary of these recommendations is provided in Table 2.4.

It can be seen that Ofcom's recommendations were generally to relax and simplify the radio ownership rules and to abolish most of the local rules concerning radio ownership and cross-media ownership. Echoing its US counterpart FCC, Ofcom's rationale was that, given the financial pressures that stations face, these changes might provide opportunities to make radio stations viable by being under common ownership, allowing more operational efficiencies. Ofcom mentioned that its research showed that a majority of consumers were not opposed to single ownership in radio, so long as they had an alternative source to their local BBC station.

Ofcom also recommended the liberalization of the local cross-media ownership rules, so that the only restriction would be on ownership of all three of: local newspapers (with more than a 50 per cent local market share); a local radio station; and a regional Channel 3 licence.

Furthermore, Ofcom recommended the removal of the national radio multiplex rule under the logic that it did little to guarantee plurality.

Meanwhile, Ofcom recommended retaining the national cross-media ownership rules. As the regulator put it, despite the rise of the Internet and the growth of digital media as news sources, television remained an important source of news. Additionally, in spite of a decline in their national circulation, newspapers retain an important role in setting the news agenda. Therefore the regulator concluded that there had not yet been such significant change in national media that the cross-media ownership rules should be removed.

Ofcom also recommended retaining the restrictions on holding broadcast licences in order to continue to protect the public interest against undue influence by certain TV and radio owners (for example, political parties and religious groups). Once again, the regulator pointed to the fact that TV and radio remained influential in the digital age (ITV1 is the most watched national news provider after the BBC, with 21.7 per cent of total news hours watched in 2008, 25.9 per cent in 2006).

Ofcom recommended retaining the appointed news provider rule, which aims to ensure that the provision of national and international news to Channel 3 is independent from the BBC. This is because Channel 3 remains the most watched source of broadcast news after the BBC, exactly as it was when the rules were liberalized with the Communications Act 2003.

Finally, Ofcom recommended retaining the public interest test for media mergers in its current form. It is worth mentioning that since the introduction of the public interest plurality test the Secretary of State has intervened in the public interest over Sky's acquisition of a 17.9 per cent stake in ITV, but the case was appealed.

On 17 November 2009, having considered the responses of the consultation group, Ofcom recommended to the Secretary of State the following two main changes, which were in line with its earlier recommendations:

- Removing the rules restricting local radio service and multiplex ownership and national multiplex ownership. For local services, this meant that all commercial radio stations in a local area could be owned by one operator.

- Liberalizing the local cross-media ownership rules so that the only restriction was on ownership of all three of: a local radio station; local newspapers (with 50 per cent or more of the local market share); and a regional Channel 3 licence.

There are two broad conclusions that can be drawn from this analysis of media ownership rules in the USA and the UK. First, overall the regulatory frameworks in both the USA and the UK have failed to prevent undue concentration in the national, local and regional press. Not only that. A trend towards relaxing media and cross-media ownership rules is evident in both countries: although Ofcom appears to be keener than the FCC to maintain national cross-media ownership rules, both regulatory agencies are well on course to abolishing most of the local rules limiting radio and print ownership, as well as cross-media ownership. Echoing its counterpart FCC, Ofcom's rationale is that, given the financial pressures that stations face, these changes may provide opportunities to make local stations viable by being under common ownership, allowing more operational efficiencies.

Second, it can be observed that although the state legislatures' attention has focused on the electronic media, there has not been such a clear divergence between the press and broadcasting. The print industry is largely a regulation-free area in comparison with broadcasting, but given the trend towards concentration of media ownership the print media are increasingly subject to anti-monopoly rules designed to ensure fair competition and a pluralistic output. As said, the trend towards concentration in the press sector (as in other media sectors) has been seen over a considerable period of time. The rapid commercial growth and the strong trend towards monopoly that the press has experienced since the early part of the twentieth century in both Europe and the USA have raised questions over the public task and public responsibility of the medium. The 1947 Report by the Commission on Freedom of the Press in America (Chafee, 1947) and the three Royal Commissions on the Press[10] in Britain made specific recommendations for standards of press performance based on the 'public interest' criteria of accuracy, fairness, integrity, access to information by the public, truthfulness and diversity. Because concentration in the written press has become more marked in the Western world in recent years, there has also been regulation of press ownership in most countries, which typically take the form of mono-media or cross-media ownership rules.

There is evidence, then, of a certain degree of government intervention concerning the structure of the press sector. Nevertheless, the 1990 report of the Calcutt Committee[11] in Britain, which dealt with 'sensational' reporting and the invasion of privacy, demonstrates that governments also intend to intervene in the content of the press. In his first report in 1990, the late Sir

David Calcutt complained about the ineffectiveness of the PCC and called for statutory regulation, but the government envisaged instead a further series of reform to the PCC. The issue of media self-regulation is discussed in more detail in Chapter 10.

The print industry is also a recipient of subsidies. As Picard (2007: 236) notes, in the 1970s governments across Europe and in North America began to supplement existing state intervention in press economics to provide a wide array of support designed to improve the finances of newspaper companies.

Press subsidies

Because there is a link between public interest in press diversity and democracy, there have been various forms of government intervention in the sector. Positive policy instruments and support measures such as tax and postal concessions gave, during the 1970s and 1980s, some economic protection to the press, and therefore some privilege, which was justified according to 'public interest' principles concerning the quality, independence, diversity and volume of information available to society (McQuail, 1992a). The various support measures for the print media in the USA and a number of Western European countries include direct subsidies, indirect incentives (for example fiscal incentives: reduced VAT rate, loans on preferential terms, fiscal incentive mechanisms for investment in production) and even support for training. By the late 1970s, newspapers in many nations benefited from preferential tax rates, reductions in postal and telecommunications rates, reductions in rates for distributing newspapers, funding for research in industry problems, and in some cases exemptions from regulations on other industries and operating subsidies (Smith, 1977, cited in Picard, 2007: 236).

All these press support schemes have been designed both to allow publications to weather the crisis which the sector is experiencing as a result of competition from other media (mainly television and the Internet) and to maintain the diversity of publications in the face of the strengthening of concentrations. According to Picard (2007: 236), Nordic nations created, in the 1970s, the most extensive and interventionist system of state support to address newspaper industry problems, which is often referred to as the 'Nordic model' in comparative studies of media and media policy. However, Picard observes a diminishing need for the subsidies for various reasons, including that numerous political papers are choosing to become commercial, nonparty publications, thereby losing their prominent roles in information delivery and public discourse among large sectors of the population. Second, Picard (ibid.: 243–4) argues that newspaper subsidies are also a risk because they have many of the characteristics of state support for public service broadcasting that have run afoul of national and

European competition law in recent years (see Chapter 7 for an analysis of state aid for PSB).

Indeed, press subsidy schemes are increasingly called into question and any attempt to subsidize is scrutinized by competitors in national markets as well as at EU level. A recent example is the EU's investigation of the best-known press aid scheme, the Swedish one, which has been in place since 1971, before Sweden's accession to the EU. The scheme allows, among other things, support for the production of subscription newspapers that fulfil a number of criteria, with the aim of contributing to media pluralism. Such aid can be compatible with the Single Market if it pursues a goal of common interest, is proportionate and does not give beneficiaries an undue advantage over their competitors.

All press aid schemes are assessed under EU state aid investigation rules but in fact the EU had received complaints against the Swedish scheme. The European Commission (EC) looked at the case and, while not calling into question the objective of media pluralism pursued by Sweden, it found that the press aid scheme did not meet the proportionality test and initiated a procedure for bringing the aid in line with EU rules. Following concessions by the Swedish government – in particular, a change in the method for calculating state support to metropolitan newspapers and a significant reduction in aid levels – the EC concluded in July 2010 that Sweden's changed regime to support newspapers was now in line with EU state aid rules (see http://www.eubusiness.com/news-eu/state-aid-sweden.207/?searchterm=None, accessed 23 October 2010).

The following section summarizes the major technological, political, sociocultural and economic developments in the global media market since the 1980s in order to provide the background for the analysis of the public interest in the new era.

Developments in media and communications since the 1980s

Since the mid-1980s the global media market has undergone upheaval. The rapid development of new communication technologies and the relaxation of strict ownership and content rules have allowed new players to enter the industry, changed the dynamics of the market and led to privatization and commercialization. The gradual convergence of different communication sectors, combined with the development of the Internet and online services, has led to the creation of new market structures, as well as new roles for the owners of communications companies. This has resulted in the concentration of capital and of control of information flow in an ever smaller number of multinational conglomerates. These factors – political, economic, technological, sociocultural and regulatory – have all had a great influence on the development of public interest policies. They will be summarized below.

Political and economic developments

Political and economic factors have affected the structure and functioning of the media. During the past three decades or so the media sector has been characterized by a trend towards reregulation, privatization and commercialization. The process, as well as the speed, of these developments was not uniform in all countries. In some places, for example the USA, there was complete deregulation of the electronic media sector. Elsewhere, for example in the UK, a regulatory framework was applied to liberalization in a predetermined way, with built-in transitional stages. Despite these differences, the impact of the trend on the media industry, particularly broadcasting, was decisive, as it moved out of a protected environment into a competitive one. Broadcasting liberalization has intensified over recent years, coinciding with the globalization of communications and the impending technological convergence of audiovisual media, telecommunications and information technology. All these multifaceted pressures have affected the status and influential position previously enjoyed by incumbents, including PSBs.

Technological changes

The introduction of new technologies – more specifically the development of cable and satellite transmission systems in the 1980s, as well as the introduction of digital technology and the rapid development of broadband Internet in the 1990s and 2000s –resulted in an unprecedented proliferation of commercially driven channels and other sources of information, education and entertainment. The digitalization of information has multiplied the possible means of communication and prompted the appearance of thematic electronic media that focus on specific issues. Although the stages of technological development may differ from country to country (for example the adoption of digital TV and the use of the Internet are more widespread in the USA and the countries of Northern Europe than in southern European countries), inevitably digital technology will penetrate people's lives and broadband Internet will offer an alternative way of accessing audiovisual material. In the UK, for example, multichannel development is already a reality as the total number of households with access to new digital media increased from just over 3 million in 1993 to over 22 million in 2009 (see Table 0.2 in the Introduction).

Sociocultural shifts

Parallel to these politico-economic and technological factors, a wide spectrum of social and cultural changes is shaping the role and influencing the status of the media sectors. At individual level, citizens are increasingly becoming customers, motivated in their choice and behavior more by individual needs and preferences than by civic duty or responsibility (Nissen,

2006: 22). Globalization, the free movement of capital, goods and services, and migration from other continents on a hitherto unseen scale, are all forces that have disrupted integration and eroded social cohesion. Increasing individualism and rapid change in Western lifestyles have combined with a general climate of discontent with traditional media, including PSBs, which are no longer able to reach out to satisfy all viewers. Reregulation has provided the benefit of many more sources of information, empowering audiences, enabling them to select services to satisfy their increasingly varied demands. This has left traditional, mainly public, broadcasters with the difficult task of trying to reverse these trends by reestablishing the lost societal and cultural commons.

Regulatory changes

As described above, many countries have introduced new regulatory regimes, which aim to abolish previous restrictions on business development. For example, with the Communications Act of 2003, British broadcasting saw the introduction of new legislation that liberated media markets and extended 'light-touch' regulation. Also, changes in French law during the 1990s, in particular the raising of maximum holdings in TV channels, were followed by higher levels of concentrated ownership in the television sector. Other large European countries, such as Spain, Germany and Italy, but also the smaller territories of Ireland, Sweden and Greece, have followed the same route towards relaxing broadcasting ownership rules observed in France and Britain (Iosifidis, Steemers and Wheeler, 2005: 71–5; Iosifidis, 2007). Furthermore, the EC has developed a 'light-touch' approach towards industry consolidation over the years, as evidenced by initiatives like the introduction of the new regulatory framework for electronic communications applied in July 2003 (see Chapter 7).

Media market concentration

The powerful economies of scale and scope generated by new digital technology have led to mergers, acquisitions and other business alliances between previously separated media companies. Corporate development in the American and European media markets has been facilitated by the introduction of liberal regulatory regimes and has inevitably resulted in higher levels of concentration, which can endanger media pluralism and diversity (Iosifidis, 1999). The market has witnessed the emergence of large companies with a transnational orientation, which cannot easily be monitored. Important phenomena are horizontal concentration across the value chains of different parts of the media industry and vertical integration of the media value chain from the development and creation of concepts and formats and content production to channel management, distribution and consumption (Nissen, 2006: 10).

Narrowing the public service aspect of public interest: the public interest and free market competition

The shift to a neoliberal communication policy regime combined with the reregulatory moves of the 1980s has challenged the traditional trusteeship model of the electronic media and resulted in a narrower definition of the concept of the public interest. The term neoliberalism refers to the prevailing assumptions that most aspects of societal development should be governed by unhindered market mechanisms. The neoliberal public policy and regulatory changes that began in the 1980s included the liberalization of the broadcasting markets, the privatization of the telecommunications markets and the reregulation of policies towards more relaxed regulatory regimes for all media and telecommunications sectors. The rise of cable and satellite TV undermined the 'scarcity of the spectrum' argument as the new system could potentially support unlimited channel capacity. Policymakers reconsidered the balance that should be struck between the various aspects of public intervention and the dynamics of the free market.

In his account of broadcast deregulation in the USA, Streeter (1996) suggests that the shift in policy process was driven by technology and economics but also ideology, as corporate liberalism underpinned the regulatory attitudes of those in government and business managers. Referring to the Canadian telecommunications market, Rideout (2003) observed that in a liberal environment market criteria foreground public interest communication. Humphreys (1996) attributed the change in policy philosophy in Europe towards more open media systems to the prevalence of pro-market ideas. Similarly, Hesmondhalgh (2005) and Freedman (2008) asserted that neoliberal values increasingly inspired US and UK policymakers. Jakubowicz (2010) went even further to argue that the traditional notion of the public interest in European broadcasting had been dethroned by commercial and individual interests.

One definition of the public interest in today's neoliberal world is free market competition – meaning an unregulated media market or, to put it more precisely, regulation to ensure free market competition. Discussions over the economic control of competition are also said to be public interest arguments. The argument is that the market produces the best outcome for the largest number of people. This is best expressed through the reregulatory philosophy of the Report of the Committee on Financing the BBC (The Peacock Report, 1986), which was conducted under the Thatcher administration. On the other side of the ocean, Horwitz (1989) noted how the concept of the public interest was shifted by the deregulatory trends in US broadcasting and telecommunications markets during the 1970s and 1980s from a focus on social equity to a concern with market efficiency.

By the same token, Aufderheide (1999) explained that while in the early capitalism the public interest in US communications policy was equated with peace, prosperity and universal service, since the passing of the 1996 US Telecommunications Act it had been associated with competition and the marketplace. More recent works (Napoli, 2001; Lloyd, 2006) echo these developments in regulatory thinking in the last decades by arguing that the contemporary American communications infrastructure serves corporate, rather than democratic, purposes. Lloyd in particular has produced a historically based critique of US communications policy and concluded that whereas in the past there was emphasis on stronger regulation, nowadays US communications are dominated by private power and there is a tolerance of monopoly or oligopoly control over national communication systems. But it is not only academic studies that mark this shift in the foundation of US communications policy in relation to the public interest. Then pro-market FCC Chairman Mark Fowler challenged the 'common good' interpretation of public interest and instead pursued the idea of identifying the 'wants of the audiences' through market forces. For him, market signals might be used to calibrate consumer needs, preferences.

As mentioned by Streeter (1996), corporate players have also called for the relaxation of regulatory regimes and the 'privatization' of the public interest in media and communications. In 1989 Rupert Murdoch, the founder of News Corporation/News International, in his landmark MacTaggart lecture, argued against state regulation in the media and dismissed PSB. Twenty years later his arguments were echoed by James Murdoch, heir to his father's media empire, who said that 'private enterprise should be allowed to go about its business unfettered by regulation'. He took a critical stance against the super-regulator Ofcom for over-regulating the media industry and argued that in the era of technological convergence the 'all-media market', in which the distinction between print and broadcasting is being blurred, should not be regulated at all. James Murdoch targeted the BBC's online operation, bbc.co.uk, for giving out news for free, thus making it difficult for commercial operators to make money from news journalism in a falling economy. Many attendees of Murdoch's speech described Murdoch's attack – on what Peter Bazalgette, the former Creative Director of independent company Endemol, called the 'twin terrors' of Ofcom and the BBC – as predictable (see Robinson and Brown, 2009).

In support of PSB

The size and scope of the BBC – funded by a compulsory licence fee (£145.50 per household as of April 2011) that guarantees a steady income at a time when the financial sector is forced to cut budgets – has always been an issue. The BBC has a turnover of £4.8 billion, which makes it the second largest UK broadcasters (the largest terrestrial commercial operator, ITV, has a turnover of £1.9 billion). But satellite network British Sky Broadcasting (BSkyB) is already larger than the BBC with a turnover of £5.9 billion (Sabbagh,

2010). While there are many supporters of the corporation, including myself, who argue that the public money guarantee programming diversity and quality, there are those (commercial channels, struggling independent producers, pro-market evangelists, the political right) who have a general antipathy towards public institutions and, among other things, want to see the BBC's licence fee cut (see Iosifidis, 2010b) and the corporation confined to its core activities and required to stay clear of the online world. The current Conservative–Liberal Democrat coalition government, led by David Cameron, has repeatedly made it clear that it wants the corporation to recognize the difficult economic environment and has put intense pressure on the BBC to cut its licence fee and identify alternative sources of funding. This was a widely expected development, as downsizing the BBC was announced even before the new government's election.[12] As a result, in September 2010 the corporation announced that it would freeze the licence fee at £145.50 until 2013, but warned that this might mean a cut in programming budgets, while some commentators (Barnett and Seaton, 2010a, 2010b) have expressed concerns over the impact of the licence fee freeze on the BBC's independence.

It is not my intention to develop the merits and demerits of public service media here, partly because they have been explored convincingly elsewhere (see Tambini and Cowling, 2004; Lowe and Bardoel, 2007; Iosifidis, 2010a; Jakubowicz, 2010), but let me take the example of online news and provide a brief assessment of whether it is the free market or a public source that is better suited to provide quality and trusted online news. I would share James Murdoch's concern about the vital role news plays in the democratic process, but can one put faith in the power of the market for producing high-quality news, including 'hard' news such as financial and educational news? At least three factors strongly indicate that the answer to this question is negative. First, driven by profits/ratings, commercial players would be inclined towards distributing sensationalist news and information, rather than important knowledge, to the citizenship.[13] Second, presenting facts accurately would be problematic, as priority would naturally be given to breaking news without always double-checking the credibility of sources. Third, commercial news organizations will most certainly in time start charging customers for news consumption in order to get a return on investment, whereas the BBC provides online news and other services for free.[14]

Despite Murdoch Junior's attempt to present the BBC as an anticompetitive entity (precisely because it gives out online content for free), it should be said that the corporation's news website is well respected and visited regularly because it provides public service journalism, bringing people all around the world stories of national and international interest. The trustworthiness of the source combined with free, widely accessible content are guarantors that the public interest is being served. In a direct challenge to James Murdoch's thesis, the BBC's business editor Robert Peston said, in

May 2009, at the Richard Dunn Memorial Lecture at the MediaGuardian Edinburgh International Television Festival that commercial news media could not always be relied on to give the public the information they needed. This is mainly because the new paid-for online model does not inform and educate on hard issues that matter to the BBC – financial matters, but also medicine, the environment and education. Peston took a hard line on deregulation and reminded his audience that the commercial digital market in news would distribute information in the same way as financial resources had been distributed unequally and inefficiently prior to the current financial crisis (Peston, 2009).

A main question is how in the capitalist era of mass politics, mass communication and the dominance of reregulatory philosophy collective goods can be best safeguarded. Another is whether they will survive at all. Therefore, the divestiture of telecommunications monopolies, the multiplication of channels of communication, and the relaxation of regulatory controls over broadcasting in particular, pose important questions about the nature of the modern public sphere. Are the attempts to move the emphasis from public to private sector in the 'public interest'? The free market competition philosophy declares that it can deliver diversity and a free marketplace of ideas, essential goals for the creation and maintenance of a public sphere of communication. But are public argumentation, freedom of speech and other desirable objectives such as quality of content guaranteed in an age of information abundance and online media?

If the answer to this question were positive, one would probably argue that publicly funded media are no longer needed. However, even free market press (*The Economist*, 2006) argue that online media fail to deliver much new quality content, while pro-market regulatory bodies such as Ofcom point out that commercial broadcast media may be less able to deliver content quality and variety due to rising competition and lack of resources as advertising spending gradually moves to the Internet (see Ward, 2006). The UK's last, New Labour, government asserted that the future provision of a wide range of public service programming in radio, television and news programming may be in jeopardy (DCMS/DBERR, 2009: 45). Given the highly partisan content that is delivered via the Internet (Humphreys, 2008) it appears that public media have an important democratic role to play in the multichannel digital age.

A public interest approach to Internet governance

The evolution of the Internet from a research and academic facility into 'a global facility available to the public' (WSIS, 2003), alongside the development of other new media, has coincided with the processes of globalization and technological convergence, which have in turn challenged traditional national policy and regulation regimes. Although the terms globalization and convergence will be examined more thoroughly in later chapters, it is worth giving a preliminary definition of convergence here as the delivery of similar, existing or new media, telephony and Internet services via the same transmission platform. It can be present at three different, albeit interrelated, levels: the technological level (mainly due to the digitization of broadcasting, print, information technology and telecommunications networks), the structural level (as a consequence of corporate alliances across different sectors) and the services and markets level (the new multimedia services) (see Iosifidis, 2002: 28; Latzer, 2009). Globalization refers to a context marked by the diminishing role of national governments, the increasing transnational concentration of corporate power, the shrinking of constraints of time and space, challenges to conventional thinking about identity, the emergence of new global networks, and the progressive establishment of a new political system of global governance (Raboy, no date).

While media policy in relation to telecommunications, broadcasting and the print media has been evident, albeit in various forms and degrees, media policy in relation to the Internet is largely nonexistent, for there is still reliance on the self-government of the Web. It is true that the Internet brought about a new area of study, dubbed Internet governance, which, contrary to the traditional policies for other media with a national focus, extends beyond the domain of governments to embrace a broad range of social institutions, including private and civic sectors. According to the 1999 Human Development Report of the United Nations Development Programme (UNPD) 'governance does not mean mere government. It means the framework of rules, institutions and established practices that set limits and give incentives for the behavior of individuals, organizations and firms' (UNDP, 1999: 8). The report went on to assert that strong governance is a prerequisite in the combat against global conflicts, global crime, civil conflicts and financial volatility.

Working group on internet governance

But how can the Internet be overseen so as to ensure that it serves the public interest? A public interest approach to Internet policy should focus on strengthening the medium's approach to good governance and accountability, though there is little agreement about the possible scope and mechanisms of Internet governance. The Working Group on Internet Governance (WGIG), which was established by the Secretary-General of the United Nations in accordance with the mandate given to the UN during the first phase of the World Summit on the Information Society (WSIS), held in Geneva in 2003, has developed the following working definition of Internet governance as part of its June 2005 report:

> Internet governance is the development and application by Governments, the private sector and civil society, in their respective roles, of shared

principles, norms, rules, decision-making procedures, and programmes that shape the evolution and use of the Internet. (Internet Governance Forum, WGIG, 2005)

This working definition reinforces the notion of inclusiveness of *governments*, the *private sector* and *civil society* in the mechanisms of Internet governance. It also acknowledges that with respect to specific issues of Internet governance each group will have different interests, roles and participation, which in some cases may overlap (ibid.). Following the WSIS, an Internet Governance Forum (IGF) was set up in July 2006 as a multi-stakeholder forum for policy dialogue on issues of Internet governance and was first convened in October 2006. The IGF, whose main themes are openness, security, diversity and access, is considered an important development of the WSIS since it involves various stakeholders in the policy framework. Therefore, it could be argued that a public interest approach to the Internet should include the following: enhanced accountability, independence, access to information, broad reach, freedom of expression and diverse content. A multitude of governmental and nongovernmental agencies are involved in governance arrangements.

Although the IGF is a much appreciated venue where governments and nongovernmental stakeholders from all over the world meet to discuss issues relating to the Internet, its future is currently uncertain. The General Assembly of the United Nations was expected to decide at the end of 2010 whether it should extent the IGF's initial five-year mandate. At its meeting in September 2010 in Vilnius, Lithuania, several speakers acknowledged the IGF's success and growth over the years (see Chairman's report at http://intgovforum.org/cms/2010/The.2010.Chairman's.Summary.pdf, accessed 10 November 2010). Indeed, over the last few years many regional and national IGF-type meetings have been held in different countries, contributing to debates between governments, politicians, industry and civil society. This activity has changed the nature of Internet governance in those countries and has resulted in moves toward cooperative models of regulation.

The multi-stakeholder model, largely initiated at the IGF, has certainly advanced the discussion on issues relating to global Internet governance. However, one of the themes discussed at the Vilnius meeting was the need for a more results-oriented IGF as the Internet Governance Forum typically involves open discussions between various actors. Some speakers favored a more results-oriented approach, while others saw in the IGF practice of non-negotiating outcomes one of its strengths, as it allows for open discussion free from the pressure of negotiations.[15]

3
Media Policy and Regulation in the Public Interest: Looking Ahead

Introduction

In identifying and assessing the academic literature on public interest in media and communications, the previous two chapters showed that communications policies are generally guided by and legitimized in the name of the 'public interest'. The literature review attempted to outline the terms in which the field is defined, but it was far from comprehensive in terms of geographical reach, for it was limited to English-language publications with examples mainly drawn from the USA, the UK and the mainland European terrain. The public interest philosophy in the Western world is generally based on freedom of communication (expression and opinion), universal access to information and knowledge (inclusiveness), diversity (plurality of ownership and content diversity), and accountability. Until three decades ago or so the means to promote these public interest goals were state intervention in the media market (but not state control, as was – and still is, to varying degrees – the case in most Eastern European countries), although lately the politics of neoliberalism have led to the 'marketization' of the public interest notion.

This commentary moved quickly from a distant past when only a few media were available and there was general agreement on basic values to an evolving multimedia present era and uncertain future with a multiplicity of players and operators where there is less agreement on basic principles but one thing is apparent: media policy in the public interest is in a recession, as the concept has been marginalized and commercialized, as evidenced by the relaxation of media ownership rules and the general trend towards reregulation in the media and communication industries, triggered by technological development. However, it is this author's view that media policy and regulation will be more important than ever in the digital age in order to counterbalance the declining scope of public content so as to ensure that the views of all societal groups are represented, quality standards are maintained and national and societal cultural identities are promoted in the face of growing globalization. This chapter closes the trilogy on the concept of the public interest in media and communications by summarizing the scholarly literature and the key issues surrounding the notion of the public interest. Unavoidably, certain points mentioned in previous chapters resurface here, but there is a clear attempt to make some forward-looking observations of what counts as being in the public interest in communications today in the light of technological, economic, political, ideological and regulatory shifts.

Difficulty in defining the contemporary public interest

First, it has to be spelled out that today's communications policymakers find it difficult to define the concept of the public interest and therefore establish goals for policy. This difficultly stems partly from the fact that any policy is scrutinized and questioned because of potential limitations on the freedom of people and partly from the changing character of the concept itself. Ways to address the tremendous methodological diversity that characterizes the field include:

- Looking at the public interest in terms of the medium in question and its technological orientation (but technological convergence has rendered this distinction obsolete).
- Investigating the public interest in relation to the field of study or discipline concerned with normative principles as common denominator (suggested method).

Looking at the public interest in terms of its technological orientation

Let us look at these in turn. Traditional print media (newspapers and magazines), 'old' electronic media (radio and television), telecommunications and the Internet have all incorporated public interest ideals, albeit different in the scope and type of policy that is possible. Attention to public interest advocacy has tended to focus on mass media, chiefly broadcasting, and more recently the Internet, with less attention to telephony and telecommunications. To be sure, telecommunications policy has attempted to defend the public interest by regulating the airwaves and paying attention to infrastructure, market conditions and anti-monopoly regulation. The sector has been subject to general competition law, which is thought to guarantee open markets and low entry barriers – incentives for providers. A robust competitive marketplace, then, rather than regulation, is believed to be the protector of the public interest in telecommunications, which has been guided by the principle of universal service.

In contrast, media policy has tended to analyze the public interest partly in terms of economics but mostly in terms of politics and culture because of the wider policy concerns of symbolic representation, national and civic identity, and media influence on public opinion. The means for preserving these socio-cultural principles have typically been sector-specific structural and content rules, rather than generic competition law, due to the special significance attached to mass media in the formation of public opinion. The dominance of neoliberal thinking in public policy since the late 1980s has resulted in reregulation (relaxation of strict regulatory frameworks), but in general this sector, particularly television, has been subject to excessive sectoral regulation compared with other terrains, both because of the scarcity of physical resources and because of its political importance.

This contrasts sharply with the print industry in territories such as the USA and Western Europe, in which light regulation and/or self-regulation are standard currency. A noninterventionist policy and adherence to the principle of freedom of speech are best thought to guarantee the social responsibility of the press. Press policy has been marginal, ensuring the principle of freedom of speech yet ineffective at limiting press concentration.

Print policy may differ from broadcast policy, but the development of the Internet and the accompanying convergence of technologies have challenged policy processes that have traditionally dealt with separate media. The new 'paradigm' of communications policy involves an increasing convergence of policy areas under the rubric of the 'Information Society',[1] the increasingly important role of transnational corporations and the development of new communication technologies including the Internet (all of these are issues that are examined in the course of this volume). The Internet, arguably the most transformational communications breakthrough since the printing press, has started as an open medium that provides freedom for everyone to innovate without permission. There are no rules that attempt to challenge this openness, although according to the current Chairman of the FCC, Julius Genachowski (2009), there are compelling reasons to be concerned about the future of the Internet's openness: limited competition among service providers; economic incentives to broadband providers whose interests may diverge from the broad interests of consumers in competition and choice; and the explosion of traffic on the Internet.

The FCC's Chairman, though, is categorically against imposing any such rules, which would quickly become outdated, and has instead announced various Internet principles, which can be summarized as: network operators cannot prevent users from accessing the Internet content, applications and services of their choice, nor can they prohibit users from attaching nonharmful devices to the network. As these principles were initially articulated by Chairman Michael Powell in 2004 and later endorsed by the FCC under Chairman Kevin Martin, it appears that the USA has been following a consistent noninterventionist policy as far as the Internet is concerned. The rest of the world appears to follow similar public policy related to this domain, which is dubbed Internet governance. The globalization and convergence of media policy around the world resembles the major American and European deregulatory moves of the 1980s, which spread to other parts of the world (Katz, 2005: 251) and posed fresh challenges to policymakers.

Convergence – the delivery of similar, existing or new media, telephony and Internet services via the same transmission platform – can be present at three different, although interrelated, levels: the technological level (mainly due to the digitization of the broadcasting, IT and telecommunications networks), the structural level (as a consequence of corporate alliances across different sectors) and the services and markets level (the new multimedia services). However, the adoption of a common approach across all sectors seems problematic, for different sectors have developed under different regulatory regimes. Can technological, industrial and market convergence result in regulatory convergence? There are three separate issues related to this question: the merging of regulatory bodies, the growing tendency to rely on competition policy (as a uniform approach) to deliver optimum economic and social efficiency across all converged sectors, and the tendency to pay greatest attention to industrial matters, thereby neglecting the social/cultural aspect of the public interest.

These issues will be subject to further investigation as this book progresses, but to enable a better understanding of them at this stage it may be helpful to sketch the increasing role of the European Union (EU) in media affairs. Since the mid-1980s the EU has attempted to implement a policy of 'Europeanization' (European integration) with regard to the communications industry, with increasing reliance on competition policy and a strong emphasis on industrial policy. Competition policy considerations have included making the media and communications sector competitive not only in the internal European market but also in the global market. In the context of this policy the EU has taken a more favorable stance on mergers and acquisitions between EU firms to allow them to grow and compete at an international level, chiefly with US firms. Meanwhile, this policy has sought to protect European cultural identity, mainly from the 'American challenge', through an essentially remedial policy process imposing rules on TV advertising and programme quotas, the definition of European works to protect cultural and linguistic diversity, copyright protection and protection of minors, to name but a few.

At the same time, industrial policy considerations have included the harmonization of the telecommunications and broadcasting regulatory frameworks (including new digital media) to enable companies to invest across Europe without having to overcome regulatory barriers to entry. The EU has also implemented regulatory reform towards more liberalized and relaxed regimes on the basis of the need of the European continent to remain economically competitive, but the increasing role of the EU in the media field, which primarily takes an economic focus, does not necessarily result in more pluralistic media systems. On the contrary, there is evidence to suggest that the more active competition and industrial policy role of the EU may lead to the resurfacing of a number of sociocultural concerns, including pressure on the finances of public broadcasters and the decline of newspapers, especially in the aftermath of the 2008–2009 financial crisis and the EU's policy to allow member states to tighten subsidy entitlement criteria. The EU's media policies have in some cases (technological convergence, harmonization of rules) led to more choice and more content for consumers as well as new forms of content in terms of production and of consumption, but there are public interest concerns over pluralism, diversity, media consolidation and the survival of the traditional mass media.

Investigating the public interest in relation to the field of study or discipline concerned with normative principles as common denominator

It can also be argued that the notion of the public interest can be defined differently depending on the field of study. While the principles of freedom, inclusiveness, diversity/pluralism form the core of communication rights of the people, these principles are likely to bear different weight when applied to different contexts and situations. For example, the main concerns when it comes to concentration of media ownership are a reduction in political pluralism and cultural diversity (or 'diversity of voice'), whereas the principle of universal service has long governed state intervention in post and telephone services. While all these goals are apparent when referring to other areas, still the tangible issues where journalism makes a real life contribution to democratic and civic life may be slightly different. Referring to the democratic deficit of lost journalism, Barnett (2009) identified the following four areas that primarily need addressing: *informing, representing, campaigning* and *interrogating*.

Citizens need to be kept *informed* about issues such as the economy, crime and the environment in order to understand them fully and participate in their local communities or at national/global level. Such information raises awareness and forms the basis of community knowledge, local identity and individual action. *Representing* is the conveying of citizens' and voters' voices to local and national elites. The role of the media is crucial in facilitating the expression of opinion. *Campaigning* is a more proactive version of representation that encompasses the media as instigators of public interest campaigns. At both local and national levels, newspapers in particular have a tradition of identifying issues relevant to their readers and demanding political action; at national level such campaigns may address broad political issues such as European matters. At the same time, an integral part of the media's contribution is its *interrogating* (watchdog) role, holding public authorities and private corporations to account and conducting independent investigations to uncover wrongdoing (ibid.).

The new media technologies (online, mobile, interactive) that are undermining the long-established business models of traditional media offer journalistic opportunities such as citizen journalism and user-generated material, which provide a greater quantity and wider range of information more widely, as digital optimists have predicted, but there are many areas in which new media present new concerns with regard to the public interest. In the case of the Internet and other online media, suitable broad areas in which the public interest could be considered to operate include defence for intrusion of privacy, crime, health and national security, and harm from defamation. Each field of study has specific dynamics, many of them bound up in prevailing understandings of the social functions of the media. The application of public interest ideals depends on the strategic objectives of specific disciplines/fields. However, the common denominator is the emphasis on particular substantive communication requirements that define the broad public interest, such as pluralism and diversity, freedom of expression and privacy. This suggests that whatever the field of study, media policy is firmly grounded in the political, social and cultural dimensions of communicative processes.

Increased reliance on competition regulation

As briefly stated above, the prevalence of neoliberal ideology has resulted in shifting policy and increased faith in competition rules for tackling matters like media concentration, whereas sector-specific limits on ownership are gradually losing ground. In the USA, a country arguably empowered by the idea of freedom, the FCC under the chairmanship of Michael Powell stated in 2003 that media ownership rules were anachronistic and were at odds with freedom of speech and the freedom to acquire and hold lawful property. This statement echoed the ideas of industry lobbyists, who had been arguing vigorously that the maintenance of ownership rules violated First Amendment freedoms.[2] The previous chapter showed that in the UK the 2003 Communications Act provided for substantial intra-media (within individual media markets) ownership liberalization as well as a reduction in cross-media ownership rules to enable players to expand their activities.

These policy developments were influenced by trends like the shift from vertical (sector-specific) regulation to horizontal regulation as the appropriate means to oversee the converged media and telecommunications industry, and a change from protectionism to the promotion of competition at global level. Former UK Culture Secretary Tessa Jowell expressed her willingness to see ownership regulations reduced, to extend self-regulation and allow the media to depend more on competition law (cited in Freedman, 2008: 116). This shift in regulatory thinking was also influenced by progressive technological convergence, which was blurring the boundaries between different media and telecommunication sectors (see the last section of this volume). In view of this, corporate players are pursuing further relaxation of ownership rules to enable them to be present in various terrains across sectors. Indeed, policy shifts can in large part be attributed to pressures exerted by the corporate interests of groups such as News International and Carlton/Granada. For example, in October 2002, the two big UK independent television companies, Granada and Carlton, agreed a £2.6 billion merger in a bid to combine broadcasting, distribution and production operations in order to combat a downturn in advertising revenue. Competition authorities cleared the merger shortly afterwards.

At the time of writing, and following a referral from regulator Ofcom, competition authorities are investigating News Corporation's £12 billion bid to take total control of satellite broadcaster BSkyB – basically to acquire the 61 per cent of BSkyB it does not already own. The Competition Commission will have to undertake a detailed 'plurality' inquiry into whether News Corporation's common ownership of BSkyB and News International newspapers such as *The Sun, The Times, The Sunday Times* and *News of the World* would threaten media plurality. By subjecting the matter to a 'plurality test' or 'public interest test', the UK authorities are expected to establish whether the bid would result in an excessive concentration of power in the hands of a single media owner. EU competition authorities will also provide a verdict.

But it is not only the area of media concentration that is increasingly subject to competition and antitrust regulation. The Competition Directorate of the European Commission has set up rules concerning various fields, such as the definition of state aid with regard to public service broadcasters (PSBs). The EU has sought to encourage the expansion of television services through the principles of liberalization and harmonization and at the same time attempted to prevent any of the possible undesirable outcomes of an unfettered marketplace (Wheeler, 2004). Therefore, an inherent tension in the EU policy process has been evident, as neoliberal values have come into collision with traditional PSB regimes. These divisions have been played out in the Competition Directorate's issuing of state aid procedures concerning the distortion of markets by PSBs through their receipt of public subsidies (Wheeler, 2010).

The Commission Directorate for competition has also dealt with the acquisition of sports rights. The recognition of sport as an economic activity and the shift from it being pure entertainment justifies the application of competition rules to the sporting industry. In 2003, an EC decision was passed which would end commercial satellite broadcaster BSkyB's monopoly status in the UK television market for live English Premiership football coverage. The EC ruled that from 2006 onwards the rights would have to be sold to at least two broadcasters (EC, 2006). Although BSkyB's stranglehold on live Premier League football has only loosened and not ended, mainly as a result of the collapses of commercial rivals (see Setanta[3]), still the increasing involvement of the EU's competition authorities in national matters is evident.

This involvement is complemented by the prominent role of national competition authorities in determining national policies. In the UK, for example, the Office of Fair Trading (OFT) and the Monopolies and Mergers Commission (MMC, replaced in 1999 by the Competition Commission) have been playing an increasingly important part in television policy. More particularly, in 1999 the MMC prohibited the proposed merger between a broadcaster (BSkyB) and a football club (Manchester United) on the grounds that the outcome would bring reduced competition in the pay-TV market, would damage competition for future TV rights and would adversely affect football 'by reinforcing the trend towards growing inequalities between the larger, richer clubs and the poorer, smaller ones'. More recently, in 2008, the Competition Commission blocked the so-called Kangaroo project,[4] a video-on-demand (VOD) plan by the terrestrial broadcasters BBC, ITV and Channel Four, on the basis that it would 'restrict competition in the supply of VOD services in the country'.

The public interest has been quantified

Another observation is that the public interest has been quantified and increasingly subjected to measurable targets. As van Guilenburg and McQuail (2003) put it, there has been a change from discourse that is guided by the public interest towards one where professional expertise and economic logic underpin aspirations and ideas. Indeed, the exercise of policy has become more complex, technical and pragmatic, preoccupied with matters of market economics rather than with broad principles of sociopolitical theory. Contemporary communications policymaking increasingly involves efforts to systematically assess the impact of individual policies and to test the underlying assumptions upon which individual policies rely (Napoli, 2007).

The 'burden of proof' in the assessment of individual policies has become commonplace. In this sense, there is a subordination of social and cultural beliefs to technological and economic necessity. The UK regulator Ofcom's reports, whether on PSB or on competition policy for sports rights (see below), take a purely fact- or evidence-based approach. This would perhaps be welcome if it meant that value judgments were absent, but policymakers at Ofcom, like those in other regulatory agencies, are not purists; they are instead preoccupied with subjective, political views on broadcasting or competition matters.

With reference to the measurement of media concentration and pluralism in the USA, economy-based criteria have been developed, such as the Concentration Ratios (ratios of the total output of an industry to a given number of firms in the industry) and the Herfindahl-Hirschman Index (HHI) (a measure of the size of firms in relation to the industry and an indicator of the level of competition between them), which run the risk of failing to measure adequately relevant aspects of political culture, art and science, minority opinions, and cultural identity. The connection between plurality of ownership and diversity of content now increasingly depends more on developing quantitative measures around market share issues. Likewise in Europe, the year 2009 witnessed the publication of the *Independent Study on Indicators for Media Pluralism in the EU Member States – Towards a Risk-Based Approach*, which aimed at simplifying the complex issue of pluralism and diversity and putting the results of the research into operation.

This *Independent Study* (2009), which forms part of the European Commission's three-step approach for advancing the debate on media pluralism within the EU, can be perceived as a monitoring tool that includes indicators of a legal, economic and socio-demographic nature. These indicators relate to various risk domains, including media ownership and/or control, media types and genres, political, cultural and demographic pluralism. Thus pluralism could now be proved, quantified and legitimized according to this data. Furthermore, the EC encourages member states to introduce a dual test to ensure that, with regard to public service media, new media services fit within the public service remit. On the one hand, the public value of the new media services must be evaluated, while on the other their potential positive and negative effects on the market should be calculated. On this basis governments would be called upon to approve the launch of new Internet and on-demand services by PSBs.

Attempts to quantify the public interest have been evident elsewhere. As mentioned, in the UK the Communications Act 2003 introduced a new approach to determine media diversity, the so-called *public interest test*[5] or *plurality test*, which applies to major players who wish to increase their interests in other areas of media by buying newspapers, radio or television assets. The test examines whether such a deal would damage the plurality of media voices and owners. Ofcom makes an initial assessment and, if concerns arise (as was the case with New Corporation's bid to take total control of BSkyB), it passes the case to the Competition Commission or Office of Fair Trading for an in-depth examination. In Germany a *three-step test* has been launched, which initially evaluates the contribution of a service to public interest objectives, then assesses the contribution of the service to quality and pluralism, and finally evaluates the cost of the service in terms of its public value and market impact. Likewise, Italy has introduced the *Sistema Integrato Delle Comunicazioni* (Integrated System of Communication, SIC), which defines the communication market too broad, thus making it unlikely that a firm will have a dominant position under this scheme. As Just (2009) noted, this newly introduced communication policy verifies the trend (noticeable on both sides of the Atlantic) toward reduced ownership regulation and the promotion of competition in the digitally converged communications market.

Policy and regulation have been professionalized

While the public interest has been quantified, policy and regulation have been professionalized. In the UK, Ofcom, which was the result of a merger of five regulatory agencies, was set up in December 2003 and since then has been involved in a bewildering range of technically and financially complex telecommunications issues relating to cable, satellite, television, radio, advertising, the Internet and mobile communications. In practice, Ofcom defines and measures PSB; it has asked the BBC to take a more quantified approach to policy and planning, which means that its trustees must more clearly state the sums that are spent, particularly on new digital services. As Tunstall (2010) argues, the emergence of the professional media regulator was exemplified by the careers of four men – Stephen Carter, James Purnell, Ed Richards and Andy Burnham – all four of whom had economics and/or financial expertise. With regard to the BBC they believed that the corporation could be split into defined components, each of which could then be measured. Ofcom's numerous reports are packed with data and statistical tables. Tunstall is convinced that in the Ofcom era PSB has been quantified.

In the same vein, Schlesinger (2009a) points out that think tanks – and other forms of expert group, such as policy advisers and industry players – have contributed significantly to the professionalization of the policy process. Echoing Tunstall, he refers to key individuals who have moved from advocacy in think tanks into positions of strategic influence in the Prime Minister's office, the Department for Culture, Media and Sport (DCMS) and other ministries, Ofcom and the BBC. Schlesinger mentions the careers within the New Labour project of the following figures to prove his point that they have shaped the policy framework in practice: Patricia Hewitt, David Milliband, James Purnell, Geoff Mulgan, Matthew Taylor, Anthony Burnham, Stephen Carter and Ed Richards.

The domination of the policymaking process by advisers who are preoccupied with empirical approaches may result in the marginalization of academics, who typically do not make a *practical* contribution to media policy debates. In situations where empirical approaches outweigh conceptual and normative approaches it is hardly controversial to argue that policy is increasingly formulated by government and industry researchers and the policymaking process dominated by corporate interests. In the past, debates took place in contexts of political dissent and enquiry. As Freedman (2003) recalls, in the UK in the 1970s plans for the restructuring of broadcasting and proposals for the setting-up of a fourth TV channel involved the participation of leading academic figures, but in more recent years there have been far fewer opportunities for academics to intervene in communications policymaking.

The view that contemporary public policy is increasingly driven by an economic and commercial logic is reinforced by an Economic and Social

Research Council-funded study undertaken in 2005 by Freedman. The study argued that UK media policy was centralized and controlled by a small number of advisers and experts (a 'cosy cartel'), while the public remained largely passive in media policy decisions. The study referred to key decisions concerning media ownership and concentration, PSB and the digital switchover, which, despite involving public consultations, were made by industry lobbyists and government insiders occasionally against the wishes of the public. The government's overt reliance on 'hard data' such as economic analysis, even in subjective areas such as public service television, inevitably handed the debate to 'experts'. The call for 'scientific data' was a means of marginalizing the public from the public policy process and safeguarding it for the economists, lawyers and executives who are in a prime position to furnish the sort of information that policymakers are seeking (see Timms, 2005).

The same trends are observable on the other side of the Atlantic. Frieden (2008) noted that the efforts of academia had little influence on the regulatory agency FCC and also generated limited recognition. Instead, the agency displayed a bias toward empirical data and a results-driven decision-making process to support preferred policies. Frieden provides a number of examples to validate his point. First, the FCC established a low bit-rate threshold to support the conclusion that robust high-speed broadband competition exists in the country. Second, the FCC sought to demonstrate that *à la carte* access to cable TV programming would foist higher costs on consumers but later reversed its position, possibly because of reassessment of the political liabilities from its initial findings. Frieden suggested that the FCC could seek out and sponsor peer-review academic research, as it has done recently in assessing the impact of concentrated media ownership (see http://www.fcc.gov/mb/peer_review/peerreview.html, accessed 13 October 2010). This could assist the agency to arrive at more informed decisions, which would better serve the public interest.

Media policymaking at supranational level

A final observation, and central to the theme of this book, is that media policymaking is increasingly taking place at supranational rather than national level as a direct consequence of the trends towards commercialization, globalization, networking and the development of new technologies. Satellite television and the Internet know no boundaries. Internet networks, particularly in the social spaces of the Web 2.0, as exemplified by Twitter, Facebook, YouTube, MySpace and the growing blogosphere, are said to create a global public sphere in which procedures of political representation take place. These new media are essential in fostering social dialogue and providing a vehicle via which the global civil society could move to the forefront of the policy debate (Castells, 2010: 44–5). *Technological capacity* is complemented by *institutional capacity*, referring to reregulation, liberalization and privatization of the rules and procedures adopted by nation-states or supranational bodies to keep control over media and communications activities. At the same time, *organizational capacity* refers to the ability to use networking as a flexible, interactive, borderless form of organization of any activity in any domain (ibid.: 38).

There is now a multiplicity of actors involved in policymaking, alongside nation-state representatives, including corporate interests, global and regional institutions like UNESCO, the WTO and the EU, network users, and nongovernmental actors – be they private sector players or public interest advocacy groups. Nonstate actors can influence public opinion and social policy and foster change through global media and Internet networks. As mentioned in the Introduction, global media policy is not a well defined discipline, as attempts to conceptualize it and define its boundaries began only recently. It is worth mentioning the efforts of the IAMCR[6] Working Group on Global Media Policy, the overall goal of whose ongoing Mapping Global Media Policy Project is to build capacity to understand and act in the ever-changing media policy environment by

- Defining the boundaries of the media policy domain, developing appropriate conceptual frameworks and methodologies, and analyzing emerging trends in media policy where – among other aspects – the relationship of content to process seems to anticipate features of future (possibly more participatory) governance arrangements.
- Establishing an empirical base from which to observe the interplay between actors, issues, levels and sites of media and communication policymaking, taking account of corporate globalization, multilateral politics, the changing role and nature of the nation-state, and the emergence of civil organizations as actors on the world stage.
- Defining the practical challenges posed to all of the actors concerned (policymakers, economic interests, civil organizations, and relevant institutions).

The Mapping Global Media Policy project has developed the following working definition of the term 'global media policy':

> what we refer to as 'global media policy' includes all processes, formal and informal, where actors with different degrees of power and autonomy define and express their interests, produce relevant knowledge and cultural practices, and engage in political negotiation while trying to influence the outcome of decision-making in the domain of media and communication.

Where does this leave the public interest notion? Traditionally, media and communication policy has been driven by the idea of public interest with a distinctive national approach. But as globalization has spread, American and continental Europe's media and telecommunications reregulatory moves to other parts of the world, and as technological convergence is increasingly resulting in global regulatory convergence, the concept of the public interest should be revisited to incorporate these changes. I argued previously that the public interest cannot be treated as a static term. The overarching principles of pluralism/diversity, freedom of expression, access to information, choice, accountability, and so on, remain relevant, but they need to be dealt with in the light of new developments, such as channel abundance, commercialization, globalization and the development of the Internet and various new media. Meanwhile, the growth of the Internet, with its global reach, and the resulting networked environment brings to the fore new issues such as safeguarding the privacy of personal data and information, decency, copyright of digital content and so on. It follows that policies 'in the public interest' should look at an increasingly global domain that cuts across local, regional, national and transnational fields.

It was William Melody who, as early as 1990, looked at media policy from an international perspective and posed the question of a global public interest.[7] Two decades later we are yet to develop an appropriate model of communication governance that would define the public interest with respect to global media. An inherent problem has been that the idea of 'regulation' and the principle of 'freedom' have always been considered contradictory. The situation has become increasingly complex in the digital, converged environment characterized by a multiplicity of actors, the prominence of neoliberal logic and the prevalence of corporate interests. While it may be difficult to identify a unified global public interest, one can observe the existence of interweaving media organizations, politics, technologies and citizenship taking place on an increasingly global scale, with different patterns of inclusion and exclusion.

What lies ahead

To sum up, this trilogy has shown that the role of regulation should be to preserve and promote the public interest, which is a universal value. Throughout the last four decades or so there has been some form of national (and more recently international) regulation in the sphere of communication. Raboy (no date) points out that, in the new media environment, regulation will have to be negotiated among a range of actors, including the nation-state and corporate and civil society representatives. As will be shown in the next section of this book, the contemporary media and communications system is simultaneously local and global, meaning that the nation-state continues to be the main location where media policy and regulation debates take place, but the emerging new environment involves a process of global governance (without, however, a global government). As

Castells (2010: 45) put it, we live in a globalized, interdependent world, so the space of political co-decision is necessarily global. The new environment incorporates global governance institutions and organizations such as the United Nations Educational Scientific and Cultural Organization (UNESCO), the World Trade Organization (WTO), the International Telecommunications Union (ITU), the Organization for Economic Cooperation and Development (OECD), multilateral groups and supranational bodies such as the World International Property Organization (WIPO) and the Internet Corporation for Assigned Names and Numbers (ICANN), as well as regional bodies such as the European Union (EU) and European Broadcasting Union (EBU) or regional trade accords like the North American Free Trade Agreement (NAFTA). These multilateral groups have an increasing say in policy definition and enforcement alongside the nation-state. The involvement of these fora requires the reframing and refocusing of traditional communication policy issues. It is to this area that I now turn my attention.

Part II

Global Communication Theories and the Nation-State

4
Global Communication Paradigms

Introduction

In order to describe the relations between the local, the national and the global one needs to look at the various theories to trace established ways of how thinkers have approached the issue. This chapter provides a brief historical account of global communication and an assessment of the various paradigms that have dominated the field in the past half-century or so: modernization theory; cultural or media imperialism; critical political economy and cultural studies; media globalization. The short sections on the theories of modernization, cultural imperialism, political economy and cultural studies are followed by an analysis of the cultural, economic and political dimensions of globalization, which has become a catchphrase of scholars, politicians and media regulators.

There is a growing body of research on the phenomenon of globalization, but this chapter will examine the topic from the perspective of the media and communications. The main objective of this chapter is to contribute to the understanding of the evolution of global information flows by summarizing the key field of study of global communications. At the same time the work aims to prepare the reader for an assessment of the impact of globalization on national media policymaking, which will be the focus of the next chapter. My approach to the subject of media and communications policy derives from the presumption that the nation-state should retain a significant role in the terrain of global policy.

Modernization theory

Traditionally the discipline of international communication has been dominated by the national considerations (Chalaby, 2007). The discipline's first paradigm, modernization theory, emerged in the 1950s to describe the then modern transformations of social life. This evolutionary theory asserts that underdeveloped nations can 'modernize' and develop to the same extent as 'modern' countries. Modernization theorists aim to identify the sociopolitical variables that lead to societal development and seek to explain the process of social change by looking at social and cultural structures and the application of new technologies. They view traditions as obstacles to economic growth and see radical shifts in cultural and religious institutions and habits as means to economic growth and prosperity. In his classic study in the field, *The Passing of Traditional Society*, Lerner (1958) examined how people in the Middle East coped with the growing irrelevance of their traditional ways and adopted new forms of social organization. Lerner closely associated the process of 'modernization' with 'Westernization', by which he meant adopting the secularization and rationalization characteristics of Western Europe and the USA.

The author pointed to two sets of problems that confront the development process: *mobility*, referring to the problems of societal dynamism; and *stability*, meaning the problems of societal equilibrium. His central thesis was that only insofar as individuals change their place in the world, their position in society and their own self-image does societal change occur. Lerner identified as key motors of modernization the media of radio and television, which bring fresh and different ideas to all classes of people. In fact, at the heart of modernization theories is the notion that communication is used to diffuse the message of modernity and transfer Western political and economic models to the newly independent countries of the global south (Thussu, 2010: 2). According to Lerner, the mass media can be used to mobilize people by the rational articulation of new possibilities and, flanked by schools and community leaders, can simultaneously induce a new process of socialization among the rising generation.

The applicability of the Western model of development to less developed countries was also celebrated in Schramm's work. In his 1964 study *Mass Media and National Development* the scholar advocated an integration of mass media with local activity, although in a later self-criticism (Schramm, 1979) he admitted that he should perhaps have paid more attention to the social requirements and uncertainties of development, and in particular the cultural differences that make development almost necessarily different from culture to culture, country to country. In his 1979 study Schramm acknowledged that developing countries have come to realize how history-specific the Western model was, as it was tailored to a situation considerably different from those of, say, India or Ecuador, which were types that he focused on. In fact, modernization theory has been subject to much criticism from both communist and capitalist thinkers, as well as world systems theorists, who assert that the adoption of Western values by developing countries is likely to bring about social disorganization and personal discontentment.

Although modernization theory has lost much of its appeal and prominence among academics, Chalaby (2007: 64) stresses that the paradigm remains popular in development circles and that various United Nations agencies and nongovernmental organizations are involved in projects in the developing world incorporating information and communication technologies.

Not surprisingly, modernization theory influenced many of the debates that took place in 2003, and again in 2005, when the international community was called upon to take part in a World Summit on the Information Society (WSIS) (see Chapter 6). This two-phase United Nations summit placed an unprecedented global spotlight on information and communication issues. In their 2005 study *Civil Society, Communication and Global Governance*, Raboy and Landry provided a portrait of the players, structures and themes of the WSIS, as well as a critical analysis of the summit's first phase, the issues it raised and the groundbreaking role, in raising awareness, played by civil society. According to the authors, modernization theory informed a great deal of the debates during these international deliberations.

Cultural imperialism theory

This theory asserts that a handful of 'advanced' nations dominate the global economic system, leaving 'peripheral' countries with little control over their social, political and economic progress. Much of the basic analysis of the concept of media or cultural imperialism is indebted to the works of Marx, Lenin and Rosa Luxemburg (see Boyd-Barrett, 1977). The central argument is that the production and consumption of goods and services is becoming increasingly unified because of the capitalist mode of production and the standardized way of producing commodities. Major corporations and trading relations are seen to be promoting capitalist and Western cultural values. The Marxist analysis of imperialism was revisited by academics in the 1970s wanting to examine the dependence of postcolonial states on previous imperial powers within a context of post-Second World War US dominance. Political independence had to be assessed within a framework of continuing economic and cultural dependence – through education, ideas, media language – not simply on specific ex-imperial power, but on a US-dominated capitalist world order (Boyd-Barrett, 2010: 139–40).

Boyd-Barrett (ibid.) claims that there are two principal models of media imperialism, both generated by scholars in the 1970s. The first, emerging in Latin America by Mattelart (1979) but also US academic Schiller (1976), understood media imperialism in terms of its functions of selling culturally related US software and hardware, promoting an image of the USA and of the world that was favorable to American interests, and of advertising American goods and services. Schiller located media imperialism in the continuing US dominance across time and space. Schiller's 1969 book *Mass Communications and American Empire* made a case for an international movement towards the commercialization of broadcasting driven by the rise of the US entertainment, communications and information industries.

Likewise, Latin American scholar Mattelart argued that first-world econo-mies, led by the USA, stunted the development of those in the third world. These studies coincided with the publication of Tunstall's seminal work *The Media are American* (1977), which, despite acknowledging the existence of some important centers of independent production, nevertheless explored a broader Anglo-American wind of influence. However, in his later work *The Media Were American* Tunstall (2007a) argued that in recent years the US media had been in decline.

Boyd-Barrett (2010) identified an alternative model of media imperialism, developed in Europe, and called it the 'generic' model. The generic model of media imperialism was rooted in Marxist theory, which interpreted capi-talism as a 'homogenizing cultural force' (see Tomlinson, 2002: 228). Yet, according to Fejes (1981: 283), it would be a mistake to label this approach Marxist in any detailed and precise sense of the word. While the motivation and sources behind the work on media imperialism are varied, such work can be better understood, both as a research approach and as a theoretical endeavor, by putting it in the larger context of the work and thinking done on the questions and problems of third-world development in general.

Boyd-Barrett (2010) also argued that Marxist theory interpreted capital-ism as the process of media colonialism. The processes of colonialism ena-bled Western cultures to impose their values on people in the less developed continents of Asia, Africa and the Americas. The discourse of colonization was based upon the cultural superiority of the 'West over the Rest', and the Western notions of economic progress and liberal democracy frequently provided the benchmarks against which other cultures were supposed to measure their sense of being (Hall, 1992). Broadly speaking, though, cul-tural imperialism refers to the situation where a foreign culture invades an indigenous one.

Like modernization theory, the cultural imperialism paradigm lost much of its appeal as an analytical tool. The main reasons were the capitalist rhetoric and the reregulatory developments of the 1980s, the emergence of the 'tiger economies' of Southeast Asia, and the decline of the communist East, all of which fed a scepticism as to the validity of imperialism (and dependence) theories, which, alongside the significant increases in media production within some developing nations (see Tunstall, 2007), popula-tion mobility and the intensification of trade, disguised 'the inevitability of global concentration behind a smokescreen of local proliferation' (Boyd-Barrett, 2010: 152).

Sparks (2007: 126) noted that the imperialism paradigm had been replaced by the concept of globalization as the prevailing way of thinking about glo-bal media. But unlike modernization theory, the concept of cultural impe-rialism can still be considered relevant, for it incorporates some of the key issues of globalization theory, including hybridism (the emergence of new transcultural models resulting from colonization) and the weakening role of the nation-state. Furthermore, the cultural imperialism thesis is close to cultural globalization theory, which argues that media globalization is not necessarily leading to the homogenization of global culture under the auspices of Western consumerism (see section on globalization below).

Critical political economy paradigm

Within the domain of political economy, *critical political economy* takes a different stance than *classical political economy*, the former providing a critique of the impact of market mechanisms and the economy on society and the latter considering market forces as a positive trend, offering enhanced choice for consumers (Harrison, 2006). Since its inception in the 1970s, the critical political economy approach has been concerned with the structural development of the media under capitalism. It focuses on themes such as media growth and power, the expansion of corporate reach and influence, and the trends toward media privatization, commercialization and reregulation. The central thesis of the theory is that there exist dominant economic structures in the media and communication sectors that impact negatively on the range of views and opinions disseminated by the media. As a result, what prevails in a given society is a hegemonic set of ideas, or put another way a 'dominant ideology'.

Critical political economy asserts that privately owned media are instruments of class domination whose purpose is to maintain the status quo. A key text illustrating the arguments for this stance is Herman and Chomsky's *Manufacturing Consent* (1988), which argues that the American news media conform to a 'propaganda model', incorporating five filters that determine news content, ownership, funding, flak, and sources and ideologies. Some scholars have criticized this model on the grounds that ownership, as a dominant factor, does not necessarily determine news content, as

> owners, advertisers, and key political personnel [...] cannot always do as they wish [because] they operate within structures which constrain as well as facilitate, imposing limits as well as offering opportunities [and] analyzing the nature and sources of these limits is a key task for a critical political economy of the future. (Golding and Murdock, 1991: 16)

Herman and Chomsky have defended the validity of their model by arguing that it focuses on media behavior rather than media effects (see Herman, 1996, 2000). In a broader perspective, critical political economy attempts to incorporate historical and contextual aspects, without, however, underestimating the significance of vested interests and other commercial considerations in media production and consumption. According to Flew (2007: 31), the political economy theory relates to the rediscovery of the Marxist stance on capitalism, which connected this critique of media in liberal-democratic societies to a wider conceptual understanding of the bases of social order in class-divided societies. In this perspective, the theory asserts that developments in international media could be understood as one dimension of the transformation of contemporary capitalism.

In his classic study in the field, *The Political Economy of Communication*, Mosco (1996) argued that the tradition of political economy puts emphasis on three issues: an analysis of historical transformations and social shifts; an examination of the social world as a whole, in which the media occupy a large part; and the promotion of social values and the democratization of media systems. So, from a critical political economy stance, the role of the media in global capitalism needs to be viewed from an angle which combines historical, structural, political and cultural criticism.

First, the media should be assessed in the context of the broad developments and processes of capitalism: systemic crises such as the recession of the mid-1970s or the 2008–2009 economic slowdown; the production of new types of commodity and endless commercialization; the growth of multinational corporations; advances in technology, marketing and advertising, which reduce the time between production and consumption.

Second, a structural analysis of the media – political economy's core theme – is needed to get a grasp of the changing institutional arrangements of the media sectors as a result of mergers, acquisitions, joint ventures, and other types of integration and amalgamation that could lead to high levels of concentration of media ownership and threaten political pluralism and cultural diversity. Garnham (1995) referred to structures of domination based upon class relations and argued that political economy views class (the structure of access to the means of production and distribution) as the main reason to the structure of domination. Political economists have called for a transformation of the media and their underlying structures to make them more open and accountable. Murdock and Golding (2000) provided a critique of the changing balance between public and commercial media, the reduction of government regulation, and the 1980s/1990s privatization of state-owned media and telecommunications enterprises.

Third, the role of the media in global capitalism should be informed by an understanding of the cultural issues that result from the economic logic of media commercialization. This, according to Ampuja (2004: 73–4), requires a renewed focus on commodification and consumerism, two phenomena that formed the main target of the Frankfurt School's critique of the culture industry. Strange (1988) and Flew (2007: 32) have added another element: critical political economy must be *global*, as the insistence upon a global perspective has been central to the development of the theory.

Cultural studies theory

Cultural studies and political economy as competitors

Cultural studies have primarily been concerned with questions of cultural power and the issue of how cultural forms develop, disseminated and interpreted through media and communications. Like political economy, cultural studies constitute a critical alternative to mainstream media sociology and an attempt to understand social reality derived from critical theory. Cultural theorist Raymond Williams (1980) sought to identify dominant forces in the media and cultural domains and argued that cultural practice by groups such as state administrators and media professionals has a close connection with the dominant culture of a given society.

However, cultural studies and political economy have frequently considered each other as competitors, rather than allies. The differences between the two paradigms have revolved around the question of how to articulate developments in the economic and cultural spheres. The debates between scholars representing the two disciplines have been fierce and focused on whether one theory overemphasizes the economic sphere (cultural studies' criticism of political economy) or the cultural sphere (political economy's criticism of cultural studies) (see Grossberg, 1991, 1996; Garnham, 1995).

Grossberg (1991) has summarized cultural studies' key criticisms of political economy as follows: its denial of the specificity of cultural practices; its focus on the economic base of cultural texts and their monolithic interpretation as merely commodities; and the lack of study of media reception. Barker (2000) notes that the cultural studies discipline has gained much prominence and become a mainstream in media research by denying economic reductionism and instead looking at a broad range of issues – culture, representation, consumption, language. During the 1980s and 1990s there were several key cultural studies of media, which broadly examined the process of encoding/decoding media messages and texts (Morley, 1980, 1992; Hall, 1982; Fiske, 1987; Ang, 1991). However, the discipline has been criticized for overlooking the issue of how the economy and the state shape cultural production and for the way in which it represents the relationship between media power, policy and culture.

Structuralism and culturalism

One can detect two dominant paradigms within the realm of cultural studies: 'structuralism', mainly influenced by the works of Althusser (1971) and Levi-Strauss (1958), stressing the determination of consciousness and communications by economic, political and social frameworks; and 'culturalism', influenced by scholars such as Williams (1962), referring to culture as a relatively autonomous practice. As Jensen (2002) notes, the work of Gramsci on hegemony bridged the gap between these two paradigms.

Gramsci, a leading Marxist thinker, used the term hegemony to denote the predominance of one social class over others. Like Althusser, he rejected 'economism', insisting on the independence of ideology from economic determinism, but at the same time he was sceptical of crude materialism and focused on human subjectivity in an attempt to offer a humanistic version of Marxism.

Cultural policy

Flew (2007: 47–50) noted that in recent years there has been a rethinking of how to understand state agencies in connection with global media, influenced by institutional theories and cultural policy studies, an emerging field especially in Australia, where it is informed by scholars such as Stuart Cunningham (1992), Tony Bennett (1992) and Lewis and Miller (2003). Cultural policy theorists have introduced more institutionally oriented and pragmatic directions than cultural studies advocates by undertaking critical, policy-focused analyses of cultural institutions. These theorists have identified opportunities for cultural politics that can impact upon government agencies and institutions.

With regard to these slippery issues and propositions about the differences between various theories, the nature of media commodities, and the main features of media policy, Flew (2007: 50) made a couple of points that could help to put things into perspective. First, 'by demanding a more institutionally delineated and context-sensitive understanding of state capacities in the cultural sphere, cultural policy studies have drawn attention to the need to recognize the agency and capacity for independent initiative on the part of policy-makers'. Although more often than not cultural policy is not formally defined, the introduction of the agency has made cultural policy more explicitly defined through a formal process. For instance, a ministry of culture or arts agency might draft a policy articulating its goals and operating principles in supporting theatre companies in various regions (see http://www.wwcd.org/policy/policy.html, accessed 12 December 2010). Second, 'the cultural policy studies perspective remains resolutely national, and in doing so is reflective of both its roots in cultural studies traditions that have tended to be national, and the focus of policy studies upon the nation-state as the primary focus of decision-making' (Flew, 2007: 50).

In fact, all the theories examined so far understand media and communications from a national perspective and largely neglect the global element. But before analyzing in more detail the relationship between the local and the global (between the nation-state and global forces) in media decision-making, let me turn my focus to the theory of globalization, which heralded the shift away from a nation-centric approach towards a post-national perspective and an international remapping of media spaces.

Media globalization

Globalization broadly refers to the spread and interconnection of production, communication and technology across the globe. When considering the concept of globalization most scholars are quick to make references to Marshall McLuhan's metaphor of the 'global village' (see McLuhan, 1964) or to more recent views of the global 'network society' developed by Manuel Castells (1996). What characterizes the phenomenon of globalization is the spread and speed of communication and cultural exchange, the complexity of the networks and corporations involved, and the huge volume of trade, interaction and risk. Although most references about globalization relate to economic issues and processes (for example, the focus on international trade and the mobility of capital), the term is also used to describe a wide array of technological, political, social, cultural and environmental practices.

There are many different definitions, classifications and meanings of globalization, informing the debate in different ways depending on the theoretical stance of the researchers – whether they are global-enthusiasts (for example, Castells, 1996) or global-sceptics (for example, Hirst and Thompson, 1996) – although some appear to be neither strong supporters of media globalization nor fierce opponents. One such is Scholte (2000, 2005) whose thesis, as a reviewer (Shaw, 2000) put it, can be termed global-transformationist. In reviewing the relevant literature, Scholte found five broad definitions of globalization.

First, globalization can be viewed as internationalization, simply describing cross-border relations between nations and the growth in international exchange and interdependence. But globalization should not be confused with internationalization, for it is in fact something different: while internationalization refers to the increasing importance of trade, relations, cultural alliances and treaties between nations, globalization reflects the economic, cultural and technological integration of various national sectors into a global one.

Second, globalization is equated to liberalization, referring to the process of relaxing or abolishing government-imposed restrictions on media products and services for the purposes of establishing an open, borderless world economy. True, liberalization, reregulation and privatization in the media and telecommunications industries gained momentum in Europe and other parts of the world through foreign investment from mostly American companies, but the corporate expansion enabled by these trends is but one aspect of globalization.

Third, globalization can be seen as universalization, referring to the process of spreading media technologies across the universe, but again this is a narrow definition of globalization that neglects sociocultural and political aspects. A fourth definition of globalization offered by Scholte equates it with Westernization or modernization – a dynamic process whereby modern social structures such as capitalism, rationalism, industrialism and bureaucratism are spread to all parts of the world, thereby influencing local cultures. But globalization is something more than modernization or Westernization (or mere market liberalization, as stated above), for it puts greater emphasis on international integration and stresses the powerful effects of the free flow of resources, information, individuals and services across national boundaries.

Fifth, globalization can be viewed as deterritorialization, whereby social space is no longer defined in terms of territorial spaces, distances and borders. It is in fact this last concept of supra-territoriality that, according to Scolte, provides a comprehensive definition of the phenomenon of globalization, for it allows the exploration of shifts in the ways people understand and experience social space (see also Giddens, 1990 and Held et al., 1999).

The globalist thesis incorporates technological change and the rise of transnational corporations (TNCs) with internationally dispersed production and distribution facilities (see Table 4.1 for a list of media conglomerates). McChesney (1999) argued that a few TNCs have stakes in many types of media, ranging from newspapers to television and the Internet and located in different parts of the world. Sparks (2007) made reference to the growth of supranational organizations and the rise of entrepreneurs like Bill Gates (Microsoft), Rupert Murdoch (News Corporation) and Steve Jobs (Apple) as distinct characteristics that underlie the most prominent theories of globalization. In his globalization theory, Sparks also mentioned the absence of controlling power, with multiple production centers and complex programme flows, regional markets, and the emergence of global 'hybridized' media products.

Alongside the role of new technologies, globalization is associated with economic dependency and the diminishing role of national economies, which have been transformed to the extent that they now share their sovereignty with bodies responsible for global governance and international law.

Table 4.1   Global communications conglomerates, 2004–2008 (in US$ billion)

World ranking by media turnover	2004–2005	2008–2009
Time Warner (1)	42.1	47.0
Walt Disney (2)	30.3	37.8
News Corporation (3)	23.9	30.4
NBC Universal (4)	12.9	17.0
Bertelsmann (5)	17.0 (euros)	16.1 (euros)
Viacom (6)	8.1	14.6
CBS Corporation (7)	14.1	14.0
Sony (8)	N/A	7.9

Source: Information gathered from various market reports.

Culturally, globalization is said to result in the decline of national cultures, the spread of Westernization and, globally, more homogenized cultures (see Robertson, 1995),[1] whereas politically nation-states are seen to be superseded by international organizations like the World Trade Organization, United Nations and International Monetary Fund, global social movements, or even global civil society (see Keane, 2001; Martell et al., 2001).

Manning (1999: 138) summarized the different aspects of globalism as follows: while *cultural globalization* generally refers to the spread of Western ideas, values and cultural practices to the rest of the world, *economic globalization* refers to the expansion of international trade and investment and *political globalization* to the organization of transnational governmental and regulatory institutions and the diffusion of liberal political ideology and institutional forms.

The media have been instrumental in the creation of the new globalized environment characterized by free trade and the free flow of information, technological advancement and technologically mediated communication, and new institutional arrangements. As mentioned above, the complexity of the media networks and communications corporations involved in the global scene and the speed of their expansion on an international scale is unprecedented. This has put pressure on the current regulatory framework, which is thought to be inadequate to address issues such as the shift in state sovereignty to the international level in media regulation resulting from increased trade and new technologies, and there are increasing calls to reform it.

As Raboy (2007) put it,

> [T]here is a sense that we are witnessing the emergence of a global media system which appears to elude control, unlike the national media systems where the rules governing the media were clearer. Media issues are increasingly transnational, hence require international interventions and fresh regulatory mechanisms of various types to shape them and drive their development and social responsibilities.

The identification of the main features of global media policy and regulation will form the basis of later chapters.

Conclusion: the national versus the global media system as the lead player

It can be seen that the media have been influential in globalizing processes in contemporary societies and that media globalization challenges assumptions about the relationship between territory, politics and culture. There are many, though, who sound a note of considerable caution about theories of globalization in relation to the media, among them Tunstall (2007b), who argues that the strength of media globalization today has been exaggerated and that it is the national level that remains most important. Tunstall reminds us that the flood of globalization books began in the late 1990s – a time when US media dominated the world and Ted Turner and CNN[2] were widely quoted as pioneers of news globalization – but even during that era of supposed 'media globalization' Hollywood and the US media were losing market share because of a huge growth in national media output that had been taking place since the 1980s. Tunstall writes that the national issue prevails and that national media are closely linked to national education systems, to national languages, to national political power and to national culture. 'Most people prefer to be informed and entertained by people who look, talk, joke and think much like themselves' (ibid.: 323).

In an attempt to challenge the validity of media globalization theory, Flew (2007) noted that the presence of global media corporations in national markets does not always make them dominant in these markets, for empirical evidence suggests that there are only a few, most notably News Corporation, that have the ability to draw upon networks and institutional relations in a range of countries and therefore could be considered 'global' corporations in the countries where they operate. Flew (2007) developed a number of counterarguments to the thesis of media globalization. He urged that there was a need to rethink the relationship between communications media, the nation-state and cultural policy. He made a case for a twenty-first-century model of the *enabling state*, where the role of governmental authorities is increasingly promotional and informative, working with complex networks of nongovernmental authorities and agencies. Flew nevertheless challenged the idea that the modern state (the enabling state) still has the control over media flows within its territory that the *regulatory and protective state* used to have in the previous century. As will be shown in the next chapter, the notion of the *enabling state* or *managerial state* has been picked up by other scholars, such as Gray (2000), and by international organizations like the United Nations Development Programme (UNDP, 1997). This discussion is very much associated with the shift from *government* to so-called *governance*.

Close examination of the role the nation-state occupies in today's globalized media world is crucial in order to analyze global changes in media policy, evaluate the changing course of national media policymaking, and explore the effects of global technological, political, economic and cultural processes. True, globalization signifies the emergence of a system of global relations and processes not present in the traditional system of nation-states, meaning that many contemporary issues cannot be adequately addressed at the national level. General examples include social movements that spread ideas such as universal human rights, global environmental responsibility and the call for democracy across the world, while specific examples in the media and communications domain include the rise of TNCs, the rapid growth of the Internet, and broadcasting by satellite, all operating independently of national borders. While state-centrism might no longer be acceptable and the state might not be the only unit of analysis in the modern age, still national policies matter for the media and communications processes, the formation of national identity and the development of national citizenship. The complex local–global dichotomy is investigated in more depth in the next chapter.

5
Globalization and the Nation-State

Introduction

Conventional wisdom views the phenomenon of globalization as the development of a stateless world; put another way, it is a fashionable mantra that calls for the diminishing role or even 'death' of the state. Much of the debate on globalization within media and communication studies has focused on the consequences of the forces of globalization on the relevance of national policymaking. On the one hand are those who assert that technological developments in the form of technological convergence and digitization, the increased reach of corporate interests, and the expanded role of international organizations are challenging the ability of national governments to oversee their domestic media industries. Specifically, proponents of this argument see reduced national government power and ability to regulate as synonymous with the shift from *government* to *governance*, which denotes a change from a unified policy exercised by the national government to a more complex system, encompassing a number of policy actors and political institutions.

On the other hand, there are those who claim that nation-states retain key policy instruments to dictate the future of their cultural assets and are able to achieve most of their policy objectives. Another view states that governments remain the dominant policy actors as they are tasked to *manage* and *orchestrate* changes (rather than control them), *coordinate* policies and offer *consensus* (rather than imposing it), *enable* and *facilitate* developments (through, for example, the provision of a regulatory framework and political order), and ensure *accountability* of the market in a period of rapid technological and social change.

Undeniably, public policy (including media policy) in a globalized world is informed by various actors, although three stand out: the *state* (core executive), the *market* (private/business actors including the media) and *civil society* (voluntary and community sector actors). Nonstate actors like individuals, scientific networks, journalists and nongovernmental organizations

(NGOs) also contribute greatly to the shaping of the agenda for global public policy. Searching for a theoretical basis on which to interpret various phenomena related to policy, governance and the media, this chapter borrows ideas from political science. After all, public policy, in which media policy is a major component, is a subfield of political science (as it is commonly known in North America), or politics (as it is more usually known in Europe and elsewhere). Political scientists deal with issues such as public policy, the allocation and transfer of power in decision-making, and the systems of governance encompassing governments and international institutions, all of them relevant to the themes investigated here.

The chapter provides stimulation for further study rather than a comprehensive analysis of the state v. globalization theme. It starts by outlining the typologies of national political and media systems and reviewing models such those of Hallin and Mancini (2004), Bardoel (2007), Baldi and Hasebrink (2007) and Jakubowicz (2007). It then moves on to reviewing works of political scientists (among others, Rhodes, 1994, 2007; Gamble, 2000; Gray, 2000; and Skelcher, 2000) that discuss the question of the diminishing power of the government to rule. In this context it explores the influence of supranational organizations like the European Union (EU)[1] on national policymaking, the impact on power flows of the trends toward privatization of previously state-owned industries, and the growing reliance of quasi-governmental and private institutions to shape public services. The main question to address is whether the rise of the market, civil society and other actors have led to a more modest role of the national state in initiating and implementing policy.

While acknowledging the interplay between states and global forces in policymaking (the work accepts that the shift from *government* to *governance* has been facilitated by the rise of intergovernmental agencies, which increasingly influence global media policy bodies), this chapter contributes to this debate by suggesting that the power of the nation-state to regulate is still visible. The role of nation-states continues to be important, not only within their own boundaries but also as facilitators of transnational processes. In addition, the power of the state is evidenced by the significant role it plays in periods of financial crisis (like the recent 2008–2009 global economic slowdown), to the point that free-market press claim the return of 'state capitalism'.

Political systems

In political science the state can be perceived as a political and administrative entity that not only contains formal structures of governance but also considers social welfare issues, forms cultural identities and constructs collective psychologies. The sovereign state, as it was conceived at the Treaty of Westphalia in 1648,[2] is not an isolated entity as it is composed of political, social and economic interests. Gellner (1983) noted that the formation of nation-states is the inevitable outcome of industrialization, with its complex division of labor. What is more, the state is not sociopolitically neutral, for it often represents the forces that are in power. As succinctly put by Nordenstreng and Lanham (2001: 224), the state is ideologically biased, which is seen as fundamentally opposed to the ideals of freedom and democracy.

The sense of national community is created by various institutions, as well as by the collective consumption of mediated communication. The media and telecommunications are effective tools for governance, especially in the old days when they were virtual monopolies, setting rules in accordance with the sociopolitical, cultural and geographical environments of nations. This is evident in works like that of Morris and Waisbord (2001), which includes national contributions from both developed and developing territories, such as Canada, Australia, the EU, Korea and India.

But of course it all depends on the types of power one refers to and the governance arrangements that are the product of a given society. The balance of power between the state, the market, and the public differs from region to region, country to country. Before looking at the different political systems and their governance arrangements, especially in relation to the media, it is worth noting that the principle of freedom of expression makes it difficult to develop workable governance arrangements. State intervention to ensure and promote the public interest may at first sight seem justifiable when, for instance, it defends a diverse media ownership structure, albeit limiting high concentration, which may restrict political and cultural diversity. Some may argue that speech can be limited for the sake of other liberal values, particularly the concern for democratic equality and human dignity, and opposition to racism, child pornography and obscenity, and perhaps for the regulation of commercial 'speech' like advertising. These are but a few examples of limitations on free speech that could balance rights to free speech.

However, the notions of governance and freedom of expression appear contradictory when one considers that free speech should be at the forefront of liberal democracies. Mill (1978: 16) defended strongly the principles of free speech and free expression and argued that *any* doctrine should be allowed to be heard no matter *how* immoral it may seem to everyone else. Such liberty should exist with every subject matter so that we have 'absolute freedom of opinion and sentiment on all subjects, practical or speculative, scientific, moral or theological' (ibid.: 11). Most legislative regimes at national level guarantee freedom of speech and the freedom of the press, like the First Amendment in the USA, adopted as early as 1791. In fact, the Supreme Court has extended the protection of the First Amendment to the Internet and, despite attempts from Congress to regulate the content of the Internet, for example with the Child Online

Protection Act of 1998,[3] the Court has ruled that any limitations on the Internet are unconstitutional. Likewise, the European Convention on Human Rights of 1950,[4] which has been adopted by all members of the Council of Europe, guarantees a broad range of human rights, including the right to freedom of expression. In short, it could be said that legal prohibitions to limit freedom of speech are at least contentious.

Returning to political systems, there have been various attempts to classify political and media systems according to types of power, people participation, accountability and so on. Hallin and Mancini (2004) proposed a framework for comparative analysis of the relation between the media and the political system. Building on a survey of media institutions in a number of European and North American democracies, the authors attempted to identify the main dimensions of variation in media systems and the political variables that had shaped their evolution. They identified three major models of media system development: the *liberal* model, relying on an individualistic concept of representation and implemented in countries such as the UK, USA, Canada and Ireland; the *Polarized Pluralist* model, with a considerable degree of politicization, state interference and clientelism, to be found mainly in Mediterranean territories; and the *Democratic Corporatist* model, based on the role of organized civic groups, observed in the Scandinavian countries, Germany, Austria, the Netherlands and Switzerland. Despite its Western focus and the neglect of Eastern European countries, this comparative analysis in political communication provides a key theoretical statement about the relation between media and political systems, and a good overview of the variety of media institutions that have developed in the West.

The limitation of Hallin and Mancini's model (the exclusion of Eastern European countries) is addressed by Jakubowicz (2007: 303–13), who proposes a further political and media system model, the so-called *Post-Communism* model, to include nations in the following regions: Central Europe (Poland, the Czech Republic, Hungary and so on), Eastern Balkans (Romania, Bulgaria), Western Balkans (Croatia, Serbia, Albania and so on), European Commonwealth of Independent States (CIS) (Russia, Ukraine, Belarus and Moldova), South Caucasus (Armenia, Azerbaijan, Georgia), Central Asia (for example, Kazakhstan and Uzbekistan) and Mongolia. Jakubowicz acknowledges that these countries vary widely in many respects – history, culture, religion, level of development – but the significant thing they have in common is the legacy of the communist system. Parallels with the systems identified by Hallin and Mancini may be sought given that these cases identify precisely political system development as the main factor affecting the shape of the media system, including in particular countries of the former Soviet block (ibid.: 304). Jakubowicz's model highlights the dynamic aspect of media systems, which differentiates it from the largely static model developed by Hallin and Mancini.

In an effort to show that there is convergence and overlapping between different media policy models and governance structures, Bardoel (2007) combines the above national media governance mechanisms into two groups: the *Liberal and Corporatist* models; and the *Mediterranean and Post-Communist* models. Bardoel suggests that the decisive distinction between these groups is the difference between old and young democracies, with, respectively, a strong and weak legislative authority and the presence/ absence of a well developed public sphere and civil society. Furthermore, he notices a difference between the Protestant cultures of northwest Europe, with strong Enlightenment roots and individualistic reading traditions, and the Catholic cultures of southern and eastern Europe, with roots in the Counter-Reformation and more collective cultures and stronger image cultures and viewing habits. However, such a broad distinction and simplification of models presents problems, such as the erroneous assumption that southern European countries share a Catholic culture (for example, Greece has a Christian Orthodox culture).

Another important distinction between European countries has been suggested by Baldi and Hasebrink (2007), who argued that national systems could be divided as follows: *most-advanced* countries, like the UK, Germany, the Netherlands, the Scandinavian region and Ireland; *Less-advanced* countries, such as France, Italy, Spain and Greece; and *Under-construction* nations, comprising all the post-Communist countries. This typology is similar to that of Hallin and Mancini, while at the same time it borrows elements of Jakubowicz's more dynamic model in that it introduces the development or progress issue. However, the shortfalls are that it might be misleading to put in the same cluster countries such as the UK and Ireland, which have different levels of economic development. By the same token, it might be unwise to label both France and Greece as 'less-advanced countries', as France's economic and market situation is far more advanced than that of Greece.

In short, no 'perfect' or 'ideal' typologies of national political and media systems have been developed, though the attempt to assess the analogies and differences between media policy systems is certainly useful in order to advance the discussion on the future of global media policy. Equally important is the search for new governance arrangements, which include the market, the state, the public and, of course, the balance between them. It has been put forward (Bardoel, 2007) that in the era of market liberalization and globalization a transformation of statehood is occurring that can be traced by trends such as the change from protectionism to the promotion of competition, the separation of political and operative tasks (for example, the setting-up of independent regulatory agencies), the change from vertical (sector-specific) to horizontal regulation, with its greater reliance on competition law, the transition from national to supra- and international regulation, and the shift from state to self- and co-regulation, in which private and societal stakeholders are becoming more actively involved in policy and regulation. Let me contribute to this discussion by looking at the new governance arrangements and the role of the state.

From 'government' to 'governance': towards a new role for the state?

In most dictionaries the terms 'government' and 'governance', as they relate to public administration and political science, are presented as synonyms, both denoting the exercise of authority within an organization, institution or state (Cariño, no date). 'Government' is the term allocated to the entity exercising that authority, for 'to govern' is 'to exercise power and authority over a territory, system or organization'. This applies to both government and governance. The exercise of authority rests primarily in government, but not exclusively, for it now appears significant in governance. The difference is that in a regime of governance power is generally shared and authority is defined not so much by the *control* of the ruler as by the *consent* and *participation* of the governed. Does this mean that the role of the state is weak under a regime of governance?

The role of the state as governor certainly appears strong as it is the sole authority that rules and controls, but in a state of governance, the state typically *manages* and *orchestrates*. A government that rules relies on force to ensure compliance, it issues laws that are binding on all inhabitants, and also monopolizes legitimate violence. In contrast, to orchestrate is to call on everyone to play a part in society. Whereas to control is to direct what each part of the system must do (assuming a law), to manage is to be open to inputs and methods other than those originally invoked that could result in the specified objectives. Governing is an act of leadership (moving a society in a preferred direction), but governance implies leadership toward societal development. The state is the wielder of power and the principal actor in government. In governance, various actors are involved in managing public affairs (ibid.).

International intergovernmental agencies

This shift from government to governance has been facilitated by the rise of international intergovernmental agencies and global bodies that increasingly influence global media policymaking. In the last three decades or so, supranational and regional organizations with a predominantly economic focus (but also sociocultural agendas) have been playing an active role in the area of media and communications policy. These will be examined in detail in Chapter 6, but examples of the most significant ones include the free trade institution WTO, the ITU, ICANN, and UNESCO – in particular the UNESCO Convention on the Protection and Promotion of the Diversity of Cultural Expressions, which came into effect in March 2007. Regional associations like the EU and the Free Trade Area of the Americas (FTAA) also influence the media and communications policy agenda. The above bodies tackle various aspects of international systems and simultaneously affect national regulatory regimes.

Civil society representatives

Alongside these international bodies, which exemplify the supranational hierarchy existing above the nation-state, civil society representatives have become a prominent public actor that needs to be consulted on policy issues. Civil society representatives include all those who are not part of government, private enterprise or intergovernmental organizations (Raboy, 2004: 228). Nongovernmental organizations (NGOs) are examples of subnational bodies, existing within the purview of states (Kumar, 2010: 157). Transnational civil society movements and NGOs have been playing an important role lately in influencing the processes of decision-making in international media and communication policy. Through their means of action (lobbying, advocacy, service providing) these nonstate actors have an impact not merely in the domain of communications but across a range of global issues such as international health, environmental protection, security and peace-keeping, trade, and human rights.

Kaldor notes three meanings of global civil society. The first meaning refers to the 'new social movements' that have emerged since 1968 and that are concerned with issues like peace, women's rights, human rights and the environment. The 1990s marked the emergence of transnational networks focused on issues such as landmines, human rights, climate change, HIV/AIDS and even corporate responsibility. The end of 1990s brought new concerns and the anti-globalization movement. The second meaning was provided by the global institutions themselves and Western governments, who perceived it as 'a mechanism for facilitating market reform and the introduction of parliamentary democracy' (Kaldor: 2003: 589, cited in Nae, Grigore and Grigore, no date) where the social movements were actually NGOs or tamed 'social movements' as Kaldor dubbed them as referring to a respectable partner in negotiations. The distinctive element for the 1990s was that the new organisms became tamed with a global framework. The third meaning is referred to as 'postmodernism' by Kaldor and includes also the new religions and ethic movements which evolved during the last decade.

Nae, Grigore and Grigore (2006) argued that NGOs have gained an important place in international public policymaking through advocacy, public policy analysis and development. According to the Union of International Associations, the number of known international NGOs increased from about 13,000 in 1981 to over 54,000 by 2006 (cited in Nae, Grigore and Grigore, 2006). But it is not only numbers that matter. Civil society associations can make important contributions to greater democratic accountability in global governance. The above scholars provide a number of reasons as to why civil society actors need to be engaged: they can, among other things, confer legitimacy on policy decisions; increase the pool of policy ideas; support less powerful governments; and counter a lack of political will (civil society keeps its eye on the issue at stake).

The corporate sector

However, in the new media environment the negotiation of regulation involves not only public actors but also private ones, like the corporate/business sector. Business actors are typically profit oriented and pursue goals such as efficiency, the security or stability of the market, power and autonomy, and responsiveness to societal demands. In 2006, there were about 64,000 multinational corporations across the world (Nae, Grigore and Grigore, 2006). Levy and Prakash (2003: 131) proposed the *regime approach* in order to understand the interests and power of business organizations, with two dimensions: regime purpose and regime authority structure, which generate four types of regime illustrated in Table 5.1. The regime purpose dimensions are *market enabling* – extent to which the regime tends to minimize transaction costs and provide collective good, which is important to multinational corporations; and *regulatory* – extent to which it imposes constraints on aspects of behavior and tackles social costs in areas like environment and labor safety. The regime authority structure applies to authority (monitoring, enforcement, sanctions) at *domestic* and *supranational* levels.

Specifically in media and communications, the business sector acts as a powerful policymaking player, both by pursuing technical innovation and, perhaps more importantly, by lobbying for the introduction of more relaxed regulatory frameworks. The rationale behind these calls for market and regulatory liberalization is to enable multinational companies to expand in

Table 5.1 New bargains: a typology of regimes

Location of authority	Regime purpose	
	Market enabling	**Regulatory**
Domestic	Trade-related intellectual property rights (TRIPs)	ISO 14001 (environmental management standard) Forest Stewardship Council (provides a certification system for forestry and forest products)
Supranational	World Trade Organization	Montreal Protocol on Ozone Depleting Gases Nuclear Non-Proliferation Treaty

Source: Levy and Prakash, 2003: 134.

various media, communication and cultural fields. Technological, corporate and market convergence (a concept that will be examined in depth in the last section of this volume) has enabled the rise of the 'network society', which has succeeded the industrial society and introduced 'a pattern of discontinuity in the material basis of economy, society and culture' (Castells, 2000). The invention of the Internet with its global reach was a crucial milestone in this progressive disconnection.

The new digital media institutions with their network power capable of crossing national borders pose fresh challenges to the nation-state (Vick, 2001; Morris and Waisbord, 2001). According to Kumar (2010), for instance, Google represents a new modality of power, increasingly making inroads into the nation-state system and presenting itself as 'centerless', thus claiming to operate in the interests of the larger global good by ensuring a worldwide free flow of information. Kumar's study provides a concrete example of the challenge that new media present by showing how Google ignored repeated requests from governments, and highlighting the latter's lack of legal, technical or diplomatic means to influence Google. In essence, new media challenge the very concept of defined international boundaries because of their 'borderless' architecture. This compromises a state's ability to implement laws within its defined geography (Kumar, 2010: 158). In fact, some scholars have called new media entities such as Google (and Facebook) 'sovereign entities equivalent to a nation' (Conti, 2009: 4 cited in Kumar, 2010: 159).

Theorizing the process to governance and the role of the nation-state

Undeniably, international bodies, network power and civil society all interrelate and wield influence (albeit to different degrees) alongside the nation-state when it comes to communications policymaking. Keohane and Nye (1998) attempted to theorize this interdependence in the field of international relations and defined it as reciprocal effects among actors resulting from 'international transactions – flows of money, goods, people and messages across international boundaries'. The authors addressed the issue by discussing changes in the global environment resulting from the information age. Their work goes deep into 'complex interdependence' by arguing that the world is becoming increasingly 'information interdependent' and by attempting to apply the assumptions and concepts present in complex interdependence to the information age.

This process to governance and the resulting 'complex interdependence' in the information era brings more activities into an international agreements framework. The process to governance is viewed as synonymous with reduced state power, for national governments are now but one player among many in the domestic and international arena. Referring to the UK, Rhodes

(1994) used the expression 'the hollowing out of the state' to describe the impact of recent changes in UK policymaking. He suggested that the UK's membership of the European Union has seen power flow upwards from the central state to a supranational tier of government. Meanwhile, the privatization of state-owned industries and wider reforms of the public sector have seen power flow downwards, from the central government to various subsidiary bodies. Rhodes suggested that the aforementioned changes have undermined the power of the UK government to regulate and that the British state is in the process of 'being eroded or eaten away' (ibid.: 138).

In the same vein, Gamble (2000) mentioned that the shift to governance has undermined UK government control of both the policy process and policy outcomes. For Gamble, the state is becoming less united and coherent and more fragmented and diversified due to globalization, European integration, devolution and administrative reform. As decisions are being taken at many different levels and by various bodies, the policy process has become hard to understand for politicians and citizens alike (ibid.: 290). Richardson (1994) noted a move from conventional direct UK governmental involvement to a more complex model of rule-making and implementation, with fresh sets of formal and informal rules and new sets of players. Echoing these opinions, Richards and Smith (2002) argued that the fragmented nature of the contemporary UK television policymaking process is a consequence of the ever increasing variety of terrains and players involved in public policymaking beyond the core executive.

The above scholars have supported the 'loss of government control thesis' or, put another way, the 'theory of the eroding state' as a result of the emergence of various national and supranational bodies, globalization and reregulation. Yet the state continues to play the key roles of enabling and facilitating the participation of other actors in society; it creates the political and regulatory conditions that enable and help other key players, such as civil society and the market, to make their own contributions. In this sense, the state remains able to achieve most, if not all, of its preferred policy outcomes. The state as *enabler* or *facilitator* creates the setting (by, for example, making changes in the law, or offering incentive schemes, or upgrading the physical infrastructure) within which all stakeholders (citizens, the market, NGOs, voluntary groups) can overcome the confusion brought about by rapid social and technological change and assimilate rapid social and technological change and accommodate it to.

As mentioned in the previous chapter, Flew (2007) referred to a twenty-first-century model of the *enabling state*, in which the role of governmental authorities is increasingly promotional and informative, as they work with complex networks of nongovernmental authorities and agencies. By acting as a manager rather than a controller, the state can move society in a preferred direction through trust and consensus, rather than by force. In this way the state does not lose power; instead the shared accountability, consent and participation of various actors makes the exercise of state power more effective.

True, governance has resulted in the administration of public goods and services taking placing in new ways, but these services are still being overseen by the national government. For Gray (2000: 298), the shift from government to governance has resulted in the appearance of a *managerial*, rather than a *hollow* state. Even Rhodes (who never suggested that the era of the hollow state had arrived but left little doubt as to the direction of the trend), in a later work in which he reviewed the study of governance, attempted to reassess his original arguments and thesis about the hollowing out of the state. Engaging with his critics, Rhodes opened new directions of research by explaining change and the role of ideas, and by focusing on policy networks. He argued that the examination of governance should concentrate on beliefs, practices, traditions and dilemmas (Rhodes, 2007).

Skelcher (2000) suggested that the *hollowed-out state* of the 1980s had been replaced by the *congested state* of the late 1990s, when the creation of collaborative institutions had become a core strategy in all areas of UK public policy. This web of linkages arose in response to the inherent fragmentation arising from hollowing out. The resulting partnerships brought together public, private, voluntary and community sector players, all of which operated between and around the core institutions of democratic government. Skelcher concluded that these tertiary (partnership) structures had complex accountability relationships with primary (elected) and secondary (appointed) public bodies, as well as with other actors.

Braman (2009) refers to the current information society, where industrial technologies have been replaced by informational meta-technologies, and in this context she sees information-induced shifts in the nature of government. She writes that contemporary states are not going away; rather, they use information and information technologies in new ways, which lead to changes in the nature of power and its exercise via information policy. Put it another way, social and technological changes make possible the transition to an *informational state*. According to Braman (2009: 4), information policy is key both to understanding the emergence of the informational state and to analyzing how it exercises power domestically and internationally.

Braman focuses on the USA and argues that with the appearance of the informational state many of the structures of US law remain in place, and traditional processes such as elections and the passage of legislation continue. However, new policy subjects emerge (such as the Internet) alongside traditional policy subjects (for example, television) and constituencies (for example, communities and ethnic groups). Changes in the law and in how we perceive it can result in a change in the nature of the state itself, 'because the institutions, processes and policies of any given political form are but a moment of stability within a much wider, more diffuse, and constantly shifting policy field' (ibid.: 3).

In this wider context of transitional media governance, helped by the emergence of an information society, regulatory reform, the rise of the Internet, globalization and technological convergence (or interoperability[5]), the state is being transformed, not overwhelmed, and certainly it is in no way heading for extinction. States remain key actors in media policy formulation and enforcement, 'making the territorial congruence of mediascapes and nation-states a key component of media policy's development' (Abramson, 2001: 301). Here, the state's regulatory role shifts in two ways: at one level, it is confined to the position of industry referee, enforcing and arbitrating the negotiations and relationships between the market players who constitute the mediascape. The other attempts to address the thorny (and slippery) dichotomy between promoting culture and safeguarding industry concerns. Under the guise of the *promotional state*, governments try to synthesize the topographic imperatives of the nation-state with their role as facilitators, promoters and partners to industry. The role of the promotional state is to act as both industry partner and national topographer (ibid.: 316-17).

Another camp of scholars point to the emergence of the *regulatory state*. In this regard, the state may not merely act as *facilitator* or *mediator* between different interests, demands and pressures, but in fact as a *shaper* of preferences. As a consequence, the role of the state in the national and international arena is not to reflect or reconcile national/global conflicts and problems, nor negotiate agreements, but to take an active role and pursue its own interests. At European level, national governments have been careful not to restrain market developments, but they still intervene in order to maintain the conditions of open and fair competition and/or protect the interests of the public in ensuring that it has access to a variety of services. For example, governments are responsible for maintaining and promoting public interest goals like political pluralism and cultural diversity, which are considered fields of national interest where the EU has no jurisdiction to intervene (see Chapter 7).

The setting-up of super-regulatory bodies like Ofcom in the UK in 2003, replacing five separate broadcasting and telecommunications regulators, can be seen as a typical product of the regulatory state. Although at face value this regulatory overhaul might be seen as a fairly straightforward response by UK policymakers to the convergence of television, telecommunications and computing technologies facilitated by digitalization, 'this motion should not obscure the fact that the establishment of Ofcom was also the institutional culmination of a significant shift in the focus of UK television regulation, away from the allocation of spectrum to achieve public service objectives and towards the control of market power to facilitate free market competition' (Smith, 2006). As Harding (2000) noted, one of the government's objectives has been to put competition law at the center of media regulation. However, the rise of the regulatory state can also lead to a significant decline in self-regulation in media and communications, which is somewhat paradoxical (see Chapter 10).

State size matters

To conclude this rather short discussion of the process of governance and the role of the state in the era of globalization and network governance, it should be acknowledged that state size matters when it comes to communications policy and regulation. Existing research (including this volume) has mainly focused on the regulatory regimes of a few large Western industrialized nations. However, geographical and population size coupled with the structural peculiarities of smaller territories affect media regulation in various ways. Policies concerning the mission of public broadcasters, cross-ownership regulation and homegrown productions are more difficult to implement in smaller countries, which prioritize the protection of their national industries. Smaller states appear vulnerable and policies that promote sociocultural goals are difficult to implement. Trappel (2010) argued that expectations of media ownership diversity and programming autonomy in smaller states such as Austria and Switzerland are unrealistic. In the introduction to a special issue of the *International Communication Gazette*, Puppis (2009) notes that small states tend towards an interventionist regulatory approach and might even sacrifice media diversity in order to protect their domestic media landscape. Diverging economic and political conditions as well as structural factors, in addition to market size, may also affect media policy and regulation. Papathanassopoulos (2010) wrote that in countries like Greece where television was developed under a military, media policy is still struggling to come to terms with the rapid and haphazard deregulation of the broadcasting scene.

The size of the market usually defines the relative strength of a country in media and communications terms and thus the influence it can exert or that is exerted on it by neighboring countries. In the television sector, the permanent presence of foreign television programmes in smaller territories limits policy options even further. For Ireland, for example, influenced as it is by a powerful neighbor (Britain), it is more difficult to develop an independent television system (Iosifidis, 2007). Trappel (2010) observes that in the small states of Switzerland and Austria there are limited policy options available to the respective governments, as media policy has been steered and dominated by the interests of large states such as Germany. Therefore, the debates about globalization and the role of the state should take into account the analysis of small media systems and their regulation.

Finally, the debates should consider democratic versus authoritarian and totalitarian[6] regimes, the latter often providing obstacles to freedom of expression and communication by using oppression and coercion. In these cases, the presence of digital networked media and social networks like Google, Facebook and Twitter may be significant in allowing different views to be heard (see Chapter 1). However, the respective ability of nation-states to address the political, corporate and civil society challenges in the globalized world further complicates understanding of market power.

Conclusion: towards 'state capitalism'?

Throughout the 1970s and early 1980s, media policy was mainly managed by nation-states by means of state intervention – this was the era of the Fordist mode of regulation. The emergence of the Fordist welfare state in most developed countries adopted state intervention in markets and welfare provisions. Steinmetz (1999) emphasized the central role of the state as a source of power and initiator of economic regulation, while Graham and Marvin (2001) highlighted the state's role in enforcing communication policy. The Fordist era understood the state as the central institutional player in the delivery of development and policy, but its appeal diminished following the emergence of international communications policy, in which a multitude of actors was involved in decision-making.

Since the mid-1980s, the terrain of media and communications policy-making has shifted. Whereas previously the field was essentially determined by national legislative and regulatory frameworks and a minimum of international supervision, it is now characterized by a complex ecology of inter-dependent structures. Communications policy is no longer exclusively the result of national governments' actions or confined to clearly identifiable locations, but it is increasingly the outcome of a multiplicity of formal and informal mechanisms originating from many different sites. A multitude of factors has created enormous pressure on the existing media and telecommunications legal systems, although three stand out – globalization; the rise of international organizations; and technological change.

This chapter argued that in a globalized era the role of the state has not been diminished. True, national economic, political and cultural forces are being transformed, sharing their sovereignty with other entities of global governance and international law, mobile capital, multinational corporations and global social movements, but they are not being replaced by these. Although rules (on finance, security, climate change, media and telecommunications, to mention but a few) are influenced by supranational bodies, such as the World Trade Organization and the EU, and on the ever growing power of transnational corporations, national governments are far from withdrawing from the scene.

The state is affected by the emergence of multinational corporations, nongovernmental organizations and the trends towards liberalization and commercialization, but it also affects the societal national and international scene. National governments maintain a significant amount of autonomy to shape national policy agendas and meanwhile continue to influence decisions in the international environment. The modern state retains a considerable degree of control over media flows within its territory, issues binding laws and uses legitimate force to ensure compliance. In the end, it is the nation-state that decides which objectives to prioritize and consequently under which regulatory conditions the media will perform.

Whether it is for the reasons listed above or for reasons of financial crisis, environmental change, or fear of terrorism or excessive media influence, governments have maintained, and occasionally expanded, their ability to issue rules, police and supervise, not least because of market failure. This is evidenced by the key role states played in the handling of the 2008–2009 financial crisis. For example, the US government spent billions of dollars to bail out not just banks but also huge industrial companies such as General Motors. The new superpower China, although theoretically embracing capitalism, does so only to the extent that it can be used as an instrument of state power. The rise of this hybrid of *state capitalism*[7] has resulted in yet another change in the balance of power between the market and the state. In 2010, almost a fifth of global stock-market value was sited in government-controlled companies, more than twice the level in the year 2000. *The Economist* (2010d: 94–5) wrote: 'state oil companies control three-quarters of the world's crude oil reserves. Three of the four largest banks by market capitalization are state-controlled. The biggest mobile phone operator, China Mobile, is also a state company'. Recent literature (see Bremmer, 2010; Halper, 2010) provide further evidence that state capitalism may pose a threat to the market model of capitalism.

Unsurprisingly, free-market press notes that the rise of state capitalism may lead to government failure. An article in *The Economist* (2010a: 24) called for a clear distinction between economics and politics, as the subordination of economic decisions to political ones can come with a price tag in the long term: 'politicians are reluctant to let "strategic" companies fail, and companies become adjuncts of the state patronage machine'. Such concerns are being voiced with regard to the role of the Chinese state in global transactions involving Chinese firms. Most Chinese companies are going global for the typical economic reasons: to acquire new inputs, such as raw materials, labour and land; to build up technical and commercial expertise; and to gain access to foreign markets. But they are under the guidance of a state that many countries consider a strategic competitor, not an ally. As another piece in *The Economist* (2010g: 11, 85–7) argues, the Chinese state 'often appoints executives [and] direct deals and finances them through state banks'. 'Once bought, natural-resource firms can become captive suppliers of the Middle Kingdom (China Inc)'.[8]

It is not the intention of this chapter to delve into a discussion of state capitalism and elaborate on the theme of *government failure* versus *market failure*, but I wish to conclude with two remarks on this subject. First, commercial firms have played a big part in the promotion of competition and globalization and in the current global epoch there appears to be little chance of governments, however powerful and opaque, coming to dominate global capitalism. Second, the question of whether a government is 'too powerful' or 'too weak' matters less than the question of whether a government is effective and innovative and, in the end, can deliver. Government attempts to privatize national telecommunications (infrastructural reformation) in the 1970s and 1980s in the USA and Europe resulted in more choice and advanced services for users in these developed countries, whereas government attempts to reregulate broadcasting (which involves content issues) resulted in industry consolidation and concerns about pluralism. The real issue for governments and policymakers is not one of more or less regulation, but rather to decide wisely on developing policy frameworks that promote both the interests of the citizens (through, for example, promoting universal service – which implies regulation *of* the market) and the interests of commerce (for example, by encouraging competition – which can be done *through* the market).

Part III
Supranational Bodies

6
Supranational Bodies, Non-State Actors and Global Media Policy

Introduction

This chapter focuses on supranational bodies of global governance that have transformed the regulations of global communication governance because they can result in loss of national autonomy and the reorganization of state functions. The chapter attempts to shed light on the role of the largely un-scrutinized and poorly understood international bodies for global media policymaking. The key bodies in the field of trade liberalization include the World Trade Organization (WTO) and the General Agreement on Trade in Services (GATS), which have become powerful since (and were the major contributors to) the rise of the liberalization agenda in global media and trade in cultural products. The International Telecommunications Union (ITU) and World Intellectual Property Organization (WIPO) are also key organizations, which pursue multilateral cooperation in the areas of technical standards and intellectual property rights respectively, while the Internet Corporation for Assigned Names and Numbers (ICANN) is the dominant institution involved in global Internet governance.

A key player in protecting and promoting cultural diversity and freedom of expression is the United Nations Education Scientific and Cultural Organization (UNESCO), one of the suborganizations of the United Nations, especially through the Convention on Cultural Diversity. Meanwhile, nongovernmental organizations (NGOs) and other civil society and scientific networks, grassroots organizations and even individuals are attempting to bring to the fore the social aspects of the media to counterbalance commercial objectives. Special attention is being paid to the role of the World Summit on the Information Society (WSIS) in the process of global decision-making and in promoting political and sociocultural processes.[1]

125

World Trade Organization (WTO)

The Geneva-based WTO is the only international organization dealing with the rules of trade between nations (in 2010, with 153 member nations, it represented more than 97 per cent of total world trade) and aiming to eliminate national obstacles to the import and export of goods and services. It is currently the most powerful global media policy institution, as it creates pressure to liberalize and privatize state-run media and telecommunications firms and can legally enforce its rules by imposing large trade sanctions on member nations that hinder the free movement of goods or services. The WTO is the successor of the General Agreement on Trade and Tariffs (GATT), which had been set up in 1947, after pressure from the USA, with the purpose of removing tariffs and promoting trade.

The Uruguay Rounds, which began in the mid-1980s, significantly broadened the scope of the GATT to include trade in 'services', where developed nations had an obvious advantage in selling the hardware and software necessary for entry into the information society, including telecommunications, audiovisual and database services (Chakravarthy and Sarikakis, 2006: 34). The eight-year negotiations that made up the Uruguay Round also created the General Agreement on Trade in Services (GATS), which covered a broad spectrum ranging from health care to telecommunications, and the Agreement on Trade-Related Aspects of Intellectual Property Rights (TRIPs), which sets up rules on copyright, patents and other forms of information protection.

The WTO (and its predecessors GATT and GATS) is the result of a shift in the focus of international policy debates, initiated by the USA and its allies after the end of the Cold War, from the wider 'politicized' bodies like UNESCO (one of the UN's institutions especially concerned with culture, media and freedom of expression) to narrow 'technical' bodies where developed nations held more clout (ibid.; Puppis, 2008: 407). The WTO (which is not a UN agency) is perceived as a symbol of corporate globalization because of its closed-door decision-making, its massive imbalance in influence between the first and second worlds (the northern and southern hemispheres) and its antipathy to public services (Costanza-Chock, 2005). What is more, the establishment of the WTO, alongside the setting-up of authorities like the World Bank and the International Monetary Fund (IMF) and the rise of the G8 and G20 structures, has given credence to the argument that policymakers across the globe have now accepted the principle of neoliberal reform (based on market functioning and the openness of national economies to global market forces) fostered by the USA.

Telecommunications reform

The WTO is dominated by the US liberalization agenda and, since the 1999 protests that followed the ministerial meeting in Seattle, has been seen as an organization that pursues market integration and liberalization at the expense of labor rights, environmental standards and consumer safety. The Seattle clashes were largely about the effects of globalization on the nation-state's ability to regulate and the new forms of global governance. In the communications domain, the WTO is viewed as a threat to national media and telecommunications regulation. In telecommunications, the scope of the WTO has been expanded to the whole industry, from basic telephone services to long-distance and valued-added (that is, non-core services, or in short, all services beyond standard voice calls) services, for in 1998 the Agreement on Basic Telecommunications (ABT)[2] was adopted as the fourth protocol of the GATS.

This was the culmination of almost two decades of debate over the terms of the new rules of trade with the liberalization of the telecommunications services. Throughout the late 1980s and early 1990s, transnational corporations (TNCs) and telecommunications networks based in developed countries (mainly the USA) initially turned to the ITU (see below) and then to the WTO, the new multilateral agency of telecommunications governance, for permission to create trans-local services and to buy licences to operate basic telephony in emerging markets, alongside investments in broadband, mobile and satellite networks.

What happened to universal service?

An area of interest here is universal services policies, under which governments can require cross-subsidization from large business users and urban areas to domestic and small users and rural areas. As Chapter 2 showed, universal telephone service was adopted as a policy objective in telecommunications in both the USA and Europe, but the Uruguay Rounds signalled a shift in policy towards the implementation of liberalization and privatization policies. The WTO permits universal service policies only where they do not interfere unduly with competition – a vague formulation that is yet to be tested (Ó Siochrú, 2004: 6). Such policies have opened the telecommunications markets to foreign investors. States in the southern hemisphere in particular have begun to privatize national markets as a means to reduce debt burdens and bring in foreign capital and expertise (Singh, 1999).

In addition, transnational equipment manufacturers like NEC, Alcatel, Erickson, US West and British Telecom collaborated with the World Bank and the IMF to direct foreign investment to southern governments (Hills, 1998). Although this economic reform and accompanying change in regulatory philosophy could certainly be seen as a response to government failure to promote development, expansion and consumer choice, left-wing scholars such as McChesney and Schiller (2003) perceived it as a response to intense corporate pressure, backed by the USA and other wealthy nations, lobbying at the GATT for liberalization. The Uruguay Rounds ended in 1994 with most nations committing to the opening-up of value-added services, while the newly established WTO required all signatories to fully liberalize their basic telecommunications markets and set up independent regulatory bodies similar in form to the FCC in the USA, thereby fundamentally altering the domestic legal framework that had guided universal telecommunications provision (Aufderheide, 1999).

Liberalizing the audiovisual sector

As the telecommunications industry is now fully liberalized, attention is being paid to applying a liberal approach to the audiovisual sector. But while the telecommunications industry mainly involves infrastructural, industrial and economic issues, the audiovisual sector involves social and cultural ideals that are traditionally regulated within nation-states. The idea of the free movement of television programmes, music and movies, pursued by free-trade advocates like the USA during the Uruguay Round of GATT negotiations in the 1990s, faced significant resistance from countries like France and Canada, which opposed full liberalization and insisted on the right to maintain subsidies to protect their audiovisual industries. The US government might have pushed for further liberalization of audiovisual services, but other countries were more reserved and wanted to see the sector exempted from free-trade rules. Only two Western democracies opted for the full liberalization of their audiovisual markets (the USA and New Zealand), whereas the vast majority urged for quotas for local content, public service broadcasting (PSB) and programmes of support for the audiovisual sector.

The European Union (EU) as a whole has also expressed concerns, mainly because it is interested in protecting the European audiovisual industry rather than in cultural objectives (Puppis, 2008: 411). Despite adopting a liberal approach to its audiovisual industry, the EU has taken a number of initiatives in support of it, especially in areas such as film and home video production, radio and television production and distribution, and sound recording. However, the Union has been traditionally divided between economic and cultural objectives and this leads to discrepancies in media policy decision-making (Pauwels, De Vinck and Van Rompuy, 2007; Wheeler, 2010). EU policy for media and communications will be examined in the next chapter. Here, it is sufficient to say that the disagreement between rich and poor nations over the exporting of agricultural commodities has rendered uncertain the future of the trade negotiation called the Doha Development Agenda (or Doha Round), which was launched in 2001 to enhance the participation of poorer countries, which represent a majority of the world's population.[3]

Towards free-trade agreements

The US response to the breakdown of negotiations was to pursue bilateral agreements with specific countries. Freedman (2008: 204) notes that by mid-2006 the USA had concluded bilateral free-trade agreements (FTAs) with about 30 countries, including Australia, Chile, Morocco and Singapore. These FTAs now include the liberalization of audiovisual sectors and therefore limit co-signatories' ability to shape or control existing media structures and audiovisual systems as they emerge in the digital era. The rationale behind these agreements is to put an end to the 'cultural exemption' (the idea exemplified by France to protect its domestic and also the wider EU audiovisual industry) and impose free-market disciplines on key sectors of the cultural industry (ibid.: 205).

An example is the USA–Australia FTA, which was one of the several bilateral FTAs signed in the early to mid-2000s that explicitly incorporated free trade in digital content. The agreement introduced a number of policy considerations. These included the circumvention of multilateral cultural policymaking and the US insertion of intellectual property rights, which reduced Australia's ability to preserve its cultural industry in the face of the dominant power of the US media communications enterprises. More specifically, the agreement prevents Australia from imposing quotas on the import of terrestrial TV, pay-TV and commercial radio programmes. The result, according to Breen (2010: 657) is 'digital determinism', for the FTA 'negatively impacts national culture industries in the global networked context, reducing employment and creative opportunities for artists and producers, thereby challenging the human rights of workers in these sectors'.

United Nations Education, Scientific and Cultural Organization (UNESCO)

UNESCO is a specialized multilateral body established in Geneva in 1945 under the UN charter to promote economic, social and cultural human rights and deal explicitly in regulating the international media and communications industries. During the 1970s the UN's cultural organization emphasized the importance of diversity and criticized the US idea of a 'free flow of information', which led to the domination of global media, cultural and news services by the United States and Western Europe. Developing countries demanded a restructuring of information flows that would promote the interests of all people, rather than only those of a wealthy minority in the northern hemisphere.

Concerned about the potential loss of control over information flows and a drop in income from media exports, the USA (under the Reagan administration) withdrew from UNESCO and was followed shortly by the UK (under the Thatcher administration) (see Chakravarthy and Sarikakis, 2006: 30–1; Costanza-Chock, 2005). UNESCO was left crippled, as both powerful countries took with them their financial dues, although they finally reentered in 2003, at the time when the debate over global information flows regained momentum in the form of a proposed treaty on cultural diversity.

UNESCO and the Convention on Cultural Diversity (CCD)

Harvey and Tongue (2006) provide a lengthy discussion on the negotiations and preparations for a binding convention on cultural diversity, which started in 2001 when UNESCO's General Assembly unanimously adopted the non-binding Universal Declaration on Cultural Diversity (Resolution 31C/25) and resulted in the March 2007 adoption of the Convention on Cultural Diversity (CCD). The major objectives of the CCD are the recognition of the dual nature of cultural expressions as objects of trade and symbols of cultural value and the recognition of the sovereign right of governments to formulate and implement cultural policies for the protection of cultural diversity.

The convention is based on the core principles of the right to sovereignty, respect for solidarity, human rights, culture and sustainable development. As Graber (2006) notes, the ambitious role assigned to the CCD was to fill a lacuna for cultural objectives in public international law and to serve as a cultural counterbalance to the WTO in future conflicts between trade and culture. Indeed, the CCD was designed to be a legal instrument that would act as a 'counterbalance' to the WTO by concentrating on cultural matters that were marginalized in trade negotiations (ibid.).

The CCD has been ratified by more than 30 countries (outside the USA), which wanted to take measures to protect and foster cultural (including media) diversity. The US negotiators were suspicious of the convention from its inception, since it pioneered protectionism against free trade and the principles of individual choice. Although the USA and some of its allies (for example, Israel) voted against it, claiming that it was an instrument of disguised protectionism that violated freedom of expression and information, the European delegation (including the UK[4]) was overwhelmingly supportive of the convention.

Unsurprisingly, the CCD was supported by European public service broadcasters, who perceived the convention as another tool for curbing the liberalization trend of the audiovisual industry. In fact, the convention recognized the role of public media in promoting cultural diversity. Puppis (2008: 416–7) summarizes the reasons why the convention was highly relevant for the media, particularly broadcasting:

- First, the CCD acknowledged the importance of culture by stating that the 'cultural aspects of development are as important as its economic aspects' (Article 2 (5)).
- Second, the CCD legitimated the regulation of electronic media. It entitled its signatory states to adopt measures and policies to 'protect and promote the diversity of cultural expressions' (Articles 2 (2) and 5 (1)).

However, Puppis also notes that the major shortcoming of the convention was its normative weakness, for in contrast to the WTO agreements, the CCD does not impose binding and enforceable obligations on the contracting parties but merely reaffirms the right of states to protect and promote cultural diversity.

More recent actions[5]

In more recent years UNESCO has been involved in a number of social issues, such as freedom of expression, privacy and social networks. Motivated by the growing violence against journalists in many parts of the world and even a number of politically motivated killings of journalists in 2009, in March 2010 it adopted decisions on the Safety of Journalists and on Impunity, calling on governments to report to the UNESCO Director-General on their investigations into the killing of journalists.

Furthermore, at the World Summit on the Information Society (WSIS) in May 2010, the UNESCO organized a High-level Debate on Social Networking, where both the great potential and the more negative aspects of social networking were highlighted. Among the latter, participants mentioned online slander and criminal information generated by social media, as well as their challenge to privacy and data protection.

In September 2010 UNESCO also held a workshop on Privacy and Social Networking at the Internet Governance Forum (IGF) meeting. Here it was stressed that various stakeholders must contribute to protecting privacy: *governments* must enforce the law and, when there is no law, to have the principles translated into legislation; *Internet companies* must develop their privacy policies and standards; and *users* must know how to protect their privacy and freedom of speech.

Summing up so far, the two international governmental organizations – WTO and UNESCO – pursue very different agendas, the former being perceived as a champion of free trade and a threat to culture and the latter as the protector of cultural goals. It is clear that power is not equally distributed between the two organizations and that in the era of the prevalence of commercial objectives (rather than societal goals) the WTO is far more important than UNESCO in terms of decision-making.

International Telecommunication Union (ITU)

The ITU, an agency of the United Nations based in Geneva, was founded in 1865 with the aim of working towards consensus on technical standards, originally for the telegraph and later on for radio, television and satellite communication. In December 2010, its membership included 192 Member States (official designations), 547 Sector Members and 151 Associates (see http://www.itu.int/members/index.html, accessed 21 December 2010). Currently, the organization is the global focal point for governments and the private sector in developing networks and services. The ITU has the following functions (Ó Siochrú, 2004: 4–5):

• It coordinates the shared global use of the radio spectrum, terrestrially or via satellite, for the purposes of telephony, data, TV and radio. Coordination is essential to prevent interference and border 'spillover'. Since the radio spectrum is a limited public resource, its allocation between users is an important and contentious issue at international level.
• It promotes international cooperation in allocating satellite orbits, including the valuable and limited geostationary orbit.
• It establishes global standards that foster the seamless interconnection of a vast range of telecommunications systems. The standardization of equipment and protocols can be highly contentious, as it is connected with issues such as market control.
• It facilitates the so-called 'accounting rate' system, whereby telecommunications operators reimburse each other for the use of their networks for international communications.
• It works towards improving telecommunication infrastructure in the developing world.

However, according to Ó Siochrú (ibid.), the ITU has only very limited authority by which to extend telecommunications to less industrialized countries. In telecommunications, since the shift from monopoly national providers to competitive global suppliers, the trade paradigm of the WTO has come to the fore. The move to free, privatized trade in telecommunications means that the role of the ITU is diminishing and that of the WTO is increasing – for example, the ITU's accounting rate system can no longer exist, resulting in the net loss of foreign earnings for some of the underdeveloped nations.

Still, the ITU remains an important and active agency in many areas. It organizes worldwide forums, such as the ITU Telecoms World, which is held every few years and concerns the global telecommunication and information communication technology (ICT) sector. For example, the 2009 forum incorporated thematic elements to highlight the reach and role of telecommunications and ICT in areas of societal change such as the digital divide (the divide between the information haves and have-nots). With its focus on development, the event addressed issues of corporate social responsibility and provided examples of best practices.

In March 2010, the ITU set up a working group on Child Online Protection (COP) to assess, among other things, the potentially harmful effects of social networking. The group suggested encouraging social networking service providers to self-regulate with regard to the ownership of user-created content as well as to draft and publish their terms and conditions in language that could be understood by youngsters. In November 2010, the ITU launched the COP Global Initiative, which will provide a framework for coordinating existing global efforts and implementing a series of safety training and prevention activities. The Initiative will build on Guidelines developed by the ITU and partners from industry and civil society, governments, UN agencies and other stakeholders (see http://www.itu.int/osg/csd/cybersecurity/ gca/cop/guidelines/index.html, accessed 12 December 2010).

Overall, the ITU has responsibility for several critical areas of interest to governments, corporations and civil society alike. It has taken a leading role in mediating and achieving cooperation between governments, the corporate sector and users of services on a wide range of areas, including telecommunications, the allocation of spectrum and child online protection. ITU events bring together the most influential representatives of government and the telecommunications and ICT industries to exchange ideas, knowledge and technology for the benefit of the global community, and in particular the developing world, on issues such as broadband Internet, wireless technology, the convergence of fixe and mobile phone telephone services, Internet access, data, voice and TV broadcasting, and next-generation networks.

A focus on the developing world

The ITU's focus on the developing world is a response to those who have in recent years put pressure on the organization to become more open and democratic. In this context the ITU has also been pressurized to expand its membership to include more NGOs from the global south and increase its civil society participation. An important action on behalf of the ITU has been the sponsoring of the WSIS, a global gathering originally proposed in 1998 and finally occurring in the years 2003 and 2005 in Geneva and Tunisia respectively (see below).

The official ITU's objective in organizing the event was 'to define a common vision of the information society' and address global communication governance, but Costanza-Chock (2003) reveals another reason behind the ITU's actions: a crisis of legitimacy and a search for purpose. In the same vein, Raboy (2004) argues that the bringing together of states, multinational organizations, NGOs and other civil society associations to deal with issues like development, equality, poverty and human rights reflects the ITU's response to its critics that the organization neglects the social side of these issues.

In the end, private enterprises and powerful governments proved to have more clout than civil society representatives, but the inclusion of these highlighted that it is not only the former who are the legitimate actors in issues of global governance like the worldwide gap in telecommunications infrastructure between rich and poor, the digital divide and so on. The move to include civil society in the WSIS recognizes the need to broaden the scope of international politics to incorporate nongovernment actors.

Civil society: the case of the World Summit on the Information Society (WSIS)

There is increasing involvement of global civil society in global governance politics. The most common umbrella is the World Social Forum, an annual meeting taking place in Brazil that addresses all kinds of social, cultural and economic issues in a pluralist, diverse and nonpartisan manner (Raboy, 2007). In effect, the Forum is an open, nongovernmental space, building processes and alliances between movements and organizations that oppose neoliberal doctrine and support the creation of a fairer world. The past half decade or so has witnessed the emergence of a number of international non-governmental and grassroots organizations that are engaging in the policy arena. The trend, as most strikingly put by Raboy (ibid.), is for civil society lobbying of international fora.

An illustrative case is the WSIS. This was initiated in the wake of the trends towards globalization and technological convergence in order to put communication and information on the global agenda. It opened a space in which to explore new ways of dealing with global issues, which bodes well for the democratization of communication and its use as a vehicle for human development (Raboy, 2004: 231; Padovani, 2005). Although the earlier UNESCO-led international forum, the New World Information and Communication Order (NWICO),[6] also focused on global communications policy and the distribution of control over outlets and images, the WSIS occurred in an environment already characterized by the convergence of technologies, the digitization of transmission methods, global digital networks and the widespread of ICTs.

In the late 1970s, UNESCO became a battleground for the newly decolonized countries, the Soviet bloc and the United States, during what are now known as the NWICO debates (Costanza-Shock, 2005). Another important difference between NWICO and the WSIS is that the latter included a large number of NGOs pursuing political and sociocultural agendas, thereby questioning mere technological solutions to imbalances of global power (Padovani, 2005).

Flew (2007: 201–4) notes that the UNESCO agenda for NWICO became problematic during the late 1980s/early 1990s for three reasons. First, the USA was hostile to the campaign and, as mentioned above, the Reagan administration withdrew all financial support from UNESCO (it was not until in 2003 that the USA rejoined UNESCO). The US government regarded NWICO as an effort to impose state regulation on the media that was at odds with neoliberalism and the doctrine of the 'free flow of information'. The outcome of political and financial pressure from the US government was pivotal to the change in direction of international communications policy towards free trade, the reregulation of national media and telecommunications systems and the rise of private-sector investment.

Second, NWICO was the result of a dialogue between nation-states 'which could be criticized for being overly nationalistic and state-centered, downplaying the suppression of media freedoms within many of the participating nation-states'. Third, the growth of the Internet contributed to moving policy debates away from political fora like UNESCO, towards more economics-oriented, pro-market agencies (on this last point see also Ó Siochrú and Girard, 2003; Chakravarthy and Sarikakis, 2006).

An assessment

But has the WSIS made any real difference in the process of global decision-making and in the promotion of political and sociocultural processes? On the first point, Raboy (2004) notes that the WSIS experience has put information and communication firmly on the global agenda and meanwhile opened a space in which to explore new ways of dealing with global issues. The WSIS process (the sum of official and unofficial activities)

> [h]as identified the problematic issues in global communication, indicated the range of views on how to deal with them, provided various blueprints of what should and could be possible in the way of solutions, and gingerly explored ways of dealing with these questions in the future. To that extent, WSIS has crystallized a new paradigm in communication governance that has been emerging for some time now. (ibid.: 225)

Thus global media decision-making is not exclusively the terrain of states/governments, since other players like NGOs are becoming increasingly important. The WSIS became a multi-stakeholder forum that involved civil society, government and industry representatives. However, Raboy makes it clear that while global governance in communication is based on the interaction and interdependence of an array of actors and policy bodies, power is not equally distributed among them, for some bodies of decision-making are more important than others. National governments and multinational corporations are clearly more powerful than NGOs and other civil society associations.

Pickard (2007: 136) is sceptical as to whether the WSIS process has promoted political and sociocultural matters. He argues that the WSIS domain does not contest the fundamental economic order, because instead of concentrating on social inequalities and political solutions, the 'WSIS seeks to shore up the existing system by limiting debate to technical issues'. Pickard points out that while the summit's initial focus was on important social problems like the global digital divide, it gradually metamorphosed into a technical dispute over Internet governance and especially whether it should remain in the hands of a private US corporation under the US Department of Commerce's authority or be transferred to the ITU and thus internationalized through a multilateral process.

Comparing WSIS with NWICO

Pickard (2007) compares and contrasts the WSIS project with NWICO and identifies significant similarities in relation to the rise of the political economic order, that is, neoliberalism. Having historicized the two UN approaches to global media and communication, Pickard suggests that both bodies (NWICO and WSIS) have been preoccupied with pro-market, neoliberal objectives. The WSIS might have included a wider participation; however, the emphasis was not on identifying a new ideological edge but on reconciling various stakeholders within the current system where Western (read American) interests prevail. Echoing Pickard, Siochrú (2004: 7) argues that because the WSIS has been preoccupied with the pro-market, neoliberal order it is doubtful whether it can counterbalance the extensive influence of liberal forums like the WTO.

But other scholars have been more positive concerning the effects of civil society input and the democratic impact of the WSIS. Raboy (2007) notes that there are two official outcomes of the WSIS: the Declaration of Principles and an Action Plan. While the UN always drafts an official Declaration of Principles on the state of consensus 'in the world today' with regard to this issue, the Action Plan can be broken down into specific lines of how to tackle specific issues. Raboy goes on to state that the WSIS produced a set of parallel official documents, available online, as a direct result of civil society input. What is interesting, according to the scholar, is that one can see the US government, the EU and China and all the other national governments that have signed a common document representing a consensus on particular issues discussed.

In terms of concrete outcomes, Raboy notes that the Global Solidarity Fund (GSF) was set up in the wake of the Summit. The GSF is an incubator for individual donors who adopt a hands-on approach to philanthropy. It is often called 'venture philanthropy' because it applies some of the methods of venture capital funding to donations/investments in social projects. Governments could contribute on a voluntary basis with the aim of bridging the digital divide. Raboy suggests that the other major outcome of the WSIS was the Internet Governance Forum (IGF), which is basically a space for the discussion of Internet governance matters. Although the IGF is a discussion and consultative body, and therefore nondecision making, it has a mandate to direct the attention of relevant authorities to issues and problems and proposed solutions.

It remains to be seen where civil society action will lead. However, according to Raboy (ibid.), we are witnessing a paradigm shift to global media governance, from the kind of libertarian, deregulatory and closed-club/top-down model represented by forums such as the ITU, the WTO and G8/G20 to a model that grows out of the WSIS experience in what he terms the 'long march'. Spaces are being set up, either within the UN system or elsewhere, that are available to all. They are being created to accommodate what is increasingly referred to as a 'multi-stakeholder approach'. Raboy demonstrates how the WSIS presented an opportunity to work on this model. In terms of democratic concerns, or media regulation as a democratic practice, he is certain that the path of the long march is the most visible one, for the ideas of transparency, public participation and a sociocultural approach to media governance embrace a range of values that are worth promoting internationally.

But one thing cannot be disputed: the openness of the WSIS forum. The next WSIS Forum took place in May 2011, in Geneva, Switzerland and provided structured opportunities to network, learn and to participate in multi-stakeholder discussions and consultations on WSIS implementation. The Forum attracted more than 1150 WSIS stakeholders from more than 140 countries (see http://groups.itu.int/wsis-forum2011/Agenda/OutcomeDocument.aspx, accessed 20 July 2011).

Internet Corporation for Assigned Names and Numbers (ICANN)

ICANN is the dominant institution involved in global Internet governance. Governance of the Internet is a public policy priority given the way in which the Internet has transformed the lives and working environments of the citizens of the world. As mentioned in Chapter 2, 'Internet governance is the development and application by Governments, the private sector and civil society, in their respective roles, of shared principles, norms, rules, decision-making procedures, and programmes that shape the evolution and use of the Internet' (see WGIG, 2005).

ICANN is a private, nonprofit organization formed in 1998 and based in California. Its functions, as assigned by the US Department of Commerce, include the following (Mueller, 2002: 6, cited in Pickard, 2007: 126):

- Setting policy for and managing the allocation and assignment of Internet protocol addresses.
- Adding new names to the top level of the Internet domain-name hierarchy.
- Maintaining responsibility for operating root services that distribute authoritative information about the content of the top level of the domain-name space.

An assessment

The experience of ICANN in its first 12 years of existence shows that the agency has fulfilled a key objective, namely the maintenance of the stability of the Domain Name System (DNS). Meanwhile it has created a broad multistakeholder forum for policymaking. However, in the course of time ICANN has been subject to fierce criticism. Whereas it was initially conceived as a technical agency, its management of Internet Protocol (IP) addresses and of the DNS, which ultimately controls the routing of Internet traffic, has moved the agency into economic and sociocultural domains. According to Pickard (2007: 126), this process empowers ICANN politically, for its mandate to allocate domain names involves intellectual property rights and trademark issues in determining who is entitled to what name. A lack of transparent governance and an arbitrary approach to allotting highly coveted top-level domains disproportionately to Western countries are two key criticisms of the US-based organization (ibid.).

Along these lines, Ó Siochrú (2004: 6) writes that ICANN, constituted as a nonprofit, private-sector corporation under Californian law, allows the US Department of Commerce to maintain ultimate control over the DNS. ICANN is accountable only to the US government and not to the global Internet community. Moreover, the self-regulatory approach, as practised by ICANN, means that incumbent operators play a potentially inappropriate role (for example, from the standpoint of competition policy) in setting entry conditions for new competitors.

Finally, ICANN's representativeness is open to criticism as the organization has comprised the full community of states. The vast majority of Internet users do not participate in ICANN activities. In the interim, initiatives from other countries to set up their own top-level domains have met with success. For example, the EU has set up its '.eu' domain name and more than 3 million EU domain names had been registered by mid-2009 (EC, 2009b).

World Intellectual Property Organization (WIPO)

'The WIPO is a UN specialized agency based in Geneva dedicated to developing a balanced and accessible international intellectual property system, which rewards creativity, stimulates innovation and contributes to economic development while safeguarding the public interest.' It was set up in 1967 by the WIPO Convention with a mandate from its Member States (184 in 2010) to promote the protection of intellectual property across the world through cooperation among states and in collaboration with other international organizations. Intellectual property refers to creations of the mind: inventions, literary and artistic works, and symbols, names, images and designs used in commerce.[7] Intellectual property plays a crucial role in an increasingly wide range of areas, from the Internet to literature and the arts. The WIPO regularly produces publications that help to understand the role of intellectual property in these areas – many of them still emerging.

At the General Assemblies of the WIPO in September 2010, an online global intellectual property reference resource was launched, dubbed WIPO Lex (see http://www.wipo.int/wipolex/en/, accessed 10 November 2010). This centralized search facility provides up-to-date information on national intellectual property laws and treaties. Currently, WIPO Lex features the complete intellectual property legal texts for over 60 countries as well as substantial coverage of a further 100 legal systems. Consistent with the spirit of the WIPO Development Agenda, it also provides, especially for countries that do not yet have their own database of laws, an Internet platform to make information available concerning their respective intellectual property legislation.

At the General Assemblies, a number of countries took the floor to discuss enforcement issues concerning intellectual property rights. All parties appear to agree that enforcement is necessary, but there are differences in views on how it should be carried out. **The Sixth Global Congress on Combating Counterfeiting and Piracy was hosted by WIPO in Paris in February 2011. Convened by a public-private partnership including, among others, leaders from INTERPOL, the World Customs Organization (WCO) and the International Chamber of Commerce, the Congress discussed issues such as new methods of financing enforcement and respect for intellectual property rights as a key component of sustainable development.**

Comparing WIPO with TRIPs

The role of WIPO (a UN agency) was challenged in the 1980s, at a time when a private-sector alliance of pharmaceutical companies, the chemical industry, giant software firms, and the recording, broadcasting and film industries developed a plan to shift international copyright, trademark and patent law away from WIPO and into what would become the WTO's Agreement on Trade-Related Aspects of Intellectual Property Rights (TRIPs) (Costanza-Chock, 2005). The TRIPs agreement was signed in 1995 and has become a far more powerful mechanism than WIPO.

The WTO and its TRIPs signatory countries now have at their disposal policing and enforcement powers and can impose trade sanctions on countries that fail to adopt strong copyright and patent law. The industries that need copyright protection, such as film, music, books, TV and magazines, include the world's largest media conglomerates, and the WTO underwrites and enforces their rights in all the TRIPs signatory countries. The WTO is also the forum in which these rights have become, in one respect, narrower, retaining only the model used by wealthy nations, and in another, deeper, in terms of duration and depth (Ó Siochrú, 2004: 6).

However, Costanza-Chock (2005) claims that WIPO as it cooperates with the WTO/TRIPs and as such favors the privatization of collectively produced information and knowledge. For example, WIPO backs the interests of the biotechnology industry in promoting the private ownership of genetic code, including plant, animal and human genes. In the media and communications domain, the organization promotes a copyright system that gives long-term control of music and other audiovisual materials to big media conglomerates, undermining the rights of fair use and limiting the creative possibilities of artists, musicians and filmmakers. Thus WIPO may have turned into an institution devoted to promoting and enforcing an 'intellectual property rights' regime that favors corporate interests above all others (ibid.).

Conclusion

The WTO and other trade-oriented supranational authorities are clear examples of the growing institutional power of international trade agreements in spheres such as media and cultural products and services, the harmonization of technological standards and intellectual property rights. The WTO and its General Agreement on Trade in Services pose a direct challenge to national media policies, as they restrict the ability of their member states to protect their markets. The existence of these supranational bodies shows that media policy is increasingly made outside national regulatory agencies.

In the case of telecommunications, the domain of national regulation has long been linked to transnational agencies of governance, from the ITU to the WTO. Meanwhile, one can witness a greater degree of commercialization (or marketization) of all forms of public communication and the relative decline of national sovereignty over the flow of media content. This means that national media regulation, including quotas for local content and support for the audiovisual sector, is at stake, as is the future of PSB (see next chapter).

Alongside the above broad observation, there are a number of specific points to be made concerning supranational organizations and their power as against that of the nation-state. The first is that not all governments are equal – powerful governments can force others to cede their authority to an agency or treaty (Ó Siochrú, 2004: 7). The most powerful media policy bodies are US-led and therefore it is often the position of the US government that prevails in their deliberations. Most of the positions and decisions taken in these bodies represent the economic interests of the powerfully entrenched US communications conglomerates, rather than the interests of civil society (Costanza-Chock, 2005: 259–60). The impact of corporate-controlled global media policy is greatest in countries with weak domestic media, culture and communication industries. Low-income communities of the global south have been under intense pressure to liberalize their national media and telecommunications sectors and allow foreign capital to flow in (see Chakravarthy and Sarikakis, 2006).

This leads to the second point – namely that the harmonization of media policy has been achieved in a context of intense pressure from the powerful players (especially the USA) whose media and communications firms stand to benefit from the revision of other countries' media and cultural policies. The harmonization of media policy typically refers to a corporate-controlled global media policy with the following characteristics: abandonment of public investment in noncommercial media; renunciation of local language requirements or support for local ownership; imposition of US-style maximalist copyright law; dropping of subsidies for universal access to telecommunications; pursuance of media liberalization and privatization; and allowance of takeovers by the largest transnational media conglomerates (Costanza-Chock, 2005: 260).

Broadly speaking, this corresponds to what Kerr (1983: 3) has termed the 'convergence of traditional national policies' as a result of globalization. Convergence here is understood as the tendency of policies to grow more alike, in the form of increasing similarity in structures, processes and performance (see also Drezner, 2001). The next chapter will show that the EU has also emerged as a supranational organization seeking to harmonize national media policies, although EU member states retain considerable powers when it comes to cultural issues.

Third, UNESCO and other global organizations that represent the non-corporatist perspective on the media are gradually gaining momentum. This is evidenced by the Convention on Cultural Diversity, which represents a protectionist alternative to the principles of free trade and highlights UNESCO's renewed role to the arena of global media governance. However, the convention has inferior power to that of the WTO and, according to industrial lobbyists, 'it is good as a promotional instrument, but not if it interferes with the free trade spirit of the WTO' (cited in Freedman, 2008: 206).

In the same vein, the WSIS experience has shown that global media decision-making is not exclusively the terrain of nation-states and other powerful multinational organizations, for other previously neglected players like NGOs are becoming increasingly important in influencing agendas. However, Siochrú (2004: 7) observes that, in relation to media and communications, civil society has so far as a whole been largely silent, viewing the media primarily as tools to promote their own agendas, rather than as active and influential agents in their own right. It has been argued that international fora such as the WSIS (a pair of UN-sponsored conferences in information and communication with the aim of bridging the global digital divide and spreading Internet access in the developing world) have been preoccupied by pro-market, neoliberal objectives (see also Pickard, 2007).

In this sense, it remains doubtful whether the participation of NGOs and other civil society organizations in multilateral forums will be able to roll back the extensive influence of the WTO. It is indeed difficult to measure what weight civil society is being given in actual outcomes. On the one hand, civil society's participation in international fora increases transparency in the process and provides an alternative point of view to the dominant neoliberal doctrine, but on the other, civil society is disorganized compared with cohesive forums like the WTO and/or the business sector when in defence of their interests.

In an era dominated by neoliberal ideals, the pursuance of economic and free-market mechanisms in all industry sectors, including the audiovisual sector overrides societal regulation. Initiatives emanating from civil society are positive and welcome, but at this point let me share Peter Humphreys' concern that too much enthusiasm is expressed about these outcomes, as at the WSIS, and that a more critical view is needed. Another worry is that these practices are perhaps a 'cover behind which deregulation and market liberalisation is rampant' (Humphreys, 2007). Borrowing from Edelman's 1985 book *The Symbolic Uses of Politics*, where it is pointed out that US competition policy has legitimized a huge amount of industrial concentration over the years, Humphreys makes a case that it might rather be marketization that is on the long march.

On the issue as to whether there has been a shift in state sovereignty to the global level due to increased trade and new technologies, the rise of international organizations like the WTO reveals that nation-states' regulatory power is clearly affected in the era of global governance. As Siochrú (2004: 7) notes:

> Once intergovernmental agreements are reached and ratified, they exhibit a tendency to take on a life of their own, and the central role of the administering agency in interpretation and implementation lands it in the driving seat. Accordingly, the agencies are gradually carving out a sphere of influence and must thus be considered as actors in their own right.

However, national governments continue to play a primary role in preserving their cultural policy. Despite globalization, governments are still in charge of their audiovisual industries, can pursue cultural diversity and protect their public service broadcasters. The next chapter shows how the European Union, viewed as a regional agent of globalization, has attempted to intervene in areas such as PSB, and pluralism and media ownership. Through examining the range of national and supranational responses to the regulatory challenges posed by changes in the above domains, the chapter demonstrates that EU member states have maintained much of their sovereignty.

7
Media and Communications Policy in the European Union

Introduction

Media and communications policy across the European Union (EU) has been conducted at national level, with each member state developing a specific regulatory regime to oversee communication issues in its territory. While the print media in Europe have traditionally enjoyed a great degree of autonomy and self-regulation (Hutchison, 2007), broadcasting has attracted state intervention because of technical matters (spectrum limitation[1]) but also because of its capacity to influence listeners and viewers in their choices. However, the organization and functioning of the media systems are not the same across Europe, for they vary in the way they are funded and structured, their political independence, and so on (Humphreys, 1996; Iosifidis, 2007). The large variations among the media systems stem from the different traditions and political cultures as well as regulatory systems that exist across Europe.

A common theme of national communications regulatory regimes has been to promote social cohesion and solidarity and create an informed citizenship by ensuring that the media offer a wide range of content that support particular social, civil and political values. But media policy and regulation has typically been influenced by national variables such as historical experience, culture and values. National political and social conditions determine the regulation of content available through the media, either in ensuring the universality of reception or in guaranteeing that certain programming genres are made available to the public. A national focus also characterizes the structural regulation of media sectors (the regulation of 'who owns what', which intends to limit media owners' influence over citizens). Governments have adopted a wide range of tools (media and cross-media ownership rules, licensing regimes, competition law) to ensure plurality in the provision of information.

Over time these differences blur as the EU emerges as a supranational organization seeking to harmonize national media policies. This chapter looks at the processes through which the EU has progressively become a main player in national communications policy and regulation. It focuses on the European institutions of the European Commission (EC), the European Parliament (EP), the European Court of Justice (ECJ) and the Council of Europe (CoE) and assesses their influence in shaping and directing national communications practice, mainly in the areas of media ownership, pluralism, public service broadcasting (PSB) and digital switchover. It reveals that, although these institutions have different objectives and varying degrees of influence (for example, the EC as the executive body has more clout than the EP, whose role in communications is mainly consultative), there is a distinct pattern of policy convergence emerging within the EU, aimed at the following two goals: completion and the efficient functioning of the internal market, which is characterized as 'an area without internal frontiers in which the free movement of goods, persons, services and capital is ensured'.

The second goal is reregulation through 'soft' governance initiatives and an industrial policy-based audiovisual policy, especially with regard to the new online media. This aim goes hand in hand with the 'new paradigm' of media policy prioritizing economic goals over social and political welfare (Van Guilenburg and McQuail, 2003). It also reflects the broad political and ideological endorsement of market-based solutions; in other words, as succinctly put by some commentators (Wheeler, 2004; Michalis, 2007), the EU is seeking to encourage the expansion of media services through the principles of liberalization and harmonization.

Yet it is clear that the EU's competence to regulate in the arena of public interest goals and cultural matters is limited compared with its powers to intervene in the economic field principally by adopting economic instruments (competition law, merger regulation). For instance, member states are still responsible for establishing media ownership rules 'for considerations of public interest'. However, the EU has recently started playing an important monitoring role in the cultural field, as evidenced by initiatives such as the development of a tool to monitor pluralism across the EU. The initiative attempted to define media pluralism broadly to cover not only media ownership issues but also access to a wide range of information (to enable people to form opinions without being influenced by dominant operators) and transparent mechanisms (to ensure that the media are independent) (Independent Study, 2009; also http://ec.europa.eu/information_society/media_taskforce/doc/pluralism/pfr_report.pdf, accessed 30 November 2010). Another example of EU involvement has been the effort to coordinate at EU level national digital switchover plans in order to make the process open and transparent.

Furthermore, the EU has become involved with several state aid procedures concerning the funding and licensing of public service broadcasters (PSBs) and has hardened its stance against PSBs and their anticompetitive effect in terms of market distortion. While the EU recognizes the right of member states to determine the organization and funding of their PSBs in accordance with the protocol of the 1997 Amsterdam Treaty (which strikes a balance between the realization of the public service remit entrusted to PSBs and the defence of the supranational common interest in the undistorted functioning of the internal market), the criteria of market distortion and unfair competitive practice have come to define the EU's monitoring approach.

The growing involvement of the European Commission in media and communications policy

The reasons of EU's involvement in media policy

Since the 1980s, the EU has been playing an increasingly important role in the sphere of media and communications. There are three main reasons for this. First, the globalization of communications systems has contested the idea of fundamentally national media. Earlier chapters showed that the emergence of international media organizations as well as supranational bodies contributed to the globalization of communications systems. The EU has also emerged as a supranational communications policy actor, posing a set of questions about the nation-state in the era of supranational governance.. Even though the EU is not a political union, it can complement, supplement and even substitute policies of the member states (Chakravarthy and Sarikakis, 2006). The EU has become a salient actor in national regulation because it wants to harmonize national regulatory regimes. Even though each EU member state had developed a specific regulatory framework to govern its communications industry, from the mid-1980s one can observe a gradual convergence in national regulation (policy convergence) (Levy, 1999; Harcourt, 2010).

The process of *Europeanization* or *integration* of national markets is another reason for intervention by the EU legislator (European Commission (EC)) in the field of media and communications. It should be noted that scholars have attempted a conceptualization of Europeanization that distinguishes it from European integration. Olsen (2002) broke down Europeanization into five possible phenomena related to what is actually changing:

- Changes in external territorial boundaries.
- Development of governance institutions at supranational level.
- Imposing supranational rules at the subnational and national levels.
- Exporting governance procedures and policies specific to EU beyond EU borders.
- Intensifying the unification of the EU through a project of a political nature.

However, according to Howell (2004), some of these areas seem to support the concept (or thesis) of European integration. For instance, the development of supranational institutions, the formulation of legislation by these institutions and the political nature of the project could be seen as relating to (at least in part) European integration.

This volume considers European integration and Europeanization as synonyms, referring to the process of EU national governments' adapting to EU communications policy and complying with EU institutional structures and mandates. This has been most striking in the case of broadcasting. The Television Without Frontiers (TWF) Directive – now Audiovisual Media Services (AVMS) Directive – was designed with the objective of favoring the completion and the effective functioning of the internal market for broadcasting services. The text was elaborated at the same time as the European Convention on Transfrontier Television and took into consideration both the market dimension of the audiovisual services and their sociocultural aspect. But although continuing EU attention on social and cultural issues such as media pluralism and freedom of expression are positive aspects, this book argues that the EU appears to prioritize economic, industrial and competition issues. The introduction of legislative documents, such as the AVMS Directive, enacts Europeanization through reregulation and the commercialization of national policy regimes.

A third reason concerns the increased EU competence over the communications industry. While the history of media policy in Europe commenced at national level with governments interfering to various degrees in the regulation of the press, broadcasting and later digital media, the EU competence over the communications industry has been progressively achieved through the joint (but not necessarily coordinated) activity of the European Commission (EC), the European Parliament (EP) and the European Court of Justice (ECJ). As Casarosa (2010) argues, the expansion of EU competence in the media domain is primarily ascribed to the ECJ in confirming its jurisdiction over fields that might not have been thought part of the original economic scope of the European Economic Community (EEC) Treaty. For example, the ECJ defined broadcasting as a tradable service and thus subject to the rules on free movement across the member states. Such an economics-based approach placed broadcasting in the domain of economic policy to be conducted at European level and provided the rationale that has been used by the EC to push for regulatory intervention in the media industry, also pointing the legal basis that could be used for the adoption of the TWF Directive.

European Union media policy in the 1980s and 1990s

The TWF Directive

The pursuance of national media policy convergence began in the 1980s, when EU member states implemented the Television Without Frontiers (TWF) Directive, now renamed the Audiovisual Media Services (AVMS) Directive.

This policy document constitutes the regulatory pillar of the audiovisual policy because it is essentially an internal market instrument setting out the 'rules of the game' for the free circulation of audiovisual media services on the basis of the country-of-origin principle. It clarifies the approach of the EU to the audiovisual sector, mainly by providing the basis for the free circulation of broadcasting programmes in the internal market and establishing a minimum harmonization of rules on advertising. As Casarosa (2010: 24) notes, the implementation of the Directive represented a milestone in EU audiovisual policy, not merely because it was the first legislative intervention in the field, but also because it prompted a significant revision of domestic media laws and regulations that were in conflict with the provisions of the Directive.

As De Witte (2006) notes, the primary objective of the EC's policy was the completion and the efficient functioning of the internal market for broadcasting services. The creation of a single audiovisual market was envisaged through the reregulation and liberalization of cross-border broadcasting. Policy formation at national level was clearly affected, as the EC could be seen to have steered the course of the debate over the reregulation of broadcasting services at national level (Humphreys, 2009). The legislator's definition of broadcasting as a service of 'economic interest' placed it in the realm of economic policy and paved the way for the development of a large body of media case law, including the TWF Directive. As will be shown below, the recently adopted AVMS Directive is largely oriented in this direction: further consolidation at EU level and structural reformation, taking into consideration technological advances and the 'realm of convergence'. Meanwhile, the document includes sociocultural interventions.

But the policy intervention of the EU into the broadcasting arena was reactive, for in 1974 the ECJ was the first institution to intervene in the media sector. The ECJ is in fact the only EU institution with the legal competence to assess national media laws and Court decisions, and determine changes to the composition of the media industry (Harcourt, 2004: 36). Through its judgments in the Sacchi and Debauve cases,[2] the ECJ defined the transmission of TV signals as a tradable service, thereby establishing EU jurisdiction over broadcasting (Michalis, 2010: 38).

Early 1990s: the EC and the Green Paper on pluralism and media concentration

While acknowledging the EU's attention to cultural issues, most academic literature notes that EU media policy is rooted in industrial policy with a focus on regulating capital investments and the efficient provision of services within the internal market. This claim can be supported if one looks at the *Green Paper on Pluralism and Media Concentration in the Internal Market – An Assessment of the Need for Community Action* (EC, 1992). The EC's

Green Paper was an attempt to respond to the concerns of the CoE[3] and the EP,[4] which, through various interventions, had expressed the view that unchecked concentrations in media ownership could pose a threat to information, editorial independence and journalistic freedom. These two institutions have shown greater attention to the cultural dimension, whereas the European Commission's approach to concentration of media ownership has been more closely connected with the internal market perspective, rejecting pluralism as an EC objective. Both the CoE and the EP called for a legislative framework for media mergers and takeovers together with antitrust laws on the grounds that diversity of opinion and pluralism of information could not be guaranteed by competition rules alone. But instead of a Directive or Legislation, the EC came up with a Green Paper whose purpose was to present both an initial assessment of the need for Community action concerning concentration in the media and an outline of the approaches the Commission might adopt once it had consulted the parties concerned.[5]

The Green Paper identified no objective to safeguard media pluralism at EU level: 'Protection of pluralism as such is primarily a matter for the member states [...] there would not appear to be any need for action at Community level, since national mechanisms for protecting pluralism can be applied to situations with a Community dimension' (EC, 1992: 7). The document did not provide a definition of media pluralism; however, it mentioned a variety of expressions used in national legislative statutes containing the 'pluralism' concept: 'pluralism of the media', 'pluralism in the media', 'the pluralist nature of the expression of currents of thought and opinion', 'pluralism of information', 'pluralism of the press' and 'plurality of the media' (ibid.: 14). In the Commission's view the concept is imprecise but it is easily used as a reason to justify measures in support of freedom of expression or diversity of information sources. The Green Paper suggested three possible ways for assessing pluralism: a) *according to the editorial content of the broadcasts or the press*, which was considered the most logical method, albeit the most complex, data-demanding and subjective; b) *according to the number of channels or titles*, which, despite being easily measurable, was rejected as insignificant in terms of diversity of editorial content; and c) *according to the number of media controllers or owners*, which seemed to be the Commission's preferred criterion since, although it too did not reflect editorial content, 'whatever the editorial content or the number of information carriers, concentration of control of media access in the hands of a few is by definition a threat to the diversity of information' (ibid.: 20).

Part two of the Commission's Green Paper described the level of media concentration in Europe. This part was based upon a Booz-Allen & Hamilton study (1992) commissioned by the EC. The study concluded that national rules limiting the shareholdings in a channel did not appear to prevent the dominating influence of a single group.[6] Therefore, a Community-level initiative to harmonize the different rules with the aim of ensuring pluralism and checking on media concentration would be appropriate. As the main objective of the Green Paper was to assess the need for action at Community level in the light of the disparities between national rules on media ownership, the concern was that these discrepancies could create obstacles to the freedom to provide services across borders and to the freedom of establishment, thereby preventing media operators from benefiting from the advantages of the internal market.

Part three of the Green Paper presented a overview of the national measures and concluded that disparities in national ownership rules could produce distortions of competition between firms from different states by placing companies operating in liberal regimes in a better position than those established in systems with stricter rules. Differences in national legislation might also hamper media companies in the development of pan-European strategies – creating subsidiaries in different member states or investing in new media outlets across Europe.

In part four, the Green Paper proposed various ways of responding to the situation, ranging from taking no action at all to enhancing transparency in the media and facilitating the disclosure and exchange of information on media ownership between national authorities or harmonizing national restrictions in the area of media concentrations via either a Directive or a Regulation or by the creation of an independent committee.

These policy options should be considered in the light of the three EC objectives. The chief objective was (and still is) the completion and the proper functioning of the single European market. The craving for the harmonization of national media ownership rules had more to do with ensuring the smooth operation of the single market than with safeguarding pluralism as such. This is the reason as to why harmonization would affect only ownership rules and not rules related to the content of the mass media, since the latter do not normally influence the performance of the internal market. In any case, the accomplishment of this objective could, in the Commission's opinion, help to increase pluralism by providing more opportunities for media entities. Pluralism was invoked to justify the second major objective, that is, the implementation of an industrial policy to foster the competitiveness of the media industry. By making media firms competitive, the Commission sought to contribute indirectly to media pluralism. The main concern, though, was to create an economically viable media sector, boost production and assist the formation of big units able to compete internationally. Differing national regulatory frameworks on media concentrations, mergers and acquisitions might affect the competitiveness of media undertakings. The formation of an audiovisual policy to create the European audiovisual space is the third Community objective. National inconsistencies and sometimes media policy anachronisms indeed affect the operation of transfrontier channels.

To sum up, the EC's approach, as expressed through the Green Paper, was to conflate two different, though sometimes overlapping, goals. On the one hand, it tried to pursue an industrial strategy that would enable European media undertakings to become big and therefore both compete effectively globally and prevent, by their presence, the takeover of a country's media by foreign interests. The deregulatory move that this aim implied carry a price, which was the threat to the diversity and circulation of ideas that might be caused by the concentration of political power in the hands of a few. The Commission was careful to ensure that its policies 'do not adversely affect pluralism' (EC, 1992: 7). It also argued that competition law 'can also contribute to pluralism in the media' (ibid.: 60). So the Green Paper acknowledged that competition and pluralism were incompatible criteria. Yet it affirmed that there was a connection between them, since the former could have positive effects on the latter. As stated by Davis (1993: 9), however, the twin aims of competition and pluralism are safeguarded in different ways. The first is fostered by removing barriers to entry whereas the second is guaranteed by 'positive' content regulation.

True, there can be a definition of pluralism as a competition law concept, in the sense of ensuring a variety of providers to access the media market. This approach implies monitoring established media enterprises in order to prevent abuses of dominant positions and the formation of price cartels and barriers to entry. Competition law can certainly help to protect media pluralism by preventing collusive practices or mergers that could restrict consumer choice, but it can be used only sporadically, on a case-by-case basis. Yet political pluralism (the possibility for all political and social voices to be heard) and cultural pluralism (the promotion of content variety in the media) are cultural values that can be best guaranteed by noneconomic, sector-specific media regulation, which is typically tighter than general competition and antitrust law. The Green Paper itself admitted that the achievement of pluralism requires tighter regulation than that of competition (EC, 1992: 82). It is clear that the Commission had embarked upon a dubious task of conflating diverse and incompatible concerns. As will be shown below, in more recent years the EC has decided to take a monitoring role on the issue of media pluralism and has commissioned a study to define it more broadly and not merely in terms of concentration of media ownership.

EC competition law and media pluralism

The EU's competition policy framework lies in Articles 81 and 82 of the EU Treaty (2006). Competition policy is concerned first with preventing agreements between undertakings that reduce the effectiveness of the competitive process, second with restricting mergers that increase the probability of excessive market power being exercised, and third with combating anticompetitive behavior, which enables firms either to acquire excessive market power or to increase barriers to entry for newcomers. The main objectives of competition rules are first to foster technological innovation and price competition, and second to guarantee consumer choice (see Iosifidis, 2005). As a former European Commissioner for Competition Policy has asserted, this is achieved by ensuring that companies compete rather than collude, that market power is not abused and that efficiencies are passed on to end-users (Monti, 2001).

Thus competition policy rules ensure (or should ensure) that the competitive process is not threatened by either the market structure or the conduct of firms. Its application to the media industry, however, cannot always safeguard other values and objectives such as media pluralism and freedom of expression. Media policy has traditionally encompassed a much wider range of public values and objectives than simply the efficient functioning of private markets. The media play a central role as disseminators of information, opinions and culture, and policies are often founded on broad principles governing the circulation of ideas and information that are fundamental values for pluralistic democratic societies. Precisely because of the nature of the media industry, competition policy objectives are not enough for preserving such values. This is not to say that competition policy does not have a role to play in the cultural field. Policies promoting efficient competition may limit the concentration of media control and at the same time promote the presentation of diverse points of view. However, the safeguarding of a competitive environment and the promotion of diversity are different (although sometimes overlapping) objectives. The latter can be fostered only by specific media rules on either content or ownership.

The Merger Regulation

In addition to competition rules, a Regulation on the Control of Concentrations between Undertakings was adopted by the Council of the European Economic Community in 1989 and became effective on 21 September 1990. The Merger Regulation (Council Regulation (EEC) No. 4064/89, as amended by Council Regulation (EC) No. 139/2004, OJ L24/I-22) was intended to complement the EC's antitrust powers, conferred by Articles 81 and 82 (then Articles 85 and 86 of the Rome Treaty), and also give the Commission preemptive power to prevent mergers. Until 1989, the EC had had the power to act against anticompetitive mergers and acquisitions only after they had taken effect and a restrictive practice or dominant position had been established or strengthened. For many years the EC had argued that it should have pre-emptive power, which would remove the necessity for retrospective action by the parties involved. In fact, competition rules that intervene after a problem of imbalance has arisen (for example, an anticompetitive practice has been established or a dominant position has already been created) may not be able to remedy the situation. The Merger Regulation was intended to deal with that problem. This is becoming more important since the Merger Regulation because, in order to gain maximum benefit from the information society, 'gate-keeping'[7] issues require a more direct anticipation in competition law.

Under the Merger Regulation, the EC has exclusive jurisdiction over proposed mergers between firms with a 'European dimension' – an aggregate turnover of at least €5 billion and an individual turnover within the European Economic Area of more than €250 million. The Regulation therefore covers only major mergers, which significantly affect competition in the market in question. As a result, it has allowed many mergers to proceed as they fell outside its scope (Iosifidis, 1996; Just and Latzer, 2000). In the 10-year period between 1990 and 2000, the Merger Regulation vetted over 2,300 cases and cleared the vast majority of them (over 90 per cent) after a routine one-month investigation. It prohibited just 18 proposed mergers, while a further 14 were withdrawn when it became clear that regulators would veto them. Six of those cases were in the media and telecommunications sectors.[8] However, there is a specific provision that relates to mergers affecting media pluralism (Art. 21(4)), which allows member states to apply stricter legislation to these mergers. This way the EC allows member states to apply tougher national regulation where they think media pluralism might be in danger.

Mid-1990s: a more interventionist and harmonizing approach to media policy

Throughout the 1990s the EU started to develop a more interventionist communications policy, as evidenced by the issuing of the White Paper on Growth, Competitiveness and Jobs (EC, 1993), the Bangemann Report (EC, 2004), the Green Paper on the Convergence of Telecommunications, Media and Information Technology Sectors, and Implications for Regulation (EC, 1997) and the Protocol on the System of Public Broadcasting attached to the Treaty of Amsterdam (EU, 1997). The 1993 White Paper and the 1994 Bangemann Report verified the pursuance of an economic policy and set the agenda for the development of an information society, the main aspects of which, as far as the media and communication industry was concerned, were outlined in the December 1997 Green Paper. This last document envisaged the need for imposing fresh rules to maximize the benefits of digital convergence in terms of job creation, industry growth, consumer choice, cultural diversity and political pluralism. However, the Convergence Green Paper revealed the conflicts that existed (and still exist) within the EU between, on the one hand, economic and industrial issues, and on the other, sociocultural implications. The last section of this book provides an in-depth discussion on convergence and in this context it reviews the EC convergence agenda. The focus here will be on how the EC has regulated media markets with reference to PSBs receiving state aid.

The Protocol on the System of Public Broadcasting in the member states

The Protocol on the System of Public Broadcasting in the member states was introduced as an Annex to the Treaty of Amsterdam and came into force in 1999. The EU Competition Directorate licensed PSBs in accordance with the above Protocol, which enabled them to receive subsides as long as they did not distort national media markets (Wheeler, 2010: 49). It should be noted that PSBs in Europe receive more than €22 billion annually from licence fees and direct government aid, placing them in third place after agriculture and transport companies among recipients of state aid. Soltesz (2010: 36) argued that these massive donations will always make it difficult for private operators to compete with them. The Protocol focused on PSB and aimed to provide an interpretative aid for the application of EU competition and state aid law to the functioning of PSBs, which were set and organised by each member state (Casarosa, 2010: 11). The document attempted to strike a balance between the realization of the public service remit entrusted to PSBs and the defence of the common pan-European interest in the efficient functioning of the internal broadcasting market (ibid.: 11–2). The reason for EC's paying such strong attention to PSB rests upon the consideration that 'the system of public broadcasting in the member states is directly related to the democratic, social and cultural needs of each society and to the need to preserve media pluralism' (EU, 1997).

The EC has become involved with various state aid cases concerning the funding and licensing of PSBs as defined by the Amsterdam Protocol and by the ECJ's Altmark decision concerning proportionality and overcompensation (ECJ, 2003). These cases were instigated by complaints from commercial market players who argued that PSBs distort the market as they are recipients both of public funding and of commercial revenue. The inherent tension in the EU broadcasting policy process has been evident insofar as neoliberal objectives have collided with traditional PSB regimes. By the end of the 1990s, commercial channels in Spain, France, Germany, Italy and Denmark had complained about their PSBs' dual forms of funding (licence fees and advertising), which they claimed gave PSBs an unfair advantage.

Although the Amsterdam Protocol stipulated that national governments were free to determine the method of PSB funding so long as it did not distort competitive trading for the common interest (see Papathanassopoulos, 2002: 72), in 1999 the Commission opened formal proceedings regarding PSBs in Italy, France and Spain (who received revenues from both state subsidy and advertising). It found that the PSBs' collection of advertising revenues did not unfairly distort the national markets (Wheelers, 2010: 51–2). In 2001, in an attempt to end the case-by-case treatment of commercial players' complaints, the Commission adopted guidelines clarifying the application of state aid rules to PSB. The 2001 Broadcasting Communication recognized that, in line with the Amsterdam Protocol, the determination of the public service remit and funding model rests with the member states, while the Commission can only check for manifest error and possible abusive practices (EC, 2001b: para. 11).

The 2009 Broadcasting Communication on the application of state aid rules to PSB[9]

In July 2009, the EC replaced its 2001 Communication on the application of state aid rules to PSB by the Broadcasting Communication (EC, 2009a), based on experience gained in its decision-making practice and taking into consideration the technological changes in the media environment. With the Broadcasting Communication the Commission stipulated that: a) the public service remit must be clearly defined and entrusted to the public service mandate through a formal act of entrustment; b) financing must be limited to the actual costs of the public service after having deducted revenues from the commercial exploitation of the public service; and c) commercial activities must be carried out in a manner that corresponds to the market criteria. There are three core policy changes that have an impact on the legal and economic framework. The first is avoiding overcompensation (to grant an operator compensation in return of the discharge of public service obligations). The Broadcasting Communication contains a more effective control mechanism concerning possible overcompensation and the supervision of the public service mission (ibid.: para. 70). As a principle, overcompensation always constitutes incompatible state aid. The Commission considers that state funding is normally necessary for the undertaking to carry out its public service tasks. However, in order to satisfy the proportionality test, the amount of public compensation may, generally, not exceed the net costs of the public service mission.

The second shift concerns clarification of 'pay services'. Technological innovations in the audiovisual markets have raised new questions concerning the application of state aid rules to audiovisual services that go beyond broadcasting activities in the traditional sense. PSBs are increasingly turning to new sources of financing, such as online advertising or the provision of services for payment. These so-called 'pay services' are, for instance, access to archives for a fee, special interest TV channels on a pay-per-view basis, deferred access to TV programmes for a fee and paid online content downloads. A section of the Broadcasting Communication clarifies the Commission's position with respect to these pay services. PSBs may use state aid to provide audiovisual services on new distribution platforms. Although public broadcasting services have traditionally been free of charge, a direct remuneration element – while having an impact on access by viewers – does not necessarily mean that these services are not part of the public service remit and should be excluded from state aid. In effect, provided that the given service satisfies specific social, democratic and cultural needs of society without leading to disproportionate effects on competition and cross-border trade, member states may allow PSBs to operate it as part of their public service remit.

Third, *ex ante* control of 'significant new services' launched by PSB was introduced (ibid.: para. 84). Member states are now required to undertake an evaluation procedure based on an open public consultation process before any significant new services are put on the market by PSBs. In order to ensure transparency and to obtain all relevant information, this consultation must give all stakeholders the opportunity to submit their views on the envisaged new service. The member state must then consider whether the proposed service meets the requirements of the Amsterdam Protocol (for example, whether it serves the democratic, social and cultural needs of the society) while taking into account its potential effects on trading conditions and competition. The Communication makes it clear that member states can define what constitutes 'significant new services'. But to ensure that the public funding of significant new audiovisual services does not distort trade and competition, member states need to assess their overall impact on the market (among others, relevant aspects are: the market structure, the market position of the PSB, the level of competition and the potential impact on private initiatives). This market impact needs to be balanced with the value to society of the services in question. For an objective assessment, this process should be carried out by a body that is independent from the management of the public service broadcaster.

It is clear that, although the EC has so far supported PSBs in state aid cases, its reasoning has changed in recent years. Whereas in the past, 'market failure' was not regarded as an important argument in the EC's analysis, the new Communication considers PSBs' expansion into nontraditional broadcasting fields (the Internet and online and mobile media) with caution. The application of competition policy to state aid measures has meant that PSBs have to clearly define their public value and has hampered their opportunities to engage in commercial activities that could create market distortion. However, the rigid employment of such policy fails to take into account the sociocultural functions of PSBs. As succinctly put by Wheeler (2010: 59–60), competition policy in relation to state aid fails to conceive information and communication rights as a public good. This is an issue of concern, since communication must be considered as having a significant *social* worth, as well as being understood as an *economic* commodity.

EU communications policy in the new millennium

The EU's interventionist and harmonizing approach to communications policy continued in the new millennium through the implementation of the 2003 Regulatory Framework for the Regulation of Electronic Communications, the E-Commerce Directive applicable to 'Information

Society Services' (EC, 2000b), the various Commission Communications pushing for the harmonization of national digital switchover plans, and the new version of the AVMS Directive, intended to create a single market for all audiovisual media services by providing less detailed but more flexible regulation and modernizing TV advertising rules (EC, 2007).

The 2003 Regulatory Framework for the Regulation of Electronic Communications[10]

In the early 2000s, the EU reviewed progress on competitive initiatives in the communications industry across the Union and re-emphasized the importance of setting out a new regulatory framework that would simplify regulation and speed up decision-making. The passing of the new Regulatory Framework for the Regulation of Electronic Communications was intended to avoid the risk of policy being overtaken by the fast-moving evolution of markets and technology. In order to ensure legal certainty in the transition from the existing regulatory framework to the new Regulatory Framework, the EC proposed five new Directives (Framework, Access, Authorizations, Universal Service and Data Protection), which would replace existing Directives (EC, 2000a). The new Directives aimed to establish a harmonized regulatory framework for electronic communications networks and services across the EU. They sought to respond to the convergence phenomenon by covering all sectors within their jurisdiction (Iosifidis, 2002).

The E-Commerce Directive

The Electronic Commerce (E-Commerce) Directive (EC, 2000b) applies to 'information society services', which are defined as 'any service normally provided for remuneration, at a distance, by electronic means and at the individual request of a recipient of services' (see Art. 1(2) Directive 98/34/EC, as amended by Directive 98/48/EC). In effect, on-demand video and radio services and online newspapers fall within the definition, but radio and television *broadcasts* are specifically exempt from the Directive. A distinction is therefore drawn between on the one hand broadcasting and printed newspapers/magazines, which are in this respect unregulated by the EU, and on the other comparable online services, which are regulated. To fall within the ambit of these EU provisions, the services must have a commercial aspect (see Stolte and Smith, 2010). However, the 2007 AVMS Directive (described below) applies a variety of content and structural requirements to audiovisual media services, though offline print media remain unregulated.

From TWF to AVMS Directive

The AVMS Directive (EU, 2007) was adopted in December 2007 to update the TWF Directive and, in accordance with the new Regulatory Framework described above, it aimed at reflecting market developments in a communications environment characterized by technological convergence. Several factors necessitated the revision (Michalis, 2010: 43–5). First, it no longer made sense to have rules on broadcast TV only, as the same content was progressively becoming available online and was largely unregulated. Second, viewers were accessing content in both linear and on-demand formats through new technological platforms outside the scope of the TWF Directive. Finally, the development of new advertising techniques (split screen, interactive advertising) and the migration of advertising from conventional to online media, which was putting pressure on traditional advertising revenues, was increasing calls for the relaxation of the prescriptive rules in the TWF Directive. So the AVMS Directive was adapted to the new audiovisual environment in accordance with technological advances and the tendency toward convergence which necessitated the scope of application to be extended to all audiovisual media services, encompassing new platforms of delivery.

The new Directive covered all audiovisual media services, including both traditional television (linear service) and video-on-demand (nonlinear services). All audiovisual media services have to respect the basic tier of obligations in the following areas:

• Identification of media service provider.
• Prohibition of incitement to hatred.
• Accessibility to people with disabilities.
• Qualitative requirements for commercial communications.
• Sponsorship (rules on sponsorship which aim to impose similar standards on sponsored programmes on on-demand services as apply to linear television channels).
• Product placement (provisions on product placement for on-demand programmes).

The rules on advertising and protecting children are stricter for television broadcasts. Stricter rules in the areas of advertising and protection of minors are in existence for television broadcasts due to their impact on society. Regarding TV advertising, there are quality standards: existing rules on protecting consumers, children and human dignity are maintained, and new challenges are addressed (for example, potentially unhealthy foodstuffs and calls for industry self-regulation/codes of conduct). There are also different limits on quantity: these are now more flexible, but the hourly limit of 12 minutes for advertising spot and teleshopping spots remains (Article 23 (1)).

In addition to placing further restrictions on the scheduling and content of advertisements, the AVMS Directive stipulates that a majority of programming should be of European origin. These measures, dubbed 'European quota rules', were intended to promote the distribution of European television programmes and independent productions. The Directive requires member states to ensure that more than 50 per cent of programming time should be

made up of European productions and at least 10 per cent of either transmission time or of the broadcaster's programming budget should be devoted
to independent productions. The latest data from the EC (the Commission
publishes a report every two years on the promotion of European TV productions throughout the Union, one of the aims of the AVMS Directive)
show that EU television broadcasters are devoting an average of 63 per cent
of their air time to programmes made in the EU and 35 per cent to independent works created by European producers (see Table 7.1).

Table 7.1 Main indicators of EU works and independent producers
for 2007–2008 by member state (in %)

Country	European productions		European productions by independent producers	
	2007	2008	2007	2008
Austria	81.0	79.1	49.0	48.7
Belgium	74.9	69.1	54.0	46.0
Bulgaria	55.6	55.6	25.2	25.2
Cyprus	27.9	30.0	39.6	41.9
Czech Republic	64.3	65.9	32.2	34.7
Denmark	84.9	84.8	28.1	25.5
Finland	64.0	56.8	40.1	35.7
Germany	64.2	63.9	61.7	62.3
Greece	54.1	61.7	14.5	15.1
Hungary	68.5	75.3	39.7	41.8
Ireland	55.0	56.4	21.9	23.0
Italy	62.9	52.7	22.6	17.0
Latvia	62.2	62.2	18.4	19.7
Lithuania	59.3	59.1	39.0	41.5
Luxembourg	69.6	70.7	56.2	56.9
Malta	55.9	69.0	41.4	45.2
Netherlands	80.8	80.3	40.2	31.2
Poland	85.0	83.1	25.0	26.3
Portugal	72.5	63.8	39.5	24.1
Romania	63.0	67.2	28.2	25.9
Slovak Republic	66.5	67.3	24.0	23.8
Slovenia	34.1	44.6	10.9	15.9
Spain	54.2	55.7	31.3	29.6
Sweden	45.1	45.5	41.6	42.9
United Kingdom	51.7	50.7	29.8	28.3

Source: Digital Agenda: Two thirds of TV programmes seen in Europe are
of European origin, Press Release IP/10/1163, Brussels 23 September 2010.
Available at: http://europa.eu/rapid/pressReleasesAction.do?reference=IP/10/
1163 (accessed 14 December 2010).

Member states must ensure that not only television broadcasters but also on-demand audiovisual media services promote European productions. The reasons for this provision are to promote the European audiovisual industry, preserve European culture and identity, and prevent excessive flows of audiovisual materials to the continent, especially from the USA, which has by far the biggest share of the world trade in television and feature films. This policy of protectionism has provoked the fury of US multinationals, who wish to enter any market without facing regulatory obstacles. Following various challenges from the USA over the legality of quotas, the Community claimed that the quota rules were compatible with international trading rules such as the GATT (General Agreement of Trade and Tariffs) arguing, *inter alia*, that

- TV programming is a service, and thus is not governed by the GATT but by the GATS (General Agreement on Trade in Services).
- The local content requirement is not legally binding.
- TV programming falls within the existing 'Cinema Exception' in Article IV GATT.
- The local content requirement is justified under a general 'cultural exception' implicit in the GATT (see Castendyk, Dommering and Scheuer, 2008: 445).

Hence the AVMS Directive takes into consideration not merely the market dimension of the audiovisual services but also their cultural significance. This can be seen through the introduction of specific content-oriented measures aiming at promoting wider values such as the protection of minors and respect for human dignity. Indeed, one of the principles the AVMS Directive upholds throughout is the protection of minors. This is particularly relevant now that on-demand services have become available, as the content of programmes seen by children is less easily monitored when any programme can be viewed at any time. Article 3h introduced a provision requiring member states to take measures to ensure that on-demand services that might seriously impair the physical, mental or moral development of minors are made available in such a way that minors cannot normally have access to them. This complements the former Article 22 of the TWF Directive, which required that programmes that minors might be exposed to in the normal broadcasting schedule must not contain content that might seriously impair their physical, mental or moral development. If such content appeared in a programme (AVMS), the audience should be warned by an acoustic message (see http://www.twobirds.com/English/News/Articles/Pages/Audiovisual_Media_Services_Directive.Aspx, accessed 8 December 2010).

Furthermore, the new Directive embodied provisions to ensure that events that are regarded by member states as 'being of major importance for society' should be broadcast in such a way that a substantial part of the national

Table 7.2   Free-to-air listed events regime operating in the UK

Group A (full live coverage protected)	Group B (secondary coverage protected)*

Olympic Games
FIFA World Cup Finals tournament
European Football Championship
   Finals tournament
FA Cup Final
Scottish FA Cup Final (in Scotland)
Grand National
Wimbledon Tennis tournament finals
Rugby World Cup Final
The Derby
Rugby League Challenge Cup Final
	Cricket test matches played in England
	Non-finals play in the Wimbledon
	   tennis tournament
	All other matches in the Rugby World
	   Cup Finals tournament
	Six Nations rugby tournament matches
	   involving Home Countries
	Commonwealth Games
	World Athletics Championship
	Cricket World Cup final, semifinals and
	   matches involving Home Nations
	   teams
	Ryder Cup
	(British) Open Golf Championship

Notes: * Sports events protected under Part IV of the Broadcasting Act 1996; The list of free-to-air sports events is regularly reviewed and will be reviewed again after the end of the digital switchover in 2012.

Source: DCMS (Department for Culture Media and Sport), 21 July 2010, at http://www.culture.gov.uk/news/media_releases/7287.aspx#list (accessed 8 December 2010).

population could access them. In effect, major events such as the Olympic Games and the European and the World Football Cups would be broadcast on free-to-air channels like public service broadcasts. Each member state is responsible for operating a free-to-air listed events regime.

As an example, Table 7.2 shows the existing policy in the UK.

The MEDIA 2007 programme

The MEDIA 2007 programme is based on Article 157 EC ('Competitiveness') and therefore aims at strengthening the competitiveness of European audio-visual companies. By virtue of Article 151 ('Culture'), and in particular paragraph 4 thereof, the MEDIA programme (like the AVMS Directive) 'takes [ample] account of cultural aspects, particularly in order to respect and promote the diversity of its [the Community's] cultures' (EC, 2009d).

'The current MEDIA 2007 programme (2007–2013) is the fourth multi-annual programme for support to the European audiovisual industry since 1991.' Its general objectives are to

- Preserve and enhance European cultural and linguistic diversity and its cinematographic and audiovisual heritage.
- Increase the circulation and audience of European audiovisual productions inside and outside the EU.

- Strengthen the competitiveness of the European audiovisual sector in the framework of an open and competitive European market favorable to employment, by, among other things, promoting links between audiovisual professionals.

EU initiatives in digital switchover[11]

Digital switchover has been put high on the agenda of European regulators in recent years. In June 2005 the European Commission published a Communication 'on accelerating the transition from analogue to digital broadcasting', which urged EU member states to bring forward the likely date of analogue switch-off and called for a coordinated approach to making freed-up spectrum available across the EU (EC, 2005a). This Communication builds on the 2003 Communication 'on the transition from analogue to digital broadcasting', which set out the benefits of switching over to digital broadcasting and initiated the debate on the amount and future uses of spectrum potentially released at the switch-off of analogue terrestrial television transmission (EC, 2003).

The digital switchover plans may primarily be the responsibility of national policymakers, but there is also a European dimension that requires the intervention of European public authorities. As is stated in an EC Communication, beyond the advantages at national level, an acceleration of the switchover process could increase learning and awareness, and promote coherency (or harmonization?) in (of?) policy actions across member states (EC, 2005a: 8). New digital technologies and services depend to a large extend on achieving a large subscriber base at EU level and become more attractive with an increased installed base of technology in Europe. The Communication goes on to argue that the development of new services could be hampered by differing national approaches to digital switchover. The harmonization of national policies would contribute to achieving a 'level playing field' and eliminating legal uncertainty (ibid.). According to Paris-based research firm BIPE (2002: 12), the need for European action in this field derives from

- The transnational nature of spectrum allocation.
- The requirement for free circulation of goods and services in the single European market.
- The promotion of global European competitiveness in all the industries involved (television services, consumer electronics, advanced television technologies), which requires coordination and synchronization of developments.

The Commission has proposed the year 2012 as the deadline for the switch-off of analogue terrestrial broadcasting across the EU. It acknowledges that there is disparity among national switchover plans and recognizes that a binding EU-wide switch-off date common to all members may not be realistic. It could not be otherwise given that in 2010 digital television (DTV) household adoption in Northern Europe was high, with Finland, Norway and Sweden well above 70 per cent and the UK (the leader in DTV penetration) over 92 per cent, while in the Mediterranean countries of Italy, Spain and Greece it was below 50 per cent. Many Eastern and Southern European countries were lagging behind not only in terms of the penetration of digital services abut also in terms of awareness of the process of digital switchover. In 2010 the European market remained fragmented with regard to the adoption of technologies and there was little sign that Europe was developing a homogeneous DTV industry.

These variations in the national structure of the television industry create a dilemma for EC regulators in terms of the feasibility of introducing common digital switch-off dates. There is clearly a tension between the *macro* and the *micro* levels. At the macro level there seems to be pressure from the Commission for member states to hurry towards digitalization in order to create a workable internal market. In sum, the EC proposes a coordinated European approach to switchover and the setting of a common timescale. Commissioner Reding explained why: 'by recommending 2012 as EU deadline for the analogue switch-off, I would like to give a political signal to market participants and customers alike that digital TV will soon be a reality' (EC, 2005b). However, EC policy towards DTV and switchover is in tension with the micro level, that is, strategies adopted by individual member states. The EC's proposal for the 2012 deadline for completing terrestrial analogue switch-off may lead some member states to an ill-timed, insufficiently planned and unduly rapid introduction of digital terrestrial TV services (DTT) to catch up with other more advanced territories.

While policy intervention to boost DTV uptake may be justified at EU level to guarantee a coordinated approach to the switchover process and to the use of the available spectrum, the pressure exerted at the macro level for new member states to be part of the 'digital economy' may not result in positive change, for it could lead to ill-informed, shortsighted policies. This danger is particularly apparent in countries where digital terrestrial TV penetration rates are low and awareness of the digital switchover process is lagging behind. While countries adopting a digital terrestrial TV policy, such as the UK, Germany and the Nordic countries, seem to conform most closely to EC ideals in terms of speed of switchover, the smaller and Mediterranean European territories, as well as Eastern European countries, do not seem capable of meeting the EC's target switch-off date. Thus the great diversity in terms both of national levels of digital television (DTT) take-up and approaches to digital switchover may make the 2012 EU-wide deadline unrealistic. The role of the Commission should be confined to setting out the benefits of switching over to digital television and explore various policy orientations, rather than announcing an EU-wide target date for phasing out analogue terrestrial television, for national fragmentation casts doubts on the credibility of setting such deadlines.

Conclusion

EU broadcasting policy has not been static, but evolving. The balances of interests and values have varied over the decades, from predominantly cultural and democratic objectives in the early 1980s, to increasingly economic and industrial goals since the early 1990s. The EC's policies are mainly connected with the internal market perspective (or the 'single digital market', the new fashionable mantra) and differ strikingly from those of the CoE and the EP, which through various Resolutions and Declarations have paid more attention to the cultural dimension. As Michalis (2010) notes, the EC stance with regard to broadcasting has been more about negative than about positive integration, for competition and economic objectives have been prioritized at the expense of sociocultural objectives. The EC has shaped the broadcasting scene in Europe through the creation of an internal audiovisual market and through its strong competition powers where it enjoys autonomy for action. This has been achieved despite fierce member state opposition in areas such as broadcasting content and ownership. The EC has been able to regulate more effectively in the adjacent sector of telecommunications,[12] which is free of content regulation and subject only to structural regulation. Still, European broadcasting policy has been developed through competition considerations, economics-oriented policy and ECJ decisions.

The evolution of European communications policy reveals that the primary rationale for such policy is the economic imperative, developing three axes of regulation: regulation of networks (fixed and mobile telecommunications, Internet protocol, broadcasting, and cable and satellite networks); regulation of service provision (broadcasting being the most heavily regulated domain); and regulation of content (Kalimo and Pawels, 2009; Casarosa, 2009). The 2007 AVMS Directive verified that cultural concerns were overshadowed by the more pressing need for breaking down market barriers to facilitate trans-border broadcasting. The AVMS Directive was certainly a victory for liberal economic forces, but it contains cultural considerations such as 'quotas' requiring broadcasters to devote the majority of their programming to European productions. According to Michalis (2010: 42), the quota provision (itself a cultural policy tool) stands out from the overwhelmingly liberalizing provisions of the Directive, but various elements minimize its significance, most notably: the provision requiring member states to fulfil the quotas 'where practicable and by appropriate means', making it a symbolic rather than substantial provision; and the fact that it is a political agreement and thus not legally binding. However, the latest data from the EC (see Table 7.1) show that EU television broadcasters largely comply with the provision.

The objectives of an interventionist and monitoring EU role have been twofold: the completion and the effective functioning of the internal market for media services; and the steering of the course of the debate over reregulation at national level. The above analysis shows that the EU has progressively acquired a more effective role in media and communication policy matters. The EC, in particular, has deeply influenced national media policies by acting as a policy entrepreneur and by recommending best practices, models and sanctions through a 'soft law' approach, which has included the publication of Reports, Communications, Green Papers and other legislative documents. The various legislative documents addressing media and communications issues have provided member states with a useful tool, in particular benchmarking capable of steering indirectly the political choices on national governments (Casarosa, 2010: 23).

Meanwhile, member states maintain much of their sovereignty rights. The failed attempt to launch a harmonization directive on pluralism and media ownership in the mid-1990s demonstrated the political sensitivities surrounding the subject and the need for a balanced and realistic approach that would take into account the specificities of media markets in the various member states. The failure of the EC to secure sufficient political compromise to enact a Directive on the concentration of media ownership demonstrates the difficulties that European institutions face in overcoming the resistance of national governments, especially the most powerful ones, those of Germany and the UK (Humphreys, 2009: 197). The EC came back to the issue of pluralism by commissioning an independent study aiming at the development of a neutral and objective monitoring mechanism, which could enhance the audit ability of media pluralism. This instrument would equip policymakers and regulatory authorities with tools for detecting and managing societal risks in this area and provide them with a stronger evidentiary basis on which to define priorities and actions for improving media pluralism within the EU. Instead of imposing measures on member states, this mechanism would ensure a uniform basis for dealing with pluralism issues and provide a more objective basis for the often heated political and economic arguments.

In the case of setting a Europe-wide deadline for digital switchover in the year 2012, the EC is careful to point out that this is an indicative and not an absolute deadline. The Commission's pressure for member states to hurry towards digitalization in order to create a workable internal market may lead some countries to an ill-timed and insufficiently planned introduction of digital terrestrial TV services to catch up with other more advanced territories. This is why member states, especially those with low digital TV take-up, have been left with some flexibility to set a later date for analogue switch-off. Furthermore, under the new rules of the AVMS Directive, member states have maintained their right to restrict the broadcast of unsuitable content (for example, unsuitable to minors, pornographic or offensive programming) (Art. 2(4)–(6)), including the retransmission of on-demand audiovisual content that may not be banned in its country of origin. To sum up, the EU has influenced deeply the choices of national governments in their media and communications policies. But member states keep much of their regulatory power over issues such as the organization and funding of PSB, the implementation of media ownership rules, the protection of media pluralism, and the decision over switching off the analogue frequency for terrestrial television services.

So member states have managed to keep their competence in politically sensitive areas – such as safeguards for media pluralism, ownership and PSB – but the EC's increasing monitoring of the sociocultural and democratic functions of broadcasting is evident. As said, the EC intends to take a monitoring role of media pluralism in the EU member states, rather than initiating regulation (for example, a Directive) that would lack a legal basis. Another example of the EC's interventionist and monitoring role is state aid for broadcasting. It should be noted that the Commission's policy impinges on broadcasters' public service activities through the general content regulation of the audiovisual sector, the main legislative document of which is the AVMS Directive laying down rules for advertising, European programme quotas, and so on. But a more implicit means of control is via general competition law, whose most relevant part is the state aid rules, which aim to harmonize market conditions in order to create a 'level playing field' for commercial and public businesses. As a general principle, the EC recognizes the crucial role of PSBs because of their contribution to the quality of public discourse, the promotion of societal integration and national culture, and their emphasis on news and education. Yet, the 2009 Broadcasting Communication shows that the Commission has tightened state aid control in the field of PSB. Although this does not necessarily mean the end of the 'state aid saga', future practice will reveal whether the aim of the new Communication – to ensure a level playing field for PSBs and private operators – can be ultimately achieved.

The EU's growing presence in national markets is not merely visible in the media field. In the midst of an economic crisis and in order to ensure the survival of the single currency – the euro – the EU aims to ensure that the member states maintain fiscal discipline. For this purpose, in September 2010 it proposed stern new measures to give the Commission power to scrutinize national budgets and impose penalties on those countries that do not conform to these rules. In this sense the EC could act as a 'fire warden' and perhaps 'prosecutor' in cases of rule infringement. It appears that the Union envisages a type of economic integration in which the EC would be 'less of an impartial referee and more of an active player in domestic politics' (*The Economist*, 2010g: 52).

Part IV

The Convergence Phenomenon and Regulatory Reform

8
The Convergence Phenomenon in Media and Communications

Introduction

This chapter looks at the nature of the convergence phenomenon in the media and communications industries. Over the last three decades or so, convergence has been most manifest in the digital communications environment with the merging of the computing (information technology), broadcasting, print and telecommunications sectors. Nowadays, we are surrounded by a multilevel media world in which all modes of communication and information are continually reforming to adapt to the increasing demands to change the regulatory framework, 'changing the way we create, consume, learn and interact with each other' (Jenkins, 2006). It is almost impossible to follow developments in technology and communications markets without encountering the term convergence.

This chapter intends to provide a framework for understanding convergence issues. It attempts to provide a definition of convergence and outline its main features. By doing so it focuses on the technological, industrial and market issues of convergence. There is a discussion relating to the producer–consumer blending relationships. The chapter prepares the reader for the in-depth discussion on the policy implications of the phenomenon of convergence to be conducted in Chapters 9 and 10.

Conceptualization of convergence

Convergence between the information technology (IT), telecommunications and media sectors is hardly a new notion. McLuhan (1964) argued as early as the 1960s that telecommunications networks and the broadcasting of information would together create a 'global village'. During the 1970s in the USA and Europe, to a lesser extent, telecommunications and IT enterprises came together to create new products and services, such as digital switches and network services. Also, convergence between broadcasting and telecommunications has been evident since the development of copper coaxial cable (now boosted by fibre optics), which enabled cable networks to deliver TV pictures. However, more recent technological advances, such as digitalization, compression, developments and the Internet, have accelerated the scope of convergence potential.

A main element of the transformation has been the digitization of information and the packaging of data distributed by digital networks. Digitization enables formerly distinct services, like voice, data, video and audio, to be delivered over the same network, to share resources and to interact with each other (the essence of convergence). While the traditional structural model of communications is dominated by analogue technologies favoring mass production and a national market focus, the new service delivery model uses digital networks that favor mass customization and an international market focus. Analogue technology, and its physical infrastructure, does not allow the application of customized services as it is dominated at the supply side by services aimed at mass markets. But digital technology allows a multitude of services to be delivered over the same network. This allows third-party service providers and users greater control over service delivery (Australian Government, 2000). In short, the process of convergence leads to a services sector that is more fragmented, competitive, flexible and international in its outlook.

At the same time, the Internet has turned into a platform for the distribution of broadcast and other information or entertainment content. The Internet provides a full range of communication services including voice telephony and webcasting. Some observers believe that the Internet will become a substitute for broadcasting, Internet Protocol Television (the delivery of audio and video via cable) and digital television satellite distribution, while others foresee that it will be a complementary distribution network to existing platforms. While the pace and direction of technology is as yet uncertain, what is clear is that the consumption of broadcasting content online has become commonplace, especially among young people. Meanwhile, Third Generation (3G) wireless networks have enabled consumers to use wireless devices to consume online broadcast content.

The pace of convergence is influenced by a series of structural changes in the information and communication industries, such as mergers and acquisitions of previously separate enterprises. Corporate consolidation indicates that traditional entities search for new business opportunities and revenue streams through horizontal and vertical integration. As will be shown below, horizontal integration is a consolidation of companies that handle the same part of the production process, while vertical integration is that of companies engaged in different parts of the process (for example, distribution and marketing). Providers that integrate the Internet, telephony and wireless and audiovisual distribution under one corporate roof can deliver a wide range of services such as mass appeal and niche content, voice telephone and Internet access.

Convergence opens up new sales markets for firms, a case observed in many sectors including mobile telephony. As the market matures, firms look to non-voice services, such as video streaming, portals, messaging, information services and gaming, to drive revenue growth (Papadakis, no date). Convenience and simplicity are also apparent, as users find in convergence an opportunity to enjoy the benefits of many devices in one, saving on both space and ownership costs. The downside, however, is that a greater concentration of ownership of media outlets may result in a less pluralistic media market in which opportunities for audience access to the media are also affected.

The inexorable globalization of information and communication technologies, together with the tendencies towards commercialization and liberalization are additional driving forces for convergence. As mentioned in previous chapters, the rapidly developing information and communication technology (ICT) and media industries have contributed to the emergence of the phenomenon of globalization. In the process of the spread of new ICTs there are overall tendencies of convergence: similar ICT devices are adopted everywhere, with converging functions. Similar information and entertainment trends apply to global media: similar output is available and access to it is facilitated through various wired or wireless devices. ICT networks are globally interconnected and foster all types of communication and information transfer (Heller, 2008: 29–30). Liberalization and deregulation have allowed companies to expand their activities in different sectors across the world. In this sense, globalization, liberalization and ICT development result in rising levels of convergence on a global scale.

Meanwhile, a multitude of sources of substitutable products, services and applications delivered by national and international providers have fragmented the communications market. Two primary and contradictory trends are evident: consolidation and fragmentation – convergence and divergence. While there are many possibilities for horizontal convergence between different sectors and vertical integration between different levels, there is also divergence and disintegration. At a theoretical level, such divergence can be shown by referring to the multitude of public spheres that exist in a multicultural, global society (see Dahlgren, 2008; Corcoran, 2010). At a practical level, sectors that have witnessed some degree of vertical integration may experience new lines of division of labor between different sectors in the field.

Convergence/integration and divergences/disintegration can occur concurrently (WDR, 2002). Table 8.1 shows the involved sectors and the levels of activities from equipment/hardware and transport/software to content/service provision, while Figure 8.1 depicts the value chain of communication networks to illustrate how different subsections deal with the technological aspects of convergence in various parts of the value chain.

Table 8.1   Convergence/integration and divergence/disintegration

	IT	Telecommunications	Broadcasting	Other media
Content/ services	Software-based content	Telecommunications-based services and content	Broadcast programmes	Film, music, newspapers, etc.
Transport/ software	Generic software	Network services	Transmission	Cinema, video rentals, etc.
Equipment/ hardware	Hardware	Telecommunications equipment	Broadcast equipment	Reproduction of films, printing, etc.

Source: WDR, 2002.

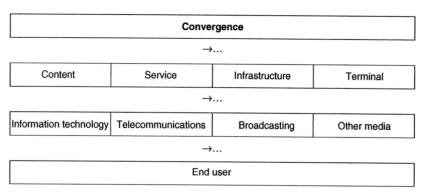

Figure 8.1   Convergence in the value chain
Source: WDR, 2002.

To sum up, convergence – the delivery of similar, existing or new media, telephony and Internet services via the same transmission platform – can be present at three different, although interrelated, levels: the technological level (mainly due to the digitization of broadcasting, IT and telecommunications networks), the structural level (as a consequence of corporate alliances across different sectors) and the services and markets level (here reference is made to the new value-added and multimedia services) (Iosifidis, 2002).

Technological convergence

Technological convergence has both a technical and a functional side. The technical side refers to the ability of any infrastructure to transport any type of data, whereas the functional side relates to consumers' ability to integrate in a seamless way the functions of computation, entertainment and integrate voice in a unique device capable of carrying out multiple tasks (Papadakis, no date). Technological convergence is made possible due, first, to the widespread introduction of digital technology, which provides new means by which moving images and sound can be processed and delivered to consumer-citizens and, second, to the compression of the signal, which enables the processing of vast volumes of information without loss of quality or functionality. Combined with digitization, compression allows efficient use of spectrum. Other key technological developments, such as the growth in computer processing power, high-speed switching and optical fibre multiwavelength transmission are also fundamental enablers of convergence because they result in efficient use of bandwidth and eventually capacity abundance (Iosifidis, 2002).

Technological convergence mostly refers to the so-called service-integrating services. Telecommunications and broadcasting media are converging thanks to the development of interactive digital broadcasting and high-speed Internet connections. Cable TV networks offer Internet services. Newspapers can be read online. Mobile phones are now TV-capable. The radio is turning into multimedia and opening up to competition from new forms of broadcasting like 'webcasting'. Apple's iPhone and Nokia's Ovi mobile can provide music, games and various Internet services. Games consoles use high-definition TV sets as their screens but can also screen material from the Net or from disc. Broadband providers offer converged packages of home phone, mobile phone, TV and Internet access (Burton, 2010: 198).

For Cukier (2008), three technology trends – blogging (types or parts of a website typically maintained by an individual with regular entries of commentary, graphics or video), mobile TV and Web 2.0 (commonly associated with Web applications that facilitate interactive information sharing and user-centered design) – are important to consider in the framework of convergence. Evans (2010) provides statistics of the most significant firms in these fields. In the field of blogging/social networking, Facebook was in 2010 by far the most important, with 500 million users around the world. The number of minutes users spend on Facebook over the course of a month was 500 billion, while the number of active applications that were available for the social network exceeded 550,000. In the field of mobile telephony, in 2010 there were 4 billion mobile phone subscribers around the world, whereas the number of Apple iPhones sold accounts for 34 million. The number of applications for the iPhone was about 150,000.

Turning to search engines, in 2010 the number of Google searches each month was an astonishing 88 billion. In partnership with Sony and others, the search giant is an example of the convergence between TV and PC.. The above constitute but a few examples of the outcomes of technological convergence, which is also termed 'multimedia' or 'TIME' (Telecommunications, Information technology, Media, Entertainment).

Shin (2005: 49) provides three key examples of the most common type of convergence, between the markets of broadcasting and telecommunications: first, internet broadcasting, also known as webcasting or streaming, which takes various forms ranging from simple chatting sites and music programme listening to media broadcasting stations storing and distributing their output and more advance forms including the generation of own content; second, video-on-demand (VOD), which is an interactive service providing customers with miscellaneous images via the general telecommunications networks. VOD users download video programmes from a server via telecommunications networks and can interactively search contents of the programme. VOD service enables market convergence both because it uses telecommunications and broadcasting networks and because it utilizes contents from the above markets. Third, data broadcasting services, often termed interactive TV or two-way TV, which provide a variety of information via broadcasting networks. Digital data broadcasting allows dialogue-type (or Internet-type) TV services like e-mail and e-commerce.[1]

Industry convergence

Technological convergence plays a leading role in the convergence process, but it may be misleading to reduce the analytical perspective of convergence to this alone, for convergence at a *structural* level (or *business organizational* or *corporate* convergence) causes a transformation of the global communication and information markets. Each of the traditional industries that are likely to be affected by convergence (IT, telecommunications and mass media) have been involved in a series of structural changes (mergers, acquisitions, joint ventures, and so on) to strengthen their position in the market. Hence, industry convergence basically means that the same corporations are now active in three sectors: the technology sector (telecommunications), the content services sector (audiovisual) and the Internet, including owning search engines and electronic betting or trading portals like eBay.

Developed countries are in an advantageous position in advancing these triple-play services. The most recent Internet World Stats report (IWS, 2010) notes that the UK remains at the forefront of media convergence in Europe. As the country's universal DSL (Digital Subscriber Line) and cable networks have been extensively upgraded, they provide a suitable delivery platform for triple-play (Internet, telephony and digital television) and emerging quadruple-play services.[2] This is complemented by high digital terrestrial, cable and satellite TV penetration,[3] which provides a good multichannel environment. Developments in VOD, IPTV (Internet Protocol Television) and VoIP (Voice over the Internet Protocol) enable the development of triple-/quadruple-play and convergent services. Virgin Media (the result of the 2007 merger between Telewest and NTL) is a combination of NTL's cable-broadband, Blueyonder (Telewest's cable-broadband operations) and Virgin.net (ADSL access). The company is a pioneer in the provision of quadruple-play services. What is more, in 2010 its broadband services had a speed of 50 mbps, which made Virgin Media the fastest broadband provider in the UK.

In order to take advantage of these opportunities, media and communication firms have embarked upon a series of consolidation strategies. In the USA and Europe, merger and acquisition activity in the information and communications industries increased significantly after the reregulatory waves of the 1980s and intensified during the 1990s (Murdock, 1990; McQuail and Sinue, 1998; Iosifidis, 1999). Although the pace of convergence at the level of ownership and control differs greatly among countries, vertical and horizontal integration appear to be the two most common strategies that communications enterprises follow in order to survive and flourish in the digital age. Table 0.1 in the Introduction provided evidence of consolidation patterns in the USA.

Vertical integration in the form of joint ownership of both distribution networks and audiovisual content has gained momentum in recent decades, the flagship case being the January 2000 $220 billion merger between the world's leading Internet firm AOL (America Online) and the audiovisual giant Time Warner.[4] The motives behind such movements are well reported in a number of works (Iosifidis, 1997; McQuail and Sinue, 1998; Gibbons, 1998; McChesney, 1999; Tambini et al., 2001; Bagdikian, 2004). They range from increasing market power and sharing the high cost of digital technologies (especially in the case of horizontal mergers) to gaining access to know-how, acquiring content, and mitigating the uncertainty of market demand (the case in vertical mergers). The common aim of these alliances is to exploit the opportunities offered by technological convergence.

However, it is the convergence between the Internet and mobile communication alongside the growth of broadband capacity that has prompted the development of networks of interactive communication that connect local and global spaces. There is clear evidence that corporate media are redirecting their strategies toward the Internet (Castells, 2007: 252–4). For example, Rupert Murdoch, owner of the global media group News Corporation, said in 2005 that his company had failed properly to engage with the online world – and risked losing its position in programming genres such as news. Murdoch had no doubt that radical change was coming and that News Corporation had to gear up for a wholesale revamp of its approach to the Internet.

As a result, in 2006, News Corporation acquired Intermix Media for approximately $580 million. The best-known asset of Intermix Media was MySpace, a social networking site, which at the time was the fifth-ranked Web domain in terms of page-views. Other examples of alliances involving new media include Google's 2006 $1.65 billion acquisition of YouTube, the consumer media company allowing people to watch and share original videos via the Web.

Alongside the recognized names of news firms such as Google, there exist emerging online giants, the most noted of these being Digital Sky Technologies (DST), accounting for more than 70 per cent of page-views on the Russian-language Internet, Napsers (Africa's biggest media group, both offline and online), and Tencent (China's largest Internet company by market capitalization – and the third-largest in the world), best known for QQ, a popular instant-messaging service with 567 million users in 2009. The three companies can be seen as a bloc, for they are financially intertwined. Napsers owns part of mail.ru and was an early investor in Tencent, of which in 2010 it held 30 per cent. In April 2010 Tencent invested $300 million in DST, giving it a stake of more than 10 per cent. Tencent also has an interest in the Indian arm of MIH, Napser's Internet division. These firms are also expanding elsewhere and making their presence felt in more recognized and perhaps 'safer' fields, as evidenced by DST's 2009 acquisition of 10 per cent of Facebook, for which it spent an estimated $800 million (*The Economist*, 2010e). High-profile deals in new-media technologies are increasingly common, for in January 2011 DST, together with Goldman Sachs, an investment bank, invested a further $500 million in Facebook, valuing it at $50 billion, making sceptics doubt that a firm whose business model is unproven is worth more than established media giants such as News Corporation and Time Warner (see Table 8.2).

But is has been argued that the king of new media is Apple. Despite the global economic meltdown of 2008–09, Apple has converted consumers' appetite for convergence into the biggest profits in the company's history, selling more than 33 million iPhones since the device's introduction in 2007 – 21 million in the 2009 fiscal year alone. In the new-media gold rush, it is selling the picks and shovels: its media business model, much like Google's, is dedicated to making it easier for users to enjoy other people's content. The iPhone represents just the latest advance in Apple's

Table 8.2 Market valuation of selected companies, in $ billion (as of 4 January 2011)

Google	185
Facebook	50
News Corporation	47
Time Warner	44
Yahoo!	20
Twitter	0.2

Sources: Thomson Reuters; press reports; *The Economist*, 2011.

convergence strategy, which dates back to the 2001 launch of the iPod music player and 2003 launch of the iTunes music store'.

James McQuivey, an analyst with Forrester Research, says that Apple can 'deliver all kinds of content to you in a way that is so seamless that you cannot pass it up,' thereby defying the conventional wisdom that people will not pay for anything they can get online free. McQuivey adds that 'it's easier to buy media from iTunes than it is to steal it' (see http://www.technologyreview.com/communications/24194, accessed 8 October 2010).

It appears that mainstream global networks coexist, interconnect and integrate well with new media and Internet sites. The increasing influence of Fifth Estate firms (to use Dutton's 2007 idea of the emergence of an Internet-enabled Fifth Estate), anchored in cyberspace, such as Google, goes hand in hand with the growing online presence of traditional Fourth Estate communications giants like News Corporation or the BBC. I have already mentioned News Corporation's plans to grow its online presence (for example, through the 2006 acquisition of Intermix Media), but public broadcasters such as the BBC also have a large online presence.

BBC Online (at bbc.co.uk) is the brand name for the Corporation's UK online service and consists of websites including, among others, BBC News and Sport, the online video and radio service BBC iPlayer, and children-oriented sites like Cbeebies and CBBC. However, following concerns from commercial rivals that the Corporation's online presence and public funding distorts the market, the BBC's online activities have been subject to various public consultations and government reviews. Responding to its critics, in March 2010 the BBC announced plans to cut 25 per cent of its online spend and close its digital radio stations 6 Music and the BBC Asian network. Also in a bid to appease the new coalition government, the BBC Trust decided in September 2010 to freeze the licence fee for two years.

As mentioned above, many communications conglomerates have been involved in a series of mergers and acquisitions, primarily taking the form of vertical consolidation (consolidation across the value chain). Vertical integration was once looked upon with alarm by governments because corporations that have control of a total process, from raw material supply through fabrication to advertising and sales, also have few motives for genuine innovation and the power to squeeze out anyone who tries to compete. This situation distorts the economy through monopolistic control over prices. However, governments today have become sympathetic to vertical corporations that have merged into ever larger total systems. This is evidenced by the passing of the US Telecommunications Act 1996 and the UK Communications Act 2003, which allowed more opportunities for companies to expand across sectors, as well as the 2003 EU legal framework for electronic communications, which provided an integrative step for convergent companies. As a result, media corporations have remained largely unrestrained and the trend towards increased integration continues unhindered.

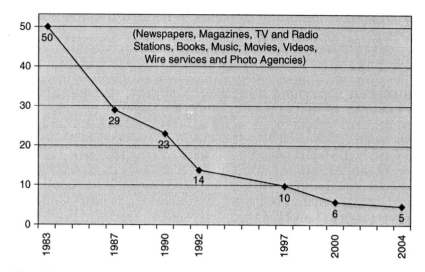

Figure 8.2   Number of corporations that control a majority of US media
Source: Bagdikian, 2004.

Renowned journalist Ben Bagdikian noted in 1983 that in the USA about 50 corporations controlled the vast majority of all news media. In his fourth edition, published in 1992, he wrote 'in the U.S., fewer than two dozen of these extraordinary creatures own and operate 90% of the mass media' – controlling almost all of America's newspapers, magazines, TV and radio stations, books, records, movies, videos, wire services and photo agencies. He predicted then that this number would eventually fall to about half a dozen companies. This claim was greeted with scepticism at the time. When the sixth edition of *The Media Monopoly* was published in 2000, the number had fallen to six (see Figure 8.2).

Since then, there have been more mergers and the scope has expanded to include new media like the Internet market. In 2004, Bagdikian's revised and expanded book, *The New Media Monopoly*, showed that only five huge corporations – Time Warner, Disney, News Corporation (owned by the Murdoch family), Bertelsmann (a German conglomerate) and Viacom (formerly CBS) – had come to control most of the media industry in the US. General Electric's NBC was a close sixth (Bagdikian, 2004).

In the same vein, media historian and political economist Robert McChesney (2005) noted that the global media market was dominated by just a few multinational corporations and provided a criticism on several grounds, among others: these corporations are increasingly becoming integrated in that they both create content and own publishing companies and/or broadcasting networks, and are able to distribute their own product; they threaten local culture by encouraging foreign investment in local media. McChesney urged for stricter regulation in the media to prevent further media consolidation.

Ferguson (2002) and Compaine (2005) are among the scholars who take the opposite view and disagree with the opinion that a few large companies are taking over the world's media and that local cultures are threatened. Compaine examined and compared international mergers and concluded that many media have divested their media assets, whilst in most cases companies are repeatedly sold and resold. Ferguson did not agree that corporate ownership results in cultural homogeneity. Both scholars rejected the argument that heavier rules are needed to guard against media consolidation.

Noam (2009: 4) undertook a systematic analysis of the concentration trend in the US media from 1984 to the mid-2000s and attempted to establish 'whether, where, and how American media are becoming more (or less) concentrate'. Noam analyzed the media, information, telecommunications and Internet industries, providing a comprehensive data analysis of market shares in each segment. Like Bagdikian, Noam found that most mass-media industries experienced gradual, but constant, increases in concentration during the two-plus decades under review (from 13 per cent controlled by the top five firms in 1984 to 26 per cent in 2005).

Noam also noted that, despite a significant number of mergers, mass-media concentration remained lower than in the information and telecommunications realms, but the gap was closing. Media subsectors that had greater electronic and digital emphasis tended to be more concentrated than those that were less dependent on electronic and digital tools. Noam believes concentration is likely to continue so that in the future the media are likely 'to be dominated by a few relatively focused integrator firms that put together elements provided by numerous smaller specialist firms' (ibid.: 6).

However, Noam argued that while mass-media industries experienced a continuing increase in concentration, non-mass-media sector concentration followed a 'U-shaped path'. In many sectors, concentration declined markedly from 1984 to 1992, during the second Reagan and George H. W. Bush administrations. During Clinton's presidency (1994–2002), concentration rose again, though not quite to the levels of 1984. Between 2001 and 2005 concentration again declined slightly. Nonetheless, only a few sectors are approaching a monopoly situation, with more 60 per cent market control by a single firm.

Noam notes that oligopoly is far more common in non-mass-media industries. According to Aronson (2010), who wrote a review of Noam's work, 'these findings may surprise those who presume that Democrats are tougher on big business than Republicans'. Another notable finding of Noam's book is that, despite the growing convergence, few companies active in one communication sector (mass media, telecommunications or IT) have moved into other sectors. But most firms from these three sectors have moved into the Internet field. The move of traditional mass media to the Internet and new media is backed up by the writings of such scholars as Castells (2007) and verified by the various aforementioned examples of alliances between traditional and new-media companies.

Market convergence

Convergence at the level of services and markets occurs as a response to technological and industry convergence. Many of the developments that are categorized as convergent trends are in fact mergers between firms in the same market segment or the same sector. Convergence in content production is most evident in various sectors such as telecommunications, IT and broadcasting, whereas convergence in distribution is most prominent in the telecommunications and broadcasting sectors. In the case of equipment production, it is essentially the IT and telecommunications sectors that are coming together (WDR, 2002).

Market analysis shows that the flexibility of digital information is creating the possibility for more and enriched conventional services, such as digital broadcasting and better quality mobile communications, as well as a range of new services and applications, from home banking and home shopping to Internet-style data services. The Internet (alongside interactive digital television) has been used as a vehicle for the delivery to customers of both existing services, such as voice telephony and electronic mail, and brand new ones, such as VoIP. The recent development of the Internet (Web 2.0) along with that of interactive digital television, wireless communication and next-generation networks (more advanced fixed and mobile networks) provide evidence that convergence is constantly advancing at all levels.

Publisher–user convergence

Technological, corporate and market convergence occur at the same time as *publisher–user* or *producer–consumer convergence*, referring to the blurring of boundaries between media companies and their audiences, itself triggered by the interactivity potential and the rise of the Internet. Many people, especially the young generation, are being weaned by new technologies away from traditional passive media and are looking for specific content through multiple platforms, such as TV (subscriber-based cable or satellite), games consoles, radio, PCs, mobile phones, iPods, WiFi, WiMAX and MP3 players. These new technologies have allowed the emergence of consumer-generated media. The Internet has given rise to 'user-generated content', which covers a wide range of activities from blog writing to participation in social networking sites, podcasting and uploading videos, photos and music. People can create news and participate in the news discourse through citizen publishing, blogging, YouTube posting, and so on. This change means that the media market itself is changing from an old and inflexible model to an environment of infinite flexibility, where content from anywhere can be viewed by anyone, and where anyone can be a publisher or producer. The terms *prosumer* (producer + consumer) and *prosumption* (production + consumption) have emerged to describe new business approaches that incorporate customers into the value-production process (Bollier, 2007). This convergence can be seen as 'recombinantly driven by an industry desperate for strong customer relationships, technologies that are increasingly cheap and easy to use, and a media culture that privileges an active audience' (Deuze, 2010: 453). User-created or consumer-generated content can be defined according to the following criteria (Wunsch-Vincent and Vickery, 2007, cited in Napoli, 2009: 33):

- Content made publicly available over the Internet.
- Content that reflects a certain amount of creative effort.
- Content which is created outside traditional professional routines and practices.

Without doubt, the converging media environment is changing the relationship between media institutions and their audiences. It also provides media owners, advertisers and agencies alike with an opportunity for more user involvement. By engaging people in user-generated content, media companies and advertisers can get people more involved in their brand, find out what they think about their product and in the process increase customer loyalty. There is indeed a need to adequately explain the process, content and implications of media production and consumption in contemporary media environment and praxis that includes both simultaneously. However, as explained in Chapter 1, there are limits to the user's ability to use the Web to produce and distribute content. The new technologies are not always accessible and cannot effectively allow the audience to participate and engage fully in the public sphere. In Chapter 10 I also provide a note of scepticism as to how quickly user habits can change to adapt to new technologies.

Most importantly, it should be noted that, despite its increasing prominence as a place where the public accesses news, the Internet remains primarily a distribution medium, not a source of original news content. Firms' investment in this medium has tended to be in technology and not in journalism. The most popular Internet sites for news remain the domain of the large media conglomerates (for example, Time Warner controls CNN and until recently it owned AOL News), while Internet sites unaffiliated with traditional media do little original local news coverage or investigative reporting (Stucke and Grunes, 2008). Napoli (2009) questions whether blogs, Twitter and other forms of user-generated content are completely adequate substitutes for more traditional forms of journalism and highlights the need for policymakers to understand why and how audience attention is migrating away from traditional journalism. Napoli asks policymakers to find new ways to preserve traditional journalistic institutions in the face of an increasingly fragmented media environment.

A short note on maximizing audience access

The main challenge for media policymakers is to ensure that the media play a positive role in a democratic society by maximizing access to audiences. In a media environment characterized by technological/structural convergence and audience fragmentation, *commercial convergence* should be countered by *public sector convergence*: public service media should become 'the central node in a new network of public and civil institutions that together make up the digital commons, a linked space defined by its shared refusal of commercial enclosure and its commitment to free and universal access, reciprocity, and collaborative activity' (Murdock, 2004). This could encompass various educational, cultural and other public institutions, libraries, universities, museums, community and alternative media, user-generated content and other elements of the noncommercial public forum and public-spirited digital commons. But an in-depth discussion on the challenges that media convergence and audience fragmentation pose to policymakers will be conducted in the next chapter.

Conclusion

This chapter attempted to conceptualize communications convergence and explore its main types and features. It argued that technology has torn down the walls between different communications media. Magazines produce video clips, while television news stations post written articles online. Technologies that are driving this media convergence are network connections, powerful mobile devices, clever interfaces, and easy-to-use software (see http://www.technologyreview.com/communications/24188, accessed 12 October 2010). Meanwhile, industry, structural or corporate convergence has intensified in recent years as evidenced by the rising number of increasingly complex corporate alliances between traditional and new digital and online media. This may result in extensive media market concentration and the reduction of pluralism and diversity, principles that media policymakers need to make steps to defend. Producer–consumer convergence is also evident due to changing consumer patterns and the possibility for everyone to become a publisher or producer. In a fragmented media market, traditional journalistic institutions are clearly affected.

The direction that technologies and industry structure will take cannot be predicted. There is no timetable for convergence, since different sectors are likely to restructure at different rates. Market adoption could be either facilitated or delayed by a range of barriers such as lack of customer confidence or restrictive technical standards. Likewise, it is uncertain which new user patterns will emerge. User habits may not change as quickly as technology or follow it unreservedly (see Chapter 10). What is certain is that policy needs to keep up with technological development and take into account the emerging market structure and changing audience needs. Regulation based on existing frameworks may not be appropriate or effective for emerging converged services. Why is that?

Prologue to the next chapter: the level of legal uncertainty and regulatory challenges

As discussed extensively in Chapter 2, the IT sector is characterized by a complete absence of regulation. IT markets have developed in an open environment dominated by global players, in which competition law has played an important part (Clements, 1998). Limited or no regulation has traditionally been applied to the print publishing industry in most parts of the world in order to ensure freedom of speech. Broadcasting and telecommunications have developed under different regulatory regimes. The content of telephone calls was generally unregulated, whereas broadcasting content has been subject to strict regulation, reflecting national concerns over the transmission of indecent material as well as the promotion of social and cultural objectives. Broadcasting policies and telecommunications policies have served different objectives. The aim of the former has incorporated sociocultural values, such as freedom of expression, cultural diversity and political pluralism, whereas the latter has been more directed at infrastructure and has mainly pursued economic goals.

The aforementioned technological, structural and market developments, together with the globalization phenomenon and political shifts (the trend towards liberalization), have called into question the existing regulatory regime covering the wider communications and information industries. It has been said that the existing fragmentation in the regulation of communications sectors might not be suitable to ensure a coherent and flexible framework to respond to convergence. The arrival of digital technology and the development of the Internet, in particular, call for rapid policy development, which could permit a common approach across all communications sectors. A new paradigm needs to pay attention to ongoing convergence between different communications spheres by adopting an integrative approach to the convergent communications/multimedia system (Van Guilenburg and McQuail, 2003). Coordination is especially important in the field of

Table 8.3   Regulatory implications caused by changes in technology and market structure

Regulation area	Regulatory implications caused by changes in technology	Regulatory implications caused by changes in market structure
Pricing	Different products offering similar facilities become available. These products may be using different pricing schemes and be subject to different types of regulation	More competition reduces the need for price regulation
Interconnection	A need for interconnection between new services such as VoIP and instant messaging	Dominance by a few international carriers. New imbalances in payments of international settlements
Licensing	It becomes more difficult to control the provision of a particular service through licensing. Service-specific licences will become a barrier to the development of new services. Coordination between the regulation of content services and broadcasting licensing is needed	Providers may easily circumvent licensing barriers in particular in the content and application markets
Universal service obligation (USO)	A definition of USO that includes only voice communication becomes less relevant as voice communication is delivered in combination with a host of other services	Provision in rural areas becomes cheaper and more economically viable
Spectrum management	Restrictions on use become more complex and hamper the development of new applications	Various actors providing different types of application compete for the same limited resources
Numbering	Need for coherence between different numbering plans facilitating communication across platforms	More competition implies the need for a fairer allocation of numbers. More competition implies a rising need for portability in numbers

Source: ICT Regulation Toolkit, 2010. Available at: http://www.ictregulationtoolkit.org/en/ Section.2396.html (accessed 10 November 2010).

spectrum management, to avoid market distortion and to increase competition between infrastructures (OECD, 2003). The scene seems to have been set, in various countries, for a new approach, with provisions for migrating from today's regulatory frameworks to a future unified regime. Since existing regulatory regimes rely on specific classifications of providers, it may be difficult to regulate new integrated services based on existing laws. Content can now be transmitted over various networks that previously were subject to separate legal regimes. Unlike telecommunications, broadcasting policy has been characterized by highly prescriptive regulation; how then should policymakers treat audiovisual content that is transmitted via the Internet? Should Internet telephony be classified as telephony and Internet TV as television, or should both services fall under the auspices of Internet law? Should new services such as VoIP be regulated at all? The above are just a few examples that show the level of legal insecurity. Some of the challenges in the digital, converged era appear to be interconnection (or interoperability), user protection, universal access, licensing and spectrum management (see Table 8.3). The regulatory implications caused by changes in technological convergence and market structure are analyzed in the next two chapters.

9
Regulatory Convergence

Introduction

While Chapter 8 looked at the nature and trends of communications convergence, this chapter discusses the policy and regulatory implications resulting from the convergence phenomenon. Expanding on the concluding remarks of the previous chapter, the chapter reviews the discrepancies between policies employed in different communications sectors and challenges resulting from convergence in policymaking and assesses the reforms adopted in reaction to convergence. Since convergence is connected to liberalization (the trend that allows new players to enter markets and form corporate alliances) and globalization (viewed by some as the process of creation of a stateless world), further important questions to be addressed are whether the process of convergence results in: a) increased opportunities to evade national law; b) overreliance on supranational regulations; and c) growing reliance on self- and co-regulation. The overall objective of the chapter is to provide an overview of the emergent governance pattern in communications and describe its main characteristics.

Before I start exploring the integrated strategies and reforms undertaken in response to convergence, it should be remembered that the use of a common approach across all sectors seems problematic as regulatory frameworks were designed for an era where clear functional differences existed between services and infrastructure. As already mentioned, in the past the telecommunications sector established itself on the basis of the common-carrier model, with the obligation to supply in the public interest, the media sector was subjected to the broadcasting public trustee model and the print sector remained free market oriented. These differences in regulatory models mainly applied to market access and content and were explained by differing regulatory aims. Economic issues prevailed in the telecommunication industry as far as infrastructure development was concerned, whereas traditional broadcasting regulation was dominated by spectrum scarcity arguments and the sociocultural consequences of the distributed programming output. It would therefore be a heroic task to collide those two different policy objectives.

Still, the broadcasting and telecommunications sectors have some common characteristics. They have both lost their monopoly status and been opened to competition from the private sector; satellite technology has enabled both sectors to enter the international arena; broadcasting and telecommunications can now be transmitted by wired or wireless means; audiovisual content can be delivered via telecommunications networks; cable companies can offer a menu of video and voice services; digital technology increasingly allows broadcasting to be a one-to-one communication (similar to telephony), offered for a price (for instance, pay-per-view and VOD services). The ultimate example of the convergence between broadcasting and telecommunications is the Internet. Using a computer, one can access telecommunications and broadcasting services, and transmit voice messages, data, words, images and music. These tasks can also be accomplished via a digital TV set or a 3G mobile phone. In sum, there is growing evidence that the separate worlds of telecommunications and broadcasting are coming together.

In view of that evidence, there are increasing calls for a new regulatory approach to include all information and communications sectors. There is an ongoing discussion at both supranational (notably European Union) and national (particularly UK) levels on whether technological convergence should result in regulatory convergence. There are two policy issues related to communications convergence: whether (or the extent to which) regulatory bodies should merge (*institutional integration*) and whether the growing tendency to rely on *competition policy* to deliver the optimum economic and social efficiency across all converged sectors is desirable.. As convergence opens up technologies that were once regarded as natural monopolies to intermodal competition (competition between different modes of transmission), it has been suggested that a side of regulation also implies an increasingly narrow side for sector-specific regulation and a greater role for competition policy (or conventional antitrust) (see Iosifidis, 2002; Latzer, 2009; Yoo, 2009). A related issue is that of maximizing access to audiences, who are increasingly turning into producers (see Napoli, 2009).

This chapter deals with institutional integration by focusing on the integrated regulatory agencies Ofcom in the UK and the FCC in the USA. In doing so it elaborates on the prominent role of competition policy and the economic imperative that has dominated the regulatory tradition. It moves on to examine European Commission (EC) policy for regulatory convergence. This chapter should be read in conjunction with Chapter 10, which assesses the continuing relevance of sector-specific content and structural rules in a convergent world and examines the cases for self- and co-regulation.

The debate over 'institutional integration'

The degree of independence

Over the past decade, in Europe and elsewhere, regulatory reform in the broadcasting and telecommunications sectors has focused on opening monopoly markets to full competition. The liberalization of communications markets has required a new set of regulatory principles, which can ensure fair competition in the marketplace. One of the most visible institutional changes was the removal of the broadcasting and telecommunications industries from public administration to the control of independent regulatory authorities (IRAs). By 2009, more than 150 countries had set up independent regulatory bodies.

Though adopted more than a decade ago, the Council of Europe Recommendation (2000) 23 on the independence and functions of regulatory authorities for the communications sector is still relevant. The Recommendation states the following regarding the appointment, composition and functioning of regulatory agencies (converged or not):

- The rules should be formulated so as to protect regulatory bodies against any interference, in particular by political forces or economic interests.
- Members should be appointed in a democratic and transparent manner.
- Potential conflicts of interest should be prevented.
- Members should be protected against arbitrary dismissal as a means of political pressure.

Regarding the regulatory agencies' financial independence, the Recommendation states that

- The funding of regulatory authorities should be clearly specified in law so as to allow them to carry out their functions fully and independently.
- Public authorities should not use their financial decision-making power to interfere with the independence of regulatory authorities.

Regarding the powers and competence of regulatory bodies, particularly in broadcasting:

- Regulatory authorities should have the power to enforce regulations and guidelines concerning broadcasting activities.
- The regulations on licensing procedures should be clear and precise and should be applied in an open, transparent and impartial manner.
- Regulatory bodies should be involved in the allocation of national frequencies to broadcasting services.

Regarding accountability:

- Regulatory bodies should be accountable to the public, for example by publishing reports on their work.
- Decisions and regulations adopted by the regulatory bodies should be duly reasoned, open to review by the competent jurisdictions, and made available to the public.

In practice, the degree of independence of the regulatory authority in the telecommunications and broadcasting sectors varies considerably across the world, depending on state traditions and structures, political policy and state reforms, to name but a few. Focusing on selected IRAs across four nations – France, the UK, Germany and Italy – Thatcher (no date) noted that officials had not used their power over nominations to pack IRAs with party politicians and that politicization has been limited in the UK, France and Germany. Italy was the exception, with a much higher level of politicization. Thatcher also observed that the formal dismissal of IRA members is virtually unknown and IRA members typically serve out their terms and have longer average tenure than politicians (see also Thatcher, 2002).

Elected politicians have made little use of their power to overturn IRA decisions. Thus, with the notable exception of Italy, delegation to IRAs in the four countries examined by Thatcher has resulted in the creation of a body of regulators independent of the state and elected politicians. However, in recently privatized markets, such as Greece, the newly established regulators have not enjoyed independence to the same degree as in the UK and Germany, where the markets have traditionally been characterized by the existence of independent bodies. For example, the Greek National Council for Radio and Television (NCRTV), which was set up in the 1989 and amended by Law 2863/2000, is an independent administrative authority that supervises and regulates the radio and television markets. Its independence is guaranteed by Article 3 of Law 2863/2000, but in practice its powers are limited in a highly politicized Greek broadcasting scene and final decisions on broadcasting matters such as the allocation of licences rests with the relevant government minister.

Converged regulatory agencies

Despite the growing trend towards convergence of technologies, most OECD[1] countries still have separate regulators for broadcasting and telecommunications (OECD, 2007), occasionally resulting in bureaucratic infighting and delays in the rollout of new services. In China, the Ministry of Information Industry and the State Administration for Radio, Film and Television share broadcast licensing responsibilities, resulting in confusion over which agency will regulate converging services like IPTV. Furthermore, content regulation is typically conducted through a separate ministry or government authority (as in India and Saudi Arabia) or by the broadcasting authority (Botswana, Chile and Colombia).

In India, there are two entities responsible for content regulation: the Ministry of Information and Broadcasting monitors content related to broadcasting and film, whereas the Ministry of Information Technology oversees content related to the Internet. Table 9.1 provides evidence that in many countries multiple government authorities are still responsible for the functions of broadcasting licensing, telecommunication licensing, spectrum allocation and content regulation.

Some developed nations have set up a joint independent regulator, separate from interested parties, in order to ensure fair and open competition in the broadcasting and telecommunications sectors. The institutional changes that governments need to consider to take into account convergence between telecommunications and broadcasting mainly relate to the establishment of organizationally integrated convergence regulators (Wu, 2004). In the USA, integrated regulation has been evident since the creation in the 1930s of the Federal Communications Commission (FCC), which has joint responsibility for broadcasting and telecommunications. This coherent vision of single regulator for the communications industry as a whole has since been pursued in other countries. Convergence regulators with horizontally integrated responsibilities for telecommunications and broadcasting already exist in a third of all OECD nations, and this trend is spreading to non-OECD counties (Latzer, 2009: 420).

According to ITU (2007), nearly 30 converged regulatory agencies were set up in the period 2000–2007. As mentioned above, the rationale for this accelerating logic is that a converged regulator is better suited to respond to an environment in which distinctions based on service and network platform are becoming blurred. Among the countries with converged regulators are the UK, Australia, Finland, Italy, Malaysia, South Africa and Singapore. In 2005, for example, in an attempt to develop a policy framework to accommodate new services and other evolutions in the marketplace, Australia launched the ACMA (Australian Communication and Media Authority), with responsibility for both telecommunications and broadcasting. South Korea provides a further striking example. Until recently, the country had four government authorities responsible for regulating the communications industry – the Telecommunications Commission, the Ministry of Information and Communication (MIC), the Broadcasting Commission and the Ministry of Culture and Tourism. This overlap in responsibilities was delaying the rollout of IPTV services, with the result that, in December 2007, the government enacted a law eliminating the MIC and calling for a unified broadcasting and communications commission, merging the Broadcasting Commission, the Telecommunications Commission and MIC's Broadcasting Policy Office.

Table 9.1 Regulatory authorities in selected countries

Country	Telecomms carriage	Telecomms spectrum	Broadcast carriage	Broadcast spectrum	Content
			Heading		
Argentina	TextNational Communications Commission (CNC); Communications Secretariat (SECOM)	CNC	Federal Broadcasting Committee (COMFER)	CNC	COMFER
Botswana	Ministry of Communications, Science and Technology (MoCST); Botswana Telecommunications Authority (BTA)	BTA	National Broadcasting Board (NBB)	NBB	NBB; BTA
Colombia	Ministry of Communications (MoC); Telecommunications Regulatory Commission (CRT)	MoC	National Television Commission (CNTV)	CNTV	CNTV
Chile	Telecommunications Secretariat (SUBTEL) within Ministry of Transport and Telecommunications	SUBTEL	National Television Council (CNTV)	SUBTEL	CNTV
Egypt	National Telecommunication Regulatory Authority (NTRA); Ministry of Communications and Information Technology (MCIT)	NTRA	Egyptian Radio and Television Union (ERTU)	ERTU	Ministry of Interior (*Internet security*); ERTU (*broadcasting*)
France	Regulatory Authority for Electronic Communications and Postal Service (ARCEP)	National Spectrum Agency (ANFR)	Higher Council for Radio and Television (CSA)	ANFR; CSA	ARCEP; CSA

(Continued)

Table 9.1 (Continued)

		Heading			
Country	Telecomms carriage	Telecomms spectrum	Broadcast carriage	Broadcast spectrum	Content
Hong Kong, China	Office of the Telecommunications Authority (OFTA)	OFTA	Broadcasting Authority (BA); OFTA	BA; OFTA	BA
India	Telecommunications Regulatory Authority of India (TRAI); Department of Telecommunications (DoT) (*licensing*)	DoT	TRAI; Ministry of Information and Broadcasting (MI&B) (*licensing*)	DoT	Ministry of Information Technology (MIT) (*Internet*); MI&B (*broadcasting*)
Jordan	Ministry of Information and Communications Technology (MoICT); Telecommunications Regulatory Commission (TRC)	TRC	Audiovisual Commission (AVC)	AVC; TRC	AVC
Mexico	Communications and Transportation Secretariat (SCT); Federal Telecommunications Commission (COFETEL)	SCT	SCT; Secretariat of Public Education (SEP)	SCT	SEP; General Directorate for Radio, Television and Cinematography (RTC) within Executive Secretariat
Pakistan	Ministry of Information Technology – IT and Telecom Division (MoIT); Pakistan Telecommunications Authority (PTA)	PTA	Pakistan Electronic Media Regulatory Authority (PEMRA)	PTA	PEMRA

Singapore	Infocomm Development Authority (IDA)	IDA	IDA; Media Development Authority (MDA)	IDA	MDA
Uganda	Uganda Communications Commission (UCC)	UCC	Uganda Broadcasting Council (UBC)	UBC; UCC	UBC
United Kingdom	Office of Communications (Ofcom)	Ofcom	Ofcom; Department for Culture Media and Sport	Ofcom	Ofcom
United States	Federal Communications Commission (FCC); various state-level public utility commissions (PUCs)	FCC	FCC; local government for cable TV franchises	FCC	FCC, Federal Trade Commission

Source: ICT Regulation Toolkit, based upon Telecommunications Management Group, Inc. research and Telecommunication Regulatory Institutional Structures and Responsibilities, OECD Paper, DSTI/ICCP/TISP(2005)6/Final, pp. 31–2.

The issue of whether and how regulatory authority over various types of communication systems should be vested in a single agency may be best exemplified by the recent debate over regulatory reform in the UK. As the then Deputy Chairman of Ofcom and Chairman of the Content Board Richard Hooper (2005) said, the new converged regulatory agency would be able to address the changing structural, institutional and ideological shifts brought about by the new, disruptive technologies of digital convergence. Hooper paid particular attention to the phenomenon of media abundance and the increasing uncertainty to centralized regulatory monopolies, the regulatory asymmetry produced by the arrival of the Internet, and the growing capacity of people in society to create and distribute content. But let me tell the story of the setting-up of Ofcom in detail.

The Office of Communications

The British government, originally through its 2000 Communications White Paper and later through its Communications Bill of 13 July 2001,[2] which resulted in the Communications Act 2003, expressed the view that the convergence of communications services was making it increasingly problematic to designate an infrastructure as being specific to a particular service. It also made it arbitrary to designate individual operators and services as falling into one category or another. The Communications White Paper acknowledged that 'the communications revolution has arrived' and therefore a new framework for communications regulation in the twenty-first century was required. The White Paper therefore made a case for merging telecommunications and broadcasting regulators into a super-body, Ofcom (Office of Communications), along the lines of the FCC in the United States. Searching for possible solutions to the current convergence problems, policymakers in the UK considered it necessary to propose the institutional integration of telecommunications and media regulations, at both organizational level (the appointment of a regulator) and normative level (the enactment of laws).

The proposal to set up a single regulator met with a mixed reaction. Some argued that this would ensure that consistent and relevant rules were adopted across all converged sectors. After all, if all communication is just zeros and ones, then it becomes impossible to sustain a regulatory system based on the application of different sets of rules for different forms of communication, such as broadcasting and telecommunications (Smith, 2006). Others raised concerns over the attempt to put economic and social issues under the same roof. Up to that point, regulatory bodies had overseen the broadcasting and telecommunications sectors under different statutes and had different roles and functions. The ITC (Independent Television Commission) put emphasis on content regulation, whereas Oftel (Office of Telecommunications) was concerned with structural regulation.

Critics of the merging of those bodies said that there was bound to be a clash between the two. Another fear was that the better resourced telecommunications sector might dominate the smaller broadcasting sector under a converged regulator. Andrew Graham (2000) argued that the new era required effective regulation, but not a single regulator combining economic regulation with issues of political voice or quality of content, which are different in kind. There was no objective way of measuring the latter, he argued, and a separate regulatory body was required to deal with these separate, public, interests.

Some British Commonwealth countries, including Australia, were also sceptical of the desirability of setting up a single regulatory body. A 2000 Australian government report suggested that competition responsibilities should remain with the Australian Competition and Consumer Commission (ACCC). It also advocated that both the Australian Communication Authority (ACA) and the Australian Broadcasting Authority (ABA) retain specialized roles, as it was difficult to identify any significant synergies that would be generated by merging them. The report continued that the cultural and social focus of the ABA had little to do with the economic and technical focus of the ACA, which was also reflected in the management skills and the membership of the boards of those organizations. While the continued separate operation of those regulators was conceived as the best approach at the time, the regulatory philosophy has since changed and Australia today is among the countries with a merged communications regulatory agency.

Foregrounding competition

Returning to the UK, almost a decade after the publication of the Communications Bill, the danger that one regulatory tradition (telecommunications) would dominate the other (broadcasting), which was then painted by many commentators, has become a reality. Ofcom has been set up as a converged regulator with responsibility both for carriage regulation and for content, products and services, whether public or commercial. The expected advantages were effectiveness and efficiency gains, synergy and lower transaction costs. As Livingstone, Lunt and Miller (2007: 613) put it, 'Ofcom was conceived as a powerful sector-wide regulator that could flexibly respond to new challenges while being "future proofed" against changes that could otherwise destabilise or impede technological innovation and market expansion'. While some of these efficiencies may have been achieved, it will be shown below that Ofcom has been dominated by one regulatory tradition (telecommunications, with its economic imperative), the sociocultural objectives of broadcasting (the social imperative) taking a back seat (Vick, 2006).

One of the key objectives of Ofcom has been to put competition law at the center of media regulation. Competition law can be defined as the set of regulatory mechanisms used to tackle market failures, typically arising from high market shares, dominant positions, corporate expansion and the creation of barriers to entry. The 2000 White Paper that paved the way for the new regulator revealed the then New Labour government's intention to 're-base broadcasting regulation upon modern Competition Act principles and give the regulator [Ofcom] concurrent powers with the OFT [Office of Fair Trading], which the ITC currently lacks' (DCMS and DTI, 2000, para. 8.9.1). Ofcom has a statutory obligation to deal with competition issues in communications markets, especially as they frequently arise in the form of regulatory disputes (which Ofcom intervenes to resolve). Most disputes are in relation to pricing: allegations of abusive/unfair pricing or the refusal to supply. As Ofcom's Chief Executive has mentioned, the regulator's powers include requiring supply, setting the price and other terms going forward and, crucially, discretion to award repayment (Richards, 2010).

Another factor that justifies the criticism of Ofcom as primarily an economic regulator is the subordination of the *citizen interest* (the long-term social benefits broadcasting brings to society, democracy, culture, identity and civic engagement) to the *consumer interest* (short-term benefits to individuals expressed through viewing choices, pay-TV services, online and Web services, and so on) (see Harvey, 2006; Livingstone, Lunt and Miller, 2007). In recent years Ofcom has chosen to deal with consumer issues online and to encourage openness in practices, process and charges for those it regulates. In an era dominated by the debate on 'network neutrality' or 'Internet traffic management' (at the heart of this debate is the concern that traffic management could be used as a form of anticompetitive behavior, for example a provider limiting the access of its subscribers to particular services), the prevailing language used by the regulator is 'protecting consumer interest' or 'consumer transparency', rather than 'citizen interest' or 'citizen rights'. Consumer policy (focusing on demand-side market failures) goes hand in hand with competition policy (focussed on the supply side) in a complex, converged communications industry. The bottom line is that the broader agenda for establishing a new converged regulatory framework in the UK foregrounds competition as the primary instrument for dealing with economic and sociocultural communication matters such as eliminating entry barriers and safeguarding plurality.

Further evidence of Ofcom's intention to accommodate commercial concerns provides the regulatory agency's ability to shape the behavior of the public broadcaster BBC. While the regulator's primary responsibility is to facilitate the thriving of the communications industry, its approach to the BBC seems to suggest a different set of political priorities (Freedman, 2008: 149). Also the government's backing of the idea of an independent, publicly funded public broadcaster, it has increased the financial stringency of the Corporation, has asked it to continuously justify the need for commercial output and to cut down its commercial enterprises. The BBC has also been asked to reform its governance structure and set up a new governing body, the BBC Trust as 'the custodian of its purposes'.

Any new services are now subject to a test that will measure their 'public value' based on 'objectivity, rigor and transparency' (http://www.bbc.co.uk/aboutthebbc/policies/text/bpv.html (accessed 29 June 2011). against their impact on the market. This reflects the then New Labour government's determination to ensure that the BBC did not unfairly distort the market. Meanwhile, the BBC has been instructed to act as a key driver of the digital revolution and facilitator of the digital switchover (Iosifidis, 2006, 2011a). As a commentator put it, borrowing heavily from Ofcom's recommendations, '[Ofcom] sees the BBC not as an autonomous proponent of public service values but as an organization that is part of an increasingly competitive, marketized environment and needs regulating according to that logic' (Freedman, 2008: 169).

The Federal Communications Commission

Likewise, competition issues and corporate interests prevail in the regulatory decisions of the FCC on the other side of the Atlantic. In the USA, the FCC, despite its long existence, strength and unified structure, has often been seen as a classic example of a regulatory body that has been 'captured' by the industries it regulates (see Dunbar, 2005; Brown and Blevins, 2008; Freedman, 2008). Over the course of time, the FCC has adopted an economic perspective to please business interests and has tended to ignore alternative perspectives that might have given greater consideration to sociocultural matters (Blevins and Brown, 2006). This is evidenced by its July 2003 decision to relax media ownership rules and in particular to raise the cap on the proportion of TV households a single corporation could reach nationally from 35 per cent to 45 per cent. The review and the ultimate relaxation of the ownership rules was prompted in part by a decision of the US Court of Appeals for the District of Columbia in the case Fox Television Stations Inc. vs. FCC (2002), which had questioned the justification for the regulation that limited the number of TV stations a single entity could control.

Despite opposition from a number of members of Congress and public media advocacy organizations (NGOs), the then FCC Chairman Colin Powell was determined to go ahead with the revised ownership rules. But following growing resistance from Congress, the public and the courts (the Third Circuit Court of Appeals in the city of Philadelphia ruled in favor of the case Prometheus Radio Project vs. FCC (2004) and eventually prevented the regulatory agency from implementing the reformation of the rules), the final outcome was a compromise of raising the cap to 39 per cent. Commentators have argued that this was not really a compromise, since the new cap allowed News Corporation (owner of the Fox network) and Viacom (owner of CBS network) to retain all their television stations (Brown and Blevins, 2008; Freedman, 2008). For Brown and Blevins (2008: 453–4), the above case reveals, among other things, the enormous power of the media corporations, the FCC's long history of ignoring the public, and the dominance of neoliberal thinking in Washington. Frieden (2008) offered more cases showing the FCC's preoccupation with competition issues and neglect of sociocultural matters (see Chapter 3).

The European Union and competition law

At EU level, convergence also goes hand in hand with a growing trend to rely on competition law rather than on sector-specific regulation to deliver economic and public policy objectives. As competition developed, a key institutional change was the growing involvement of competition authorities, especially in telecommunications regulation. The trend towards globalization and, especially in Europe, the creation of a single market, increased the role of international competition authorities (see Chapter 7). The growing involvement of the EC's competition authority reflects the need for consistent jurisdiction in the sector to enable market participants to make rational business decisions.

Competition policy objectives prevail in the broadcasting sector, too. The Competition Directorate of the European Commission has been active in setting up rules concerning the following areas (Wheeler, 2004, 2010): the definition of state aid with respect to public service broadcasters; mergers that result in the concentration of media ownership and cross-media integration; and the sale of sports coverage rights to broadcasters. Indeed, in recent decades, broadcasters in various member states have been subject to Competition Directorate investigations with regard to each of these areas (Levy, 1999).

European Commission policy for regulatory convergence[3]

Early policies

The EC offers a striking example of the political-strategic integration of communications markets. In the early 1990s, the EC was considering the possibility of setting up a European Regulatory Authority (ERA) to oversee telecommunications systems and services across the EU, although after lengthy deliberations it decided not to proceed with the creation of an ERA but instead encourage cooperation between national regulatory authorities (NRAs). The Communications Review (EC, 1999a: 9) reads: 'The Commission considers at this stage that the creation of a European Regulatory Authority would not provide sufficient added value to justify the likely costs. In addition, it could lead to duplication of responsibilities, resulting in more rather than less regulation'. The Commission considered that issues concerning disparities in the interpretation and application of Community legislation (NRA assessment of operators with significant market power) were best dealt with by improving coordination and cooperation between NRAs.

The above results, concerning NRAs, were drawn from a study commissioned by the EC into the opinions of interested parties on, among other things, the need to streamline or change regulatory structures within the EU (EC, 1999b). Since then, regulatory cooperation between NRAs both in telecommunications and broadcasting has been of primary importance, especially in view of the intrusive and borderless nature of many of the new technologies. However, the EC continued to consider combined political responsibilities. Latzer (2009: 419) notes that since 2004 the responsibilities that previously belonged to the General Directorates XIII (Telecommunications) and X (Media, Education and Culture) have been united under one roof: the General Directorate of the Information Society and Media.

But the debate over regulatory convergence gained momentum in December 1997, when the EC, through its Convergence Green Paper (EC, 1997), opened a discussion at EU level over the need to impose fresh rules to maximize the benefits of digital convergence in terms of job creation, industry growth, consumer choice, cultural diversity and political pluralism. The EC's objectives were twofold: to create an economically viable EU media industry capable of competing globally; and to promote the 'public interest' (enhanced service quality, consumer choice, access to new technologies, plurality and so on). The overall objective of the Green Paper was to support, rather than stifle, the process of change and innovation. It was viewed by the EC as a means to achieve a 'European information society'. Faith in convergence to create the information society appeared strong, and regulatory reform was viewed as a means of encouraging convergence. As stated in the Green Paper, the opportunities provided by convergence should not be hampered or constrained by inappropriate regulation. A key message from the Green Paper was that convergence should not lead to additional regulation.

However, as shown in Chapter 7, the Convergence Green Paper revealed the conflicts that existed (and still exist) within the EU between, on the one hand, economic and industrial issues, and on the other, sociocultural implications. It could hardly have been otherwise, as the Green Paper was the product of two Directorates, DGX (Directorate of Media, Education and Culture) and DGXIII (Directorate of Telecommunications) (now merged), pursuing different agendas. Although the Green Paper spelled out different regulatory options,[4] the thrust of it was in favor of the creation of a horizontal regulatory model to cover the whole range of existing and new services in the communications sector. The horizontal model meant that there should be homogeneous treatment regardless of the service carried. The move towards a horizontal approach implies, on the one hand, the primacy of telecommunications concerns over those of broadcasting and, on the other, increased reliance on competition policy rather than sector-specific rules.

The consultation process (EC, 1999c) that followed the publication of the Green Paper revealed that it was necessary to adopt separate approaches to the regulation of the transport of electronic signals (and the infrastructures used for this) and to the regulation of content. The Convergence Communication also confirmed the need for a more horizontal approach to all transport network infrastructures and associated services, irrespective of the types of service carried. The majority of respondents were also in favor of setting up a regulatory regime for new services that recognized the need for large investments in their launch and the uncertainties of the marketplace while at the same time maintaining adequate consumer safeguards. A final message from the consultation process was that there was increased faith in competition rules, accompanied by the gradual phasing-out of sector-specific regulation, as the market became more competitive. This key message related mainly to access issues concerned with communications infrastructure and associated services. The Convergence Communication noted that open and competitive markets could not contribute to public interest objectives such as the protection of minors and human dignity.

In the past decade, the emphasis in regulatory reform has been on three policies: accelerating liberalization,[5] speeding up the decision-making process and simplifying regulation. Much of the impetus for reform dates from the 1999 Communications Review, which proposed the main elements for a new framework of communications infrastructure and associated services. In line with the principle of technological neutrality, it proposed that the new framework cover all communications services, therefore applying to telecommunications networks (fixed or mobile), satellite communications, cable TV networks and terrestrial broadcast networks, which control access to services. There followed the Lisbon summit of EU heads of government (EC, 2000a), which set out a broad agenda intended to make the EU more competitive with the USA by removing burdens on European companies.

European Commissioners have emphasized on several occasions the need to improve the EU's approach to regulation, by both speeding up and slimming down its legislation. The Stockholm summit (EC, 2001a) reviewed progress on competitive initiatives and re-emphasized the importance of setting out a new regulatory framework, with the following two principles: simplifying regulation and speeding up decision-making. In that way, it would avoid the risk being overtaken by the fast-moving evolution of markets and technology. In order to ensure legal certainty in the transition from the current framework to the new regulatory framework, the EC proposed five new Directives (Framework, Access, Authorizations, Universal Service and Data Protection), which would replace existing Directives.

Contemporary policies

The Directives were aimed at establishing a harmonized regulatory framework for electronic communications networks and services across the EU.

They sought to respond to the convergent phenomenon by covering all sectors. Hence the 2003 Electronic Communications Framework (see http://ec.europa.eu/information_society/policy/ecomm/index_en.htm, accessed 20 November 2010) created a level playing field for a converging world. As is mentioned on the official EU website, 'regulation is seen as temporary, needed only until normal market conditions develop, and is applied regardless of the technology, stimulating innovation'. By creating a consistent market across Europe, the regulation would give operators the confidence to build on a scale appropriate to a community of 27 states.

Latzer (2009: 419) noted that convergence was also a key theme of Strategy i2010: European Information Society 2010 (see http://ec.europa.eu/information_society/eeurope/i2010/index_en.htm, accessed 20 November 2010). The strategy promoted the positive contribution that ICTs can make to the economy, society and individual quality of life. One of its objectives was to establish a convergence pattern between policymaking and technology. In this sense, it aimed to modernize and utilize the EU's policymaking instruments in order to advance the digital economy.

This strategy has been followed by a new initiative – the Digital Agenda. In May 2010, EC Vice-president Neelie Kroes formally launched the Digital Agenda, which is basically a grand ICT plan for Europe intended to 'maximize the potential of ICT to boost Europe's prosperity and the well-being of its citizens'. In a sense, this is a revival of the Lisbon Agenda of 2000, which boldly claimed it would create by 2010 'the most competitive and dynamic knowledge-based economy in the world capable of sustainable economic growth with more and better jobs and greater social cohesion' – an economy that has not yet materialized. The 2010 Agenda has seven priority areas for action (see http://www.computing.co.uk/computing/news/2263328/ec-sets-digital-agenda-2020, accessed 20 November 2010):

- Creating a digital single market.
- Greater interoperability.
- Boosting Internet trust and security.
- Much faster Internet access.
- More investment in research and development.
- Enhancing digital literacy skills and inclusion.
- Applying information and communications technologies in addressing the challenges facing European society, such as climate change and an ageing population.

Also, the Audiovisual Media Services (AVMS) Directive, which came into effect in 2007, replacing the Television Without Frontiers (TWF) Directive, updated Europe's broadcasting rules. It covered TV and TV-like services (such as VOD and mobile TV) across the EU and aimed to stimulate the European broadcasting industry and protect consumers. As it extended beyond broadcasting, it was expected to set convergence-like European standards for content regulation (Latzer, 2009: 419). The AVMS Directive provided an enabling regulatory framework and legal certainty in an effort to foster new-media audiovisual services. A main objective of the Directive was the promotion of open technologies where Europe has considerable assets to take advantage of the opportunities offered by the convergence of communication platforms and the transition to digital technologies.

However, the introduction of the idea of 'linear' content (programming that looks like regular TV: it reaches a wide audience, there is scheduling, it is for-profit, the station keeps a record of what appeared and when) as distinct from nonlinear content (material that may be intended for a small audience, conducted without a commercial motive, viewed by people on request, such as by clicking on a Web link as opposed to turning on a TV set) has been criticized as shortsighted. According to a market analyst (Cukier, 2008), the problem with these definitions is that they are artificial and try to reproduce the classic 'licensing' model of broadcasting in the context of a new medium that has few characteristics of the traditional TV model.

To sup up, the EC intends to:

- Establish a harmonized regulatory framework for all communications services.
- Simplify and minimize regulation.
- Separate approaches to the regulation of infrastructure and the regulation of content.
- Put greater emphasis on competition law than in the past to achieve desirable economic and social objectives in the digital universe.

Conclusion

This chapter examined the discrepancies and challenges resulting from convergence in policymaking and assessed the reforms adopted in reaction to convergence. It highlighted the prominent role of competition policy and the economic imperative in regulatory traditions at UK, US and EU levels and offered examples of converged regulatory actions in the communications industry from elsewhere. Given that the EC provides a good example of the political-strategic integration of the communications market, the chapter devoted a large amount of space to reviewing the EC's policy for regulatory convergence, which has the following objectives: the acceleration of market liberalization; the speeding up of the decision-making process and the simplification of regulation; and growing reliance on competition law rather than sector-specific regulation.

To develop an effective media policy in an era of rapid technological advancement, regulators need to look beyond traditional media policy, which applied different rules to different sectors, and towards the spaces where traditionally distinct boundaries of policy and governance overlap. Among them are the realm of technological revolution; the liberalization and reregulation of communications industries; the emergence of supranational and/or regional bodies like the EU to dictate regulatory matters; and the growing tendency to rely on competition law to deliver public service purposes. The following chapter attempts to put these issues into a context by offering guidelines for regulatory reform in world of media abundance.

10
Guidelines for Regulatory Reform

Introduction

This chapter offers guidelines for regulatory reform and makes an assessment as to whether it is sector-specific or economic regulation (or a combination of both) that provides an adequate regulatory response to the concerns expressed in the previous chapter. The chapter starts by asking whether we need regulation at all in the new multichannel global communications era – and, if so, why. In this context, it reviews the principles of media regulation and examines whether these are likely to remain important in the new age. The work then moves on to assessing the need for a new, common regulatory framework for the converged information and communications sectors and the extent to which traditional communications regulation models are applicable to new services. Next, it analyzes the balance between competition law and sector-specific regulation, such as content and media ownership regulation, before it examines the cases for self- and co-regulation that have gained momentum in recent years. The themes of privacy, freedom of expression, copyright and network neutrality are analyzed as hot issues in the current global networked era.

The rationale for regulation in the digital age

While there has been much discussion about how the process of convergence challenges audiovisual and telecommunications regulation, accompanied by calls for a 'lighter' regulatory regime, few argue that 'no regulation' is a valid option. However, limited or no regulation at all has traditionally been applied to the print publishing industry worldwide in order to secure freedom of speech. Pro-market evangelists suggest that the regulatory model within which publishers currently operate could be adopted by all players in converging markets (for example, freedom to set up a business and unrestricted access to the market, the application of general laws combined with effective competition policy, and so on). Publishing, according to the European

Publishers Council (EPC, 1998), is an example of how competition can thrive in a highly competitive market without the need for strict sector-specific regulation. In Europe, this view is in line with the wider argument that competitiveness is of fundamental importance given that European enterprises must prepare for global competition on a scale never experienced before. The problem is that the characteristics of the publishing sector are not applicable to other sectors. For example, whereas it is relatively inexpensive to launch a magazine, it is very costly to set up a TV network. The television industry involves high entry and operational costs, which prohibit many potential proprietors from launching even small or local TV stations. True, digital technology, by driving costs down, has enabled small firms to enter the broadcasting market, but very few have managed to challenge incumbents and gain a significant market share. Small and medium-sized enterprises typically lack the financial resources to acquire content that would lure an audience, while at the same time they face barriers from established companies. A striking example is Murdoch-controlled satellite operator BSkyB in the UK, which has acquired the exclusive rights for premium content (sports and the latest blockbusters), thereby leaving little room for newcomers.

Facilitation of market entry: BSkyB and televised football rights

In the UK in the last two decades, BSkyB has been dominant in the live coverage of football matches, despite the escalating costs of acquiring these rights. In 2000, the satellite broadcaster paid £1.1 billion (about a third of its total programme budget) for the live coverage of 66 Premiership matches in a three-year deal (2001–2004) and in 2003 it paid almost as much (£1 billion) for a further three-year deal (2004–2007). The four-year deal before the start of the new millennium had cost BSkyB £670 million and the five-year contract before that a mere £191 million. The British Premier League's total revenues from UK pay-TV rights for the 2010–2013 seasons reached a record £1.78 billion (about €2 billion) for all six packages (for competition reasons, and also to meet EC guidelines not to allocate all rights to one broadcaster – in this case BSkyB – the selling of rights has been split into packages). This is remarkable given the ongoing economic downturn and the fact that sports broadcaster Setanta, which had won the rights for the two packages – 46 Premier League football matches for 2009–2010, plus 23 in each of the next three seasons – informed the League on 3 June 2009 that it could not honor the deal. Disney-owned ESPN, which had been outbid by Setanta before, took advantage of Setanta's failure to keep up payments and acquired the rights, which the League had decided to resell.

The above case shows how difficult it is for any new operator to enter the UK satellite broadcasting market and establish a presence by generating a strong subscriber base. BSkyB's dominant position in the market provides disincentives for any newcomer. Undoubtedly, the presence of BSkyB has improved the live broadcasting of football matches and stimulated investment in the UK's football industry. But the Murdoch empire has sometimes crossed reasonable boundaries with overzealous business practices, especially in the acquisition of sports and film rights. Therefore, regulation should be in place to facilitate market entry, ensure nondiscriminatory access and oversee pricing. Ofcom's March 2010 ruling that BSkyB must wholesale its premium sport content to rivals was a step in the right direction, as this decision is expected to trigger a price war and cheaper packages for consumers. In particular, Ofcom ruled that BSkyB must offer Sky Sports 1 and 2 channels to cable, terrestrial and Internet Protocol Television groups at a wholesale price set by Ofcom. However, the regulator failed to make a similar ruling on other premium content such as new films.

Management of spectrum

The above discussion makes clear that regulation still has a place in the converged era in order to safeguard fair competition and break barriers to entry. Second, convergence has not eliminated the need for spectrum management. The trends towards convergence, competition and liberalization may call for a shift in 'scarcity'-based regulation to regulation tailor made for the era of abundance. Still, new services and technologies (mobile commerce, wireless telecommunications links, high-speed data links to electronic equipment) have highlighted the need for regulators, at both national and global levels, to ensure adequate spectrum for all new technologies. The radio spectrum is a finite resource. There are many competing technologies and services and the question as to which find success in the marketplace will depend on how well they meet consumer needs and preferences. But the regulatory challenge is how to make spectrum available to meet the growing and often conflicting demands of businesses, consumers and essential services at a time of rapid, unpredictable change. This will require a flexible, dynamic approach using a full range of spectrum management tools, including regulation, pricing and trading.

Universal access

The third reason as to why an unregulated market will not work is that regulation is required to ensure open technical standards and universal compatibility. Rules are needed to ensure that universal access is maximized. The principles of regulation – to protect and promote values such as freedom of expression and access to information, and balance these with acceptable restrictions, such as for the protection of minors, diversity and impartiality – continue to occupy an important place in the converged era. Because broadcasters can exert tremendous communicative influence and form public opinion, regulation is required to ensure that operators reflect a range of views and cultures in a society and contribute to rational political debate (Humphreys, 2000). The move to pay-TV may deprive some parts of the population of certain kinds of programming, such as popular sports and the latest releases. The Ofcom decision relating to BSkyB described above (in particular, the ruling that BSkyB must wholesale its premium sport content to rivals) shows that regulation can play a significant role in facilitating market entry. Another notable example is the Listed Events policy, described in Chapter 7, under which specific sports events should be shown on terrestrial free-to-air channels. To address the issue of consumer access it has also been suggested that policymakers preserve free-to-air public-service broadcasters and allow them to expand into new platforms, such as digital terrestrial television, as well as the Web. Public Service Media should launch new, on-demand services and also be available on various platforms (terrestrial, mobile, satellite, etc) in order to serve current audience needs. Cross-platform strategies and the launch of on-demand services help public-service media to reach new audiences and serve an extended form of citizenship (see Tambini and Cowling, 2004; Lowe and Bardoel, 2007; Iosifidis, 2010a). In this way, the gap between information haves and have-nots (the so-called 'digital divide') may be bridged.

The term 'digital divide' refers to the socioeconomic gap between individuals, households, businesses and geographic areas with regard both to their opportunities to access ITCs and to their use of the Internet for a variety of activities (OECD, 2000). However, as computer ownership and Internet access are rising sharply, the idea of the digital divide has lost some ground. What is more, the Internet has now been liberated from the tyranny (or gateway bottleneck) of the PC, for digital TV sets and 3G mobile phones provide alternative gateways to the Internet. Meanwhile, various projects have been launched that have constituted positive steps towards bridging the divide. These include 'One Laptop per Child' (run by a US nonprofit organization established to oversee the creation of an affordable educational device for use in the developing world) and '50x15' (launched in 2004 by Advance Micro-Devices and aimed at providing Internet access and computers for 50 per cent of the world's population by the year 2015).

Yet, it is likely that Internet differentiation will emerge along a dimension of quality. For example, high-speed broadband Internet access requires an upgrade of infrastructure – whether telecommunications, cable or wireless – but as this must be recovered through higher prices, not everyone will be able to have access. High-speed Internet access is not expected to command the same societal priority as the basic type of Internet service. Broadband will therefore be the digital divide issue for developed countries, whereby income, location and demand will be factors in bandwidth consumption (Noam, 2010: 48–9).

But the focus should not merely be 'access to the media', for 'access to audiences' is also a key area of concern in the digital converged era. As Napoli (2009) suggests, it is important to design policies to enhance the rights of individuals as speakers. The traditional component of the access principle in media policymaking has been the right of people to access various media technologies in order to obtain various types of content. Napoli argues that the concern should also be with citizens' rights as speakers, as disseminators of information, rather than only with citizens' rights as consumers of information. Moving away from citizens' consumption of information and towards thinking about access in terms of citizens' dissemination of information clearly represents a fundamental shift in policy priorities that reflects the growing trend towards user-generated or user-distributed output.

Thanks to the Internet, a large part of the population has the ability to produce, rather than merely distribute, content. Technology has provided the potential to place the organization-based speaker and the individual on a more equal footing. As Napoli (2009: 37) put it, 'a policy focus on the right of access to audiences focuses attention on whether the producers and distributors of user-generated content are able to operate on an equal footing and on identifying impediments to equality in the opportunities to take advantage of the tremendous distribution capacity of the Internet'. Policymakers should therefore take steps to remedy potential imbalances in audiences' access to speakers.

A continuous concern: concentration of media ownership

Fourth, there is a danger that the market, left alone, will favor concentration of media ownership, partly due to the high basic costs of access to the media, and partly due to the ability of powerful enterprises to penetrate any market and achieve 'synergies'. According to Graham and Davis (1997), high-quality multimedia content is expensive to produce in the first place but, once created, relatively cheap to edit or to change and even cheaper to reproduce. Put another way, it has high fixed costs and low variable costs – the natural creators of monopolies. High-quality material can be produced and yet cost very little per unit provided that it reaches a large number of people (exploiting economies of scale) and/or provided that it is used in a variety of formats (exploiting economies of scope), but the exploitation of these economies of scale and scope imply concentration of ownership.

For Graham and Davis, even though technology has removed one source of monopoly, that of spectrum scarcity, it has replaced it with another, the natural monopoly of economies of scale. It is then a small step to argue that the previously state-run media monopolies will be replaced by private monopolies with the potential of both limiting competition and damaging pluralism (see also Iosifidis, 1999; McChesney and Schiller, 2003). Central to the concentration of media ownership issue is audiences' access, as extensive concentration of ownership of media outlets results in further inequalities in access to audiences across speakers (Napoli, 2009).

Summing up: regulation retains its relevance in the digital converged era

In short, regulation retains its relevance and importance in the new digital era. It is needed for eliminating barriers to entry and creating the stability and certainty that enables the industrial sector to take rational business decisions, for example via spectrum management and the provision of technical standards (economic objectives). Also regulation is needed for delivering social benefits such as pluralism, diversity, affordability, interconnectivity and access (sociocultural objectives). However, to achieve these objectives, regulation should adopt new methods and be more dynamic so as to cope with a fast-changing environment. On the one hand, it should be flexible enough to encourage innovation, take into account technological convergence, provide for interconnection and protect against anticompetitive behavior, especially in view of the increasingly complex nature of corporate alliances. General competition law has an important role to play here. According to the EC Competition Directorate, competition rules should be the prime vehicle for regulating the electronic communications sector. On the other hand, regulation should redefine and promote the broader public interest in the new communications environment in order to maximize the social benefits associated with the digital revolution. It should continue to pursue traditional social objectives, such as pluralism and diversity of sources, but at the same time address considerations new to the digital converged era (for example, access to the Internet and provision of the necessary skills for its efficient use; the dissemination of TV content via the Internet; the protection of intellectual property on-line; consumer protection on-line; e-commerce; affordable access to digital connectivity and broadband technologies; the right of access to audience producing user-generated content, and so on). Competition law does not suffice to address the social and cultural public interest objectives. So sector-specific regulation (like media ownership and/or content regulation) is still justified to ensure that these objectives, such as political pluralism and audience access to diverse content, are safeguarded and promoted.

The convergence regulatory framework

My argument so far has been that:

- The principles of media regulation are likely to remain important in the new age.
- Competition policy alone cannot provide adequate safeguards for economic and, especially, sociocultural objectives.
- There might be a need for a common regulatory framework to accommodate all converged sectors.

However, the way regulation is shaped in the digital converged environment depends, to a large extent, on whether one considers convergence as simply an *inevitable consequence of technological and communications service evolution*, or as a *process dictated by industry and/or political decisions*. The two views have differing impacts on market development policy/policymaking. The former assumes that services using different components (digital broadcasting, telecommunications and multimedia computing) will necessarily and automatically merge as a result of technological advancements. The latter imposes a requirement for political decision-making, outlining the objectives of 'convergence policy', setting the conditions for bringing into the market new, Internet-style data services, and so on.

Although I am in favor of the latter approach, it should be noted that excessive regulation in the future media market, yet uncertain as to *which* converged services will actually find a market, creates disincentives for new actors. Also, a balance should be achieved between protection and encouraging investment as, for many decades, Europeans have gained a reputation of being 'regulation addicts', thereby stifling investment and innovation. For these reasons, it is advisable to leave service providers some flexibility as to the services they may offer. This, however, should not be done to the detriment of social and cultural values.

Once a new, common regulatory framework for the converged information and communications sectors has been realized, the next step would be to assess the extent to which traditional communications regulation models are applicable to new services as well as the balance between competition law and sector-specific regulation to be adopted. What I consider in the rest of this chapter is a dual model in which competition law could apply, supplemented by flexible sector-specific regulation, especially with reference to broadcasting. This is particularly important, given the power of the medium of television to influence public opinion.

Sectoral content and/or ownership regulation has traditionally been imposed for the protection of the audience and also as a result of spectrum limitation. There is a train of thought that digital convergence naturally leads to an end to the regulation of content and ownership, as it abolishes spectrum scarcity and blurs the boundaries between previously separated sectors. This is a strong argument, but one should perhaps raise a note of caution, for the market perspective may not go hand in hand with patterns of media usage, meaning that the market may be heading towards convergence, but without paying close attention to audience habits.

Changing audience habits? The case of TV versus the PC

Audience habits cannot change overnight! Let me take the example of the television medium and compare it with the personal computer (PC). Television has so far been a moving image-based, point-to-multipoint service and a one-way channel of communication, capable of delivering mass entertainment to passive audiences. On the contrary, the PC is a text-based, point-to-point interactive – or 'on demand' – service, mainly used for business and education. Users purchase a PC with the purpose of being able to fulfil their college coursework, surf the Internet for information, communicate via e-mail, and engage in on-line chat and electronic commerce. In contrast to a TV screen, in front of which people sit back and enjoy, a PC screen is sat close to as the user leans forward and interacts.

Therefore the TV and the PC seem to serve different purposes and apparently function in different markets, the former in the *entertainment world* and the latter in the *learning world*, where users engage with Internet-style services via the PC terminal. This suggests that the substitutability of TV and the Internet is questionable. Still, technology gurus such as Nicholas Negroponte (1995) argue that digital technology, and in particular the introduction of interactive digital television (iDTV), will change the nature and the economics of the television medium. Indeed, iDTV can offer services previously confined to the PC domain, that is, e-learning, e-commerce, e-mail, home shopping and banking and gambling, in addition to being able to offer mainstream programming. iDTV alongside mobile TV, third generation mobile telephony and other novelties, are technologies that offer the remarkable potential for widening media access, changing viewing habits, creating new types of programmes and enhancing interactivity.

However, the hype over iDTV ignores the psychology of media usage: most people want television for entertainment and relaxation. TV is a *shared medium* and watching it involves a relaxed and passive usage, in which the viewer typically consumes whatever the network delivers. In direct contrast to computing, which is seen as an active medium driven by individual 'users', television is considered a passive medium consisting of multiple 'viewers' (see Table 10.1). It may be the case that technologies are converging

Table 10.1 Differences between PCs and TVs

Personal computer	Television
Single-person experience	Any number of people can watch the same TV
User sits close to the screen	
Screens are small and high-resolution/ -quality	Users sit at a distance
Screen typically displays static images	Screens are often large but with relatively low resolution/quality
Active, controllable medium	Screen displays constantly moving images
Constant interaction via a keyboard/ mouse	Passive medium
	Little (via a remote control) or no interaction

Source: Blachford, 2003.

so that the boundaries between television, computing and telecommunications are blurring. Yet convergence is as much about *behavior* as it is about technology; it is not so much an issue of whether the computer or the television will dominate in the home, but rather what people will *do* with these devices, how they intend to *use* them. And the fact is that television has not traditionally been associated with work and learning.

The favorite TV programmes in the majority of EU countries are the so-called couch potato services, including sport (particularly football), blockbuster movies, children's programmes and news/current affairs. Despite the emergence of the multichannel environment, in most EU countries people settle down for a small range of traditional channels which capture large audiences by showing shared moments of national or international interest (see Iosifidis, Steemers and Wheeler, 2005). The increased level of choice has certainly had an impact on viewing patterns, as they are now more widely dispersed, resulting in some loss of share for traditional terrestrial channels. In the UK, for example, the share of audience for the main five terrestrial broadcasters BBC1, BBC2, ITV, Channel 4 and Five dropped from 77.7 per cent in 2002 to 61 per cent in 2007 (Ofcom, 2008).

However, the growing range of competing media does not seem to have impacted on the amount of time that people spend watching TV. Despite the available Internet options, video games and DVDs, TV watching per day has gone up, for in 2008 the average British viewer spent more than a day per week (26 hours) watching broadcast TV whereas 10 years ago, the average viewing was less than a day per week (Thinkbox, 2010). According to the UK regulator, terrestrial television remains the main source of the consumption of programming genres such as news and current affairs content (65 per cent) (Ofcom, 2007). While the Internet as a source of news and information is growing in significance, it is still seen as a source of supplementary, rather than primary information. But the behavior of the younger population shows strong signs of change. Triggered by increases in bandwidth and superfast broadband, 16–24 year olds are beginning to spend more time online than watching TV (EIAA, 2006), with a substantial amount of their use dedicated to social networking sites like Facebook and Twitter.

The other observation is that people prefer passive viewing and largely ignore iDTV, the two-way technology that permits viewers to order products and play video games. Viewers have shown little or no interest in interacting with broadcasters and have not got excited about the features and benefits of interaction. They are not prepared, for example, to choose the camera to view a football game or change the plot of a film. It follows that iDTV, like most new interactive technologies, has yet to capture a mass audience almost a decade and a half after it was introduced. Once again, the biggest indicator of change to come is the behavior of younger age groups, who consider interactivity in media (together with mobile communications) an essential part of their lives.

Currently, the social habit of watching television from a distance limits user interaction and therefore reinforces the passive nature of the medium. Viewer habits, especially those of older groups, do not change easily and it would thus be difficult to convince citizens to start using TV for work, learning and business services, such as home banking, monitoring finances or even buying airline tickets. We cannot expect to see people using the living-room television to perform complicated functions like sending e-mails or electronic shopping – this is what laptops and mobile phones are for. Technology gurus like Gilder (1992) and Negroponte (1995) predicted that future televisions will look like a PC and capitalize the power the Internet brings to television and buying habits. After all, the Internet disrupted many businesses before television, notably printing. However, and despite the rhetoric about convergence, the majority of people do not want a television that functions as a PC; what they want is better TV (Sims, 1999; Ofcom, 2004).

Behind all this hype over convergence and the launch of new gadgets, there lies a simple fact: people want to access high-quality content that is both popular and innovative. Viewers in the UK prefer to watch established channels that provide a balanced TV diet of trusted and familiar programming with innovative, quality, original output (Ofcom, 2004). Likewise, most Americans continue to get their news and information primarily from traditional media companies (Stucke and Grunes, 2008). Of course, things may change. Google TV, which was expected to be released as a set-top box and built into US television sets in late 2010, is likely to blend searches with video content by introducing a familiar search bar. At the same time, it may bring more attention to YouTube, Google's video site. In this way, the Internet will hugely increase the amount of content available to TV viewers. The problem for companies is to find a way to convince viewers, especially older ones, to take advantage of the available options.

Having made these cautionary remarks, let me now return to the theme of designing regulation for the digital converged communications environment. It should be spelled out from the outset that certain traditional restrictions still have a role to play. Technology might change the media environment, but that does not imply that concerns about pluralism, diversity and free speech, traditionally protected by sectoral regulation, are less valid.

The continuing importance of content regulation

Negative content regulation

Content regulation is country- and culture-specific and therefore mainly the responsibility of nation-states. Content issues are primarily national in nature, being directly and closely related to the cultural, social and democratic needs of a particular society. Each state has imposed regulations designed to ensure the dissemination of output that competition tends to suppress. National governments have applied both *negative content regulation* – restricting the diffusion of certain types of information, text, sound and images and imposing advertising restrictions – and *positive content regulation* – promoting access to content, guaranteeing quality, safeguarding diversity. However, the restriction or suppression of harmful, politically or socially undesirable content is at odds with the principle of freedom of speech in democratic societies and therefore it is not a straightforward task for contemporary policy to apply content rules. The principle of liberal democracies' noninterventionist approach in communications is incompatible with the imposition of restrictive media content policies.

USA

As explained in previous chapters, the commitment to free speech in the USA, guaranteed by the First Amendment, does not allow, at least in theory, for controls over information flows to citizens. An essential goal of the First Amendment is to promote the marketplace of ideas (the sphere in which intangible values compete for acceptance) by restricting to varying degrees governmental restraints on speech, and achieving 'the widest possible dissemination of information from diverse and antagonistic sources'. In practice, though, there is a delicate balance between on the one hand freedom of expression and the right to hold opinions and on the other control and commitment to protect the public interest in minimizing the risks of harm and offence to people. Despite the First Amendment in the USA, broadcasting is subject to limited content rules, particularly in the areas of obscenity, indecency and children's programming. For example, the 1990 Children's Television Act provides only for limitations on commercials between programming. There have also been some cases in which the FCC has banned obscene and/or indecent material (see Freedman, 2008: 126–34).

Since the enactment of the Broadcast Decency Enforcement Act of 2005, broadcasters have faced significant financial penalties for the broadcast of obscene, indecent or profane material. The law allows the FCC to fine broadcasters as much as $325,000 for *each* utterance of profanity or display of indecent or obscene material in a particular broadcast, up to a maximum fine of $3 million. It does not modify existing statutory regulations, under which the FCC may revoke a station's licence, issue a warning for violations of its rules, or sanction individuals who appear on air and broadcast obscene, indecent or profane material. The broadcast of obscene material also remains a federal crime, allowing the Department of Justice to prosecute broadcasters who air such material. The regulatory agency has prepared a number of guidelines to help broadcasters to meet the FCC's standards. These guidelines should be considered in concert with the information provided in the

FCC's June 2006 memorandum 'FCC Regulation of Broadcast Obscenity, Indecency, and Profanity' (see FCC, 2006; also http://www.ucop.edu/irc/services/documents/guidelines.pdf, accessed 16 October 2010).

UK

In the UK, Ofcom ensures that 'generally accepted standards' are applied to the content of broadcasting services so as to provide adequate protection for members of the public from the inclusion in such services of harmful and/or offensive material. Ofcom's relevant legislation, Section Two of Broadcast Codes: Harm and Offence (http://stakeholders.ofcom.org.uk/broadcasting/broadcast-codes/broadcast-code/harmoffence/, accessed 16 October 2010) provides that programmes must not include material which condones or glamorizes violent, dangerous or seriously antisocial behavior and/or leads to suicide attempts. Demonstrations of exorcism, the occult and the paranormal are prohibited, hypnotic techniques are banned, and broadcast competitions and voting must be conducted fairly. Broadcast content is also subject to detailed rules on fairness, balance, impartiality and accuracy. In contrast, the print media are subject only to general legislation.

Ofcom's Content Board is a committee of the main Board and it sets and enforces quality and standards for television and radio. One of the fundamental beliefs of the Content Board is that content providers in the digital age have a responsibility, above all, to label material properly. This allows people to make their decision whether or not to view content with a reasonable understanding of what the content is likely to contain. Labelling can contain ratings or classifications to help citizens to self-regulate their consumption of electronic media and protect their children from harmful content (Hooper, 2005). Labelling is European policy and has been reinforced through the AVMS Directive.

EU: AVMS Directive

The UK, like all EU member states, is a signatory to the AVMS Directive, which came into effect in 2007, replacing the Television Without Frontiers (TWF) Directive. As discussed in Chapter 7, the AVMS Directive covers all services with audiovisual content irrespective of the technology used to deliver the content, meaning that the rules apply whether news or other audiovisual content is watched on TV, on the Internet or on a mobile phone. This is the principle of *technological neutrality* or *network neutrality*, which refers to the idea that the Internet should be an 'open' and 'neutral' platform for parties to send and receive traffic, without the middleman, the network service provider, acting as either censor or tollbooth. This idea of the 'end-to-end' nature of the Internet is one of its founding principles: the network was designed to be as decentralized as possible (Cukier, 2008). Thus network neutrality ensures a level playing field for all audiovisual media service providers. However, taking into account the degree of choice and user control over services, the AVMS Directive makes a distinction between linear services (television broadcasts) and nonlinear (on-demand) services.

The distinction, which imposes 'heavy' regulation on linear services and 'light touch' regulation on nonlinear services, has been criticized by media industry players, who claim that such a distinction is untenable in the age of digital convergence. For industry figures, the multiplication of channels and other sources of communications, particularly the rising penetration of the Internet, inevitably results in more pluralism and diversity, thereby justifying minimum or no public intervention and the abolition of rules on audiovisual content. Freedman (2008: 127) recalls that during the TWF negotiations – on whether on-line audiovisual content should be regulated in the same way as television or whether TV content regulation should increasingly be reregulated along the lines of the Internet – James Murdoch, CEO of BSkyB, declared that TV content regulation should be lessened and that a new noncontent control approach was needed to recognize the new on-demand world. Firms tend to favor less regulation generally, because it is perceived to benefit their activities (Gibbons, 2008).

Positive content regulation: the role of PSB

So far I have restricted my remarks to negative content regulation, that is what broadcasters should not do. Positive objectives and regulatory instruments concerning content have included subsidies for audiovisual production and direct or indirect subsidies (in the form of a lower VAT rate, for instance) to support struggling newspapers. In Europe, positive content regulation has traditionally taken the form of the establishment of public-service broadcasters (PSBs) in each member state, with the remit of providing all citizens with high-quality and diverse material. The principle of inclusion and access (public-service broadcasting is in principle open to all at affordable prices, as households typically pay a fixed licence fee) is therefore combined with the principle of sufficient programming diversity and quality to satisfy all interests.

Most European governments have supported publicly funded PSBs and, despite sustained criticism from commercial rivals, have allowed extensive on-line public-service broadcasting (PSB) activity. In spite of financial constraints (for example, in the autumn of 2010 the BBC announced under government pressure that it intended to freeze the licence fee), PSBs in Europe remain prominent players in the digital era and greatly contribute to original domestic production. Compliance with European quota requirements for EU content is built into PSB policy and, although this is a crude indicator, saying nothing about the quality and little about the type of programming (Gibbons, 2008), it nevertheless contributes to the supporting of European production.

The presence of strong PSB has allowed the relaxation of public-service requirements for other providers. This is particularly true in Germany, where commercial broadcasters are not subject to any type of public-service obligation. The German constitutional court has even ruled on several occasions that private channels are allowed to be truly market oriented as long as PSB exists. Likewise, in Spain and Italy there are no public-service obligations for commercial broadcasters. But the main concern for regulators in these countries is to ensure that the Italian public broadcaster RAI and its Spanish counterpart RTVE really provide a public-service output, since for the last decade both broadcasters have been highly commercialized (see Iosifidis, 2010). In the UK, public broadcaster BBC receives a high degree of political and audience support due to the Corporation's role as 'national champion' and its success in international markets.

Is content regulation still applicable?

What needs to be considered here is whether content regulation has a place in an era when new digital technologies are allowing more and more citizens to become content producers and publishers, and where blogging, podcasting and file sharing are becoming common practice. It is my firm belief that content regulation remains essential in the converged media age. An emerging and progressively more competitive media industry does not warrant ignoring content rules. Such rules should aim increasingly at ensuring that public interest content reaches users in the multichannel era. Content regulation will be required to provide a framework – particularly valuable at a time of rapid change – that also allows intervention to take place when the above values are at stake.

Nevertheless, the traditional means of regulating through licensing broadcasters and imposing conditions on their licences are being challenged by the proliferation of channels of communication and the volume of material transmitted. In addition, the internationalization of television, the development of cable and satellite TV and the introduction of digitization have made it more difficult to maintain and manage content rules traditionally designed for free-to-view mass audience channels (Tambini and Verhulst, 2001). Technological convergence has made it increasingly difficult to distinguish between broadcasting and telecommunications. The Internet, the catalyst of convergence, can transmit voice messages, data and video and raises questions as to whether it should (or could) be regulated at all.

The case of the Internet

In fact, the Internet provides a good illustration of the current challenges to content regulation. There can eventually be a limitless number of websites and multiple means of delivery to the end user, and equally varied ways and means for controls to be evaded. An Internet service provider, depending on the services it offers, may be variously categorized as publisher, journalist, broadcaster or phone company, each of which has historically had different liabilities for content it produces or distributes. From a general regulatory and societal perspective, it may no longer matter whether a piece of indecent material (for example, pornography) is obtained by mail, at a store or via a TV set, mobile phone or the Internet (Levy, 1999). Of course, a distinction can currently be made between indecent material transmitted via a universally available medium, like television, a medium with fast-growing home penetration rates, like the Internet, and a medium in its infancy, like IPTV (Internet Protocol Television) and Third Generation (3G) mobile phones.

However, technological developments are likely to change things in the near future. Today's niche technologies may become mainstream in a short time. Regulation should be dynamic and flexible enough to anticipate and accommodate such changes. A consistent approach is needed to determine the types of material that are objectionable so that their dissemination can be banned regardless of the type of conduit used to obtain them, with regulation tailored as needed to fit the specific medium of transmission.

As Oswell (2007) mentioned with regard to the Internet, the medium has opened the doors to a new age of regulatory complexity, but at the same time it has led to a series of simplifications and centralizations of regulatory authorities and powers. The Internet has offered a single space in which various regulatory problems and issues of different media and communications sectors could be made visible. As a discursive concept, the Internet could provide a totalizing space, a surface around which trans-media regulatory issues are discussed. Regulatory convergence constitutes a single train of thought, understanding and problematization.

Privacy needs protection[1]

Privacy issues are a hot topic of discussion. Safeguarding the privacy of personal information is a terrain that has generated varied responses from countries around the globe. The EU has been at the forefront of the legislative response to this issue since its Personal Data Directive 95/46/EC of 24 October 1995 (EC, 1995), which attempted to strike a balance between a high level of protection of the privacy of individuals and the free movement of personal data within the EU. To achieve this, the Directive set strict limits on the collection and use of personal data and asked each Member State to set up an independent national body responsible for the protection of such data. Most countries seem to agree that legal protection of personal data is necessary. In Canada, for example, the federal Privacy Act, in place since 1983, protects the personal information collected by government institutions, while the Personal Information Protection and Electronic Documents Act (PIPEDA) addresses the collection, storage and use of personal information by organizations in the private sector. However, the USA has been resisting this policy initiative and urging for self-regulation by industry as a better alternative (Samuelson, 1999). As a result, some commentators argue that privacy is slowly slipping away from Americans (see Sullivan, 2006).

The question for policymakers is how to protect personal data in today's ubiquitous digital environment. For although legal frameworks to protect privacy exist in most parts of the world, globalization and modern technology are making these rules outdated and in need of revision, if not major overhaul. According to a recent OECD (2010b) report, new privacy protection laws have been introduced, or will be introduced shortly, in approximately 50 per cent of OECD member countries (Austria, Canada, Denmark, France, Germany, Luxembourg, Norway, Sweden and the USA have passed legislation, while Belgium, Iceland, the Netherlands, Spain and Switzerland have prepared draft bills) to prevent what are considered to be violations of fundamental human rights, such as the unlawful storage of personal data, the storage of inaccurate personal data and the abuse or unauthorized disclosure of such data.

Meanwhile, there is a danger that disparities in national legislation could hamper the free flow of personal data across frontiers; these flows have greatly increased in recent years and are bound to grow further with the widespread introduction of new computer and communications technology. Restrictions on these flows could cause serious disruption in important sectors of the economy, such as banking and insurance. For this reason, OECD member countries considered it necessary to develop Guidelines that would help to harmonize national privacy legislation and, while upholding human rights, prevent interruptions in international flows of data. They represent a consensus on basic principles that can be built into existing national legislation, or serve as a basis for legislation in those countries which do not yet have it (see OECD, 2010b).

Privacy issues were also discussed at the global Internet Governance Forum (IGF) in Vilnius, Lithuania (14–17 September 2010). One of the questions raised was how to provide reasonable privacy for individuals and entities in 'cloud computing', an increasingly prevalent practice where data is stored not in individual PCs but in remote data storage facilities and services. Just a few days after the IGF meeting, 13 privacy enforcement agencies around the world[2] joined forces to launch the Global Privacy Enforcement Network (GPEN), designed to facilitate cross-border cooperation in the enforcement of privacy laws. In developing this network, the participating agencies recognized the need for greater international cooperation in this area.

A topic of particular interest to many policymakers in 2010 was the need for more protection of privacy in social networks, not least with regard to children, who eagerly share personal information on such networks. In March 2010, the International Telecommunication Union's (ITU) recently established Child On-line Protection working group (COP) held its first meeting, at which the potentially harmful effects of social networking were one of the topics discussed. It was proposed that COP encourage social networking service providers to self-regulate in relation to the ownership of user-created content as well as draft and publish their terms and conditions in language that could be understood by youngsters.

In November 2010, the ITU launched the COP Global Initiative, which will provide a framework for coordinating existing global efforts and implementing a series of training and prevention activities. The Initiative will build on guidelines developed by the ITU and partners from industry, civil society, governments, UN agencies and other stakeholders.

UNESCO has paid a good deal of attention to this issue, too. At the World Summit on the Information Society (WSIS) forum in May 2010, UNESCO organized a High-level Debate on Social Networking, where both the great potential and the more negative aspects of social networking were highlighted. Among the latter, participants mentioned on-line slander and criminal information, as well as challenges to privacy and data protection.

UNESCO also held a workshop on Privacy and Social Networking at the Internet Governance Forum (IGF) meeting in September 2010. Here it was stressed that the protection of privacy is the responsibility of all: governments must enforce the law and, when there is no law, have the principles translated into legislation; Internet companies must develop privacy policies and standards; and users must know how to protect their privacy and free speech.

Finally, a practice often raising privacy concerns is 'behavioral advertising', in which consumers' Internet browsing patterns are mined for clues about their interests, so that marketers can show them 'relevant' advertisements. This practice is currently being investigated by lawmakers in the USA, Europe and elsewhere. Behavioral advertising was one of the topics of discussion at the 32nd International Conference of Data Protection and Privacy Commissioners (see http://www.justice.gov.il/PrivacyGenerations, accessed 12 December 2010). The EU also pays increasing attention to this issue. Recently, concern about such practices was voiced in the AVMS Directive as well as a draft EU Parliament report, which also pointed to the development of 'hidden' Internet advertising in the form of comments posted on social networks, forums and blogs, 'the content of which is difficult to distinguish from mere opinion'.

Privacy is but one area in need of protection in the globalized network society. Copyright and freedom of expression are also fundamental values in need of reformation and protection.

Reform of copyright

To many lawmakers, scholars and Internet users, calls for tougher enforcement of intellectual property rights look like desperate attempts to salvage an outdated copyright system that needs to adapt to the modern world.

'It's not about a generation that can't respect the rules, it's a problem in the design of the system. It does not make sense in the digital environment', explained the influential copyright scholar Larry Lessig at a discussion on copyright in the digital age held at offices of the World Intellectual Property Organization (WIPO) on 4–5 November. The news service Intellectual Property Watch reports that Lessig called for WIPO to lead an overhaul of the copyright system. 'If and only if WIPO leads this debate will we have a chance [of fixing the system]', he said, encouraging WIPO to form a 'blue sky commission', a group that 'has the freedom to think about what architecture for copyright makes sense'.

Other speakers at the event suggested that WIPO create and administer an international repertoire database, compiling information about who owns what rights related to specific artistic works. At the end of the meeting Trevor Clarke, WIPO Assistant Director General for Copyright Issues, said that WIPO is 'prepared to facilitate' such a commission, changes to licensing practices, a global repertoire database, and efforts to reduce antagonism between copyright and competition.

How much WIPO can do remains to be seen. In the past year, WIPO has had difficulties in finding agreement even on copyright limitations and exceptions for the visually impaired. Policymakers are discussing copyright reform at regional and national level too. One of the key actions on the EU's new Digital Agenda for Europe is to 'simplify copyright clearance, management and cross-border licensing' (see. http://ec.europa.eu/information_society/digital-agenda/index_en.htm, accessed 11 December 2010). The issue is also being discussed in the Council of Europe, which recently adopted a Recommendation (No. 1906/2010) on Rethinking Creative Rights for the Internet Age, calling on the public authorities to 'work towards restoring the balance between the rights of the various players in the process of intellectual creation while guaranteeing respect for privacy' (see http://assembly.coe.int/Main.asp?link=/Documents/AdoptedText/ta10/EREC1906.htm, accessed 11 December 2010).

In the UK, the current government is showing an interest in US copyright rules, as these were proposed in June 2010 (see http://www.whitehouse.gov/sites/default/files/omb/assets/intellectualproperty/intellectualproperty_strategic_plan.pdfIn, accessed 11 December 2010). In November 2010, UK Prime Minister David Cameron announced that Britain's intellectual property laws would be reviewed to 'make them fit for the Internet age', particularly the 'fair use' provisions, which he believes give companies 'more breathing space to create new products and services'. The prime minister said the law could be relaxed to allow greater use of copyright material without the owner's permission. Unsurprisingly, the announcement was welcomed by internet campaigners who say it will boost small business (see http://www.bbc.co.uk/news/uk-politics-11695416, accessed 3 July 2011).

Freedom of expression

In 2010, policymakers and human rights groups voiced concerns about various threats to freedom of expression. Two phenomena have particularly caused these concerns: restrictions on the free flow of information through the Internet, and the increased violence against journalists in various parts of the world. In January 2010, US Secretary of State Hillary Clinton delivered a policy speech on Internet freedom, which she affirmed was a central part of US foreign policy (see http://www.state.gov/secretary/rm/2010/01/135519.htm, accessed 11 December 2010). Ms Clinton outlined how the State Department was supporting, for example, the development of new tools that would enable citizens to exercise their rights of free expression by circumventing politically motivated censorship and providing funds to groups around the world to make sure that those tools got to the people who needed them in local languages, with the training they needed to access the Internet safely.

In February 2010, four UN Special Rapporteurs[3] adopted a joint Declaration on 10 key threats to freedom of expression in the next decade (see http://www.osce.org/documents/rfm/2010/02/42638_en.pdf, accessed 11 December 2010). With regard to the Internet they mentioned, for example, 'efforts by some governments to control or limit this medium', 'state interventions, such as blocking of websites and web domains which give access to user-generated content or social networking', and 'pricing structures which render the poor unable to access the Internet'.

Alarmed that Internet freedom in many regions of the world is increasingly under attack, an international coalition of 25 human rights NGOs adopted a Declaration on Internet Freedom at a meeting in Geneva in March 2010 (see http://www.osce.org/documents/rfm/2010/02/42638_en.pdf, accessed 11 December 2010). The Declaration says that suppression of independent thought by the filtering, monitoring and censoring of websites, on-line content, blogs and messaging services constitutes a violation of Article 19 of the Universal Declaration of Human Rights and that all countries have obligations to guarantee Internet freedom.

The subject was also discussed at the international Internet Governance Forum (IGF) meeting in Vilnius, Lithuania, in September 2010. 'Freedom of expression on the Internet remains a main concern for the international community', said several participants during a workshop on this issue organized by UNESCO. At the workshop, a report of a UNESCO-supported study was presented, entitled *Freedom of Connection – Freedom of Expression: The Changing Legal and Regulatory Ecology Shaping the Internet* (see http://portal.unesco.org/ci/en/files/30748/12837652519UNESCO-19AUG10.pdf/UNESCO-19AUG10.pdf, accessed 11 December 2010). The report, which was compiled by renowned scholars such as William Dutton, Anna Dopatka, Michael Hills, Ginette Law and Victoria Nash, shows that with growing access to information in Internet censorship and filtering has increased. This is done not only by governments, it is stressed, but also by private companies with diverse goals and values.

It can be seen that many of the discussions on freedom of expression via the Internet seem to result mainly in solemn declarations calling for change; whether such declarations have any effect on those responsible for curtailing Internet freedom remains to be seen.

Another threat to freedom of expression is violence against journalists in many parts of the world. This 'remains a very serious threat with more politically motivated killings of journalists in 2009 than in any other year in the past decade', says the joint Declaration by four international Special Rapporteurs on freedom of expression (see above), which criticizes, among other things, the insufficient attention to investigating these killings and bringing those responsible to justice. The issue has also been repeatedly raised by UNESCO, which in March 2010 adopted a Decision on the Safety of Journalists and the Issue of Impunity calling on governments to report to the UNESCO Director-General on their investigations into the killing of journalists (see http://portal.unesco.org/ci/en/ev.php-URL_ID=29751&URL_DO=DO_TOPIC&URL_SECTION=201.html, accessed 11 December 2010).

The Council of Europe has also expressed concerns about this issue. In January 2010, the Council adopted Recommendation 1897/2010 urging the Committee of Ministers to take various measures to guarantee greater respect for media freedom and the safety of journalists in the all member states, focusing in particular on countries such as Russia, Ukraine, Belarus and Turkey (see http://assembly.coe.int/Mainf.asp?link=/Documents/AdoptedText/ta10/eREC1897.htm, accessed 11 December 2010). Finally in this connection, in June 2010, the European Parliament published a Written Declaration recommending EU member states to 'support independent journalism free of any political and commercial interference at national level' (see http://www.jeanmariecavada.eu/users_files/news/file/FILE__d_claration__crite_pdf.PDF, accessed 11 December 2010).

Alongside *privacy, copyright law* and *freedom of expression*, calls for *network neutrality* and the question *who should govern the Internet* are of fundamental importance. These are discussed in the following section. Internet governance has been addressed in earlier sections of this book, but what is stressed here is that content increasingly becomes network-independent, as it can be transmitted via different networks. Thus centralized, coercive and forceful content regulation cannot apply in the new era. Although the rationale for regulation remains, centralized regulation is difficult to sustain. Therefore, new mechanisms and paradigms appropriate for a changing, multichannel, digital and on-line environment need to be considered (Tambini and Verhulst, 2001).

The cases for self- and co-regulation

Setting the scene

A case can be made here for increased reliance on self-regulation and/or co-regulation. Self- regulation is the situation where the industry regulates itself, while co-regulation involves a combination of state and nonstate regulation. Self-regulation may be understood as 'pure' regulation (self-regulation by industries) and co-regulation, or enforced self-regulation, as the situation in which the state or supranational bodies like the EU set broad policy objectives but leave the details – and enforcement – to self-regulating business groups. So the process of co-regulation implies that official legislative actors set broad principles but leave their enforcement to business groups. The state/supranational fora also set procedures, which facilitate business compliance. Both concepts – self-regulation and co-regulation – are understood not as the absence of regulation or law, but as complementary to official regulation. They are a form of indirect intervention that assumes a liaison between the state and a business interest. Under a scheme involving a mixture of official (legal) regulation and self-regulation, public authorities can specify general standards and principles, but their implementation rests with companies themselves.

The arguments most frequently pursued in support of self- and co-regulation are based on expertise and efficiency (Baldwin and Cave, 1999). Bartle and Vass (2007) elaborate the argument as follows: industry practitioners have more expertise and technical knowledge than public officials and can foster contracts within the industry and up-to-date knowledge. Practicable rules are more easily developed, which results in greater effectiveness and compliance. Alongside greater efficiency, it is argued that there are lower costs in obtaining information. In addition, disputes are more likely to be settled informally, without recourse to the law. From the state's perspective, too, regulation is more efficient, as the regulatory costs are borne by industry rather than by the state. However, Bartle and Vass have observed that in the twentieth century there has been a decline in self-regulation, which is somewhat paradoxical in that it coincides with the era of reregulation and liberalization, both representing an aversion to state intervention. The logic would therefore be that self- and/or co-regulation and reregulation/liberalization would coexist and rise (and fall) in unison.

Borrowing from Moran (2003) and Baldwin (2004), the scholars attributed the decline in self-regulation in the UK to the rise of the regulatory agency Ofcom, which has statutory powers, and the general trend toward the 'regulatory state' (described in Chapter 5), alongside the trend towards 'punitive' regulation, in which criminal sanctions feature strongly. Bartle and Vass (2007) observed that in recent years in the UK, corporate disasters and collapses had resulted in calls for stronger corporate approaches to punishment and compliance. In turn, this had led to a move away from perceived 'soft' approaches like self-regulation and towards increased reliance on statutory regulation. However, Bartle and Vass were quick to note that the modern trend towards self-regulation does not mean *laissez-faire*, for there are prominent issues of public accountability, effectiveness, efficiency and legitimacy, which mean that self-regulation is likely to be allied to public processes to guarantee the achievement of these objectives. The scholars conclude that self-regulation is likely to become one of a number of tools that can be deployed in particular circumstances and can be accompanied by varying degrees of government regulation.

The processes of co-regulation and self-regulation in the EU

Processes of co-regulation and self-regulation have for some time now been favored at EU level. Former pro-market Commissioner Martin Bungemann, for instance, in various public speeches during the 1990s, expressed his objections to strict, official regulation, on the grounds, first, that content becomes network-independent and, second, that control of content and therefore responsibility for its use shifts from government to the individual Uniform Resource Locator (URL). A European Commission Communication (EC, 1999d: 14) stated that 'whilst it is for governments and public authorities to define public interest objectives, to lay down requirements related to the level of their protection and to adopt the regulations necessary for this effect, the operators and the users/viewers concerned can nevertheless contribute to the achievement of these same public interest objectives through the development of self-regulatory measures within the overall legal framework'. Other high-profile former Commissioners, such as Erkki Liikanen and Frits Bolkesten, have repeatedly called for the traditional system of statutory – and highly protective – regulation to be largely replaced by self-regulation by business groups.

These calls for the introduction of self- and/or co-regulatory regimes in the media and communications industry have continued with increased pace in more recent years. In 2007, then Information Society and Media Commissioner Viviane Reding said that 'for the media and Internet industry to flourish responsibly, the regulatory framework needs to strike the right balance between fairness and firmness while still allowing industry to respond quickly to change. It is my firm belief that self- and co-regulation offer very real alternatives to traditional legislative approaches' (Press Release IP/07/138, 6 February 2007). A study for the European Commission presented in 2007 on Europe's 'Safer Internet Day' backed up the idea that in a rapidly evolving digital world, self- and co-regulatory models can be attractive alternatives to traditional regulation. The study, on co-regulatory measures in the media sector, was undertaken for the Commission by the Hans-Bredow institute for media research, at the University of Hamburg, in cooperation with the Institute for European Media Law in Saarbrücken, and concluded that the speed of technological, economic and social change justified the application of co-regulatory measures in media and on-line activities. According to the study, transparency and openness were found to be vital to build trust in these mechanisms, particularly where nonstate organizations are responsible for regulating, or where interest groups are not involved (Hans-Bredow Institut and EMR, 2006).

Self- and co-regulation are explicitly encouraged by the EC in the AVMS Directive, which replaced the TWF Directive in 2007. The AVMS Directive was the first legislative proposal by the Commission related to the media sector to contain such an explicit reference to self- and co-regulation. More specifically, the new rules of the AVMS Directive require governments to encourage self-regulation in certain fields, sometimes combined with government intervention (co-regulation) – where their legal systems allow (Article 4 (7)). Such regimes must be broadly accepted by the main stakeholders and include effective enforcement. As a result, various EU countries have implemented or expanded existing self-regulatory mechanisms in the communications field. In the UK, the Advertising Standards Authority (ASA), traditionally a self-regulatory body overseeing nonbroadcast advertising such as press, cinema and poster advertising, has since 2004 also been responsible for the regulation of broadcast advertising content. By 'contracting out' broadcast advertising to the ASA, the UK's independent regulator of advertising across all media, the regulator Ofcom has ensured procedures of public accountability that can include the monitoring of its effectiveness.

Self-regulation and media content rules

Media content regulation is an area that increasingly relies on self-regulation, mainly due to the proliferation of new forms of media, which makes the regulation of their content more and more difficult. As already mentioned, the ITU's COP recently assessed the potentially harmful effects of social networking and proposed to encourage social networking service providers to self-regulate in relation to the ownership of user-created content. In the UK, Ofcom encourages self-regulation of various media, for example through a code of practice for the labelling of films, DVDs, CDs, computer games and television programmes. 'As technological convergence of the various forms of media continues so lightly regulated new forms will clash with more heavily regulated old forms. A code of practice for all forms of media is therefore becoming more and more important' (Bartle and Vass, 2007: 71).

Co-regulation and telecommunications

Another area in which co-regulation could work is telecommunications. Universal service in telecommunications could be supported through a system of 'pay or play' in which enterprises may volunteer to provide universal service or, if they do not do so, are required to pay a levy to support its provision by others (Prosser, 2000). Network interoperability or interconnection could also be subjected to co-regulation. In the UK, specifications and technical standards associated with the interoperability of networks of competing firms is ensured by a telecommunications industry committee, the Network Interoperability Consultative Committee (NICC) operating under the auspices of Ofcom, to which it offers advice on the harmonization of interconnection arrangements (Bartle and Vass, 2007: 58). The committee includes representatives of network operators and public providers of communication services, and as such it can be viewed as an example of co-regulation as it involves representatives from industry and the state regulator.

Self- and/or co-regulation and the Internet

Another domain in which self- and/or co-regulation could apply is the Internet through the imposition of content ratings, whereby an agreed set of categories would be applied to websites, which would inform users of the appropriateness of a given source. The ratings could also be used for filtering 'gatekeeper' software. This approach was favored by the UK's New Labour government, which backed the establishment of the Internet Watch Foundation (IWF) in the late 1990s in order to explore ways of developing ratings measures, as well as ways of detecting breaches of rules by Internet Service Providers (ISPs) and the dissemination of illegal or unsuitable for minors, such as pornographic material. Without such ratings, sites could not get access to search engines, or be carried by internet service providers (ISPs) (Svennevig and Towler, 2000). The IWF is not statutorily constituted, but it collaborates closely with government (there is a 'partnership' agreement between the IWF, the government and the police) and the industry (particularly ISPs).

In fact, the Internet has provided momentum for the introduction of self- and co-regulatory mechanisms as it is a media platform that is not obviously subject to existing regulatory provisions. The World Summit for Regulators organized by UNESCO in cooperation with the Association of National Audiovisual Authorities at the end of 1999 in Paris, pleaded clearly for co-regulation on the grounds that it would be impossible to regulate the Internet effectively if private and public bodies did not combine their efforts. Today, ISPs, on-line content producers and advertisers are calling for such mechanisms in order to stimulate innovation and creativity and promote diversity in the on-line and on-demand terrain. An interesting issue to explore would be to view to hold Internet users more accountable through the development of innovative mechanisms. Some scholars (e.g. Johnson, Crawford and Palfrey, 2004) argue that on-line problems such as spam, invasions of privacy and network insecurity lend themselves to 'peer production of governance'. The scholars claim that traditional sovereigns have tried and failed to address these three problems through the ordinary means of governance and that new form of order on-line, brought on by private action, is emerging in response to these problems. According to Dutton (2007), the problems are typified by self-governing processes developed for successful new on-line applications, such as Wikipedia and the eBay on-line auction service, where users participate in setting up and monitoring governance rules.

Self-regulation, international cooperation and network neutrality[4]

In 2010, network neutrality was a hot issue on both sides of the Atlantic and was discussed at international level. The recurrent questions raised in the debate include: Should ISPs be allowed to prioritize one kind of Internet traffic over another? How can it be ensured that operators treat all Net traffic equally and do not block or slow down certain services for competitive or other reasons or start offering 'quality of service' guarantees to certain content providers in return for a premium fee?

In the USA, users of the BitTorrent file-sharing service challenged the cable operator Comcast that had blocked the service. The FCC ordered Comcast to stop the blocking, but in April 2010 an appeals court sided with the operator, saying that the FCC could not tell Comcast how to manage its network. In August a policy proposal by industry giants Google and Verizon sparked controversy in the USA. The firms proposed that network neutrality should be ensured for wireline Internet services but not for the rapidly growing wireless ones. 'Industry deal-making is no substitute for responsible policymaking. This latest effort by a few large companies to dictate the rules behind closed doors will not protect Internet users', commented Free Press, an organization working to reform the media.

Recently, Congressman Henry A. Waxman – Chairman of the House Committee on Energy and Commerce, which includes a subcommittee on Communications, Technology, and the Internet – sought to reach bipartisan agreement, between Republicans and Democrats, on legislation that would protect and promote an open Internet. Under this agreement, Waxman explains, phone and cable companies would be prevented from unreasonably discriminating against any lawful Internet traffic. It would also direct the FCC to formulate transparency regulations so that consumers know the price, performance and network management practices of their broadband providers (see http://www.henrywaxman.house.gov/News/DocumentSingle. aspx?DocumentID=209385, accessed 11 December 2010).

On 21 December 2010, a new regime was finally passed by the American regulator (see http://www.thesunnews.com/2010/12/22/1881959/fcc-adopts-web-rules.html, accessed 9 January 2011) incorporating three basic rules. The first prevents network operators from blocking lawful traffic, subject to 'reasonable network management' (an exception needed to ensure that spam or denial-of-service attacks can be stopped). The second rule requires network operators to be open about their network management policies, so that firms and consumers can see what might be blocked, and why. The third rule, prohibiting 'unreasonable discrimination', is more controversial. Discrimination, in this context, means letting some packets of data travel faster than others. To net neutrality purists, any kind of discrimination is unacceptable: by allowing 'reasonable' discrimination, the FCC has, in their view, left open a vast loophole. For *The Economist* (2011), however, nondiscrimination seems excessively conservative. The newspaper asks: why shouldn't a company be able to charge more for, say, faster delivery of video or special broadband links that ensure snappy connections for video-gamers?

The Economist (ibid.) argues that there are two flaws in the new regulation and a huge omission. The first flaw is that the law is not clear. Despite allowing reasonable discrimination, the FCC says that 'pay for priority' would 'raise significant cause for concern'. In other words, the FCC has not explicitly banned fast-tracking, but it does not seem disposed to allow it. So fast-tracking's fate will be decided by the courts. The other relevant flaw in the regulator's new rules is their leniency toward mobile operators, who will be allowed to block some kinds of traffic. The omission, according to the newspaper, is the failure to address the underlying lack of competition in the provision of Internet access. In other rich countries it would not matter if some operators blocked some sites: consumers would switch to a rival provider. This, according to the newspaper is because the big telecommunications companies with wires into people's homes must offer access to their networks on a wholesale basis, guaranteeing vigorous competition between providers, with lower prices and faster connections than are available in America. The newspaper concludes that politicians and regulators should do more to get the USA's phone and cable firms to open up their networks to others.

The debate about net neutrality is also current in Europe. The social goal is to ensure that consumers can reach any website they want at affordable prices and high speeds. At a recent EU Summit on this issue, European Commissioner Neelie Kroes pointed out that there is more competition in the sector in Europe than in the USA, but said that competition alone is not sufficient to avoid problems. 'To let competition work, consumers need to be effectively informed about traffic management practices and to be able to switch to alternative operators if they are not satisfied'. International cooperation on these issues is important, underlined several speakers at the summit. 'We must have real discussions about this with our American friends. What happens in the United States will affect Europe and other parts of the world', pointed out a spokesman of the EU Presidency.

Such discussions have already been held in the Transatlantic Consumer Dialogue (TADC), a coalition of USA and European consumer advocacy groups. In April 2010, the TADC issued a resolution on network neutrality saying that consumers are entitled to an Internet connection that is free from discrimination and enables them to send and receive content of their choice as well as to be informed what network management practices are employed by their network providers (see http://www.tacd.org/index2.php?option=com_docman&task=doc_view&gid=264&Itemid=40, accessed

11 December 2010). Recommendations regarding network neutrality were also included in the Best Practice Guidelines at the Global Symposium for Regulators (GSR) in November 2010. The guidelines recommend that 'when Internet Service Providers (ISPs) employ traffic management mechanisms [...] they comply with the general principles of relevance, proportionality, efficiency, non-discrimination between parties and transparency' (see http://www.itu.int/ITU-D/treg/Events/Seminars/GSR/GSR10/consultation/guidelines/GSR10_guidelines_V3-en.pdf, accessed 11 December 2010).

Other examples of self- and co-regulation

Further examples of current self- and co-regulation in the EU include:

- The signing by mobile operators of a European Framework agreement on the safer use of mobile phones by children (see Press Release IP/07/139).
- The Film On-line Charter signed by the film and content industries in May 2006 (see Press Release IP/06/672).
- The management of the.eu domain by the private, not-for-profit agency EURid, entrusted with this task by the European Parliament and European Council (see Press Releases IP/05/1210, IP/06/476 and MEMO/06/332).

A summary

To conclude this section on self- and co-regulation, two issues need to be highlighted. First, these mechanisms must be allied to public-service purposes to guarantee the objectives of public accountability, effectiveness, efficiency and legitimacy (Bartle and Vass, 2007). National governments and international bodies should develop and publish clear benchmarks for acceptable levels of transparency, accountability and due process and appeal, particularly with regard to communications regulation that may impact upon freedom of expression. Self- and co-regulatory institutions should follow the guidelines for transparency and access to information that are followed by public and government bodies according to international best practice (Marsden, 2004).

Second, effective self-regulation and/or co-regulation require active consumer and citizen consultation based upon shared responsibility at all stages of development and implementation. If the public is to bear more responsibility and indeed to be more accountable in using the Internet and other new media, it has to be aware of the role of self-regulation (Tambini and Verhulst, 2001). Therefore, there is an imperative need to educate the public in how to protect themselves. If regulation is to become reactive rather than prescriptive, then steps should be taken to raise public awareness.

Is media ownership regulation still applicable?

This volume has presented evidence showing that concentration of media ownership is increasing and that corporate alliances between communications firms have become the norm. Media concentration is as much an American issue as it is a European one. This book has provided basic information on the existing regulatory frameworks in the USA, the EU and the UK. At this point, it should be remembered why media concentration may affect socioeconomic ideals. Two concerns have traditionally been raised with regard to large media firms. First, media conglomerates may raise prices to consumers and advertisers above competitive levels. The second concern is media-specific and refers to society's sociocultural and political health, which is fostered by the existence of numerous, independent media. Excessive media concentration may threaten the access of the public to important information or viewpoints (Stucke and Grunes, 2008).

As with the case of content rules, US authorities have imposed ownership restrictions to deal with competition concerns as well as social objectives, including pluralism and diversity. However, the Telecommunications Act of 1996 lowered the ownership limits on broadcasting stations locally and nationally, permitting a single entity to control a greater number of radio and TV stations. In 2008, the US regulatory agency FCC, under Chairman Kevin Martin, voted to relax media cross-ownership restrictions, thereby loosening the newspaper–broadcast media cross-ownership ban in the top 20 cities (the vote was three to two, along party lines). As a result of this liberalizing policy, the 10 largest TV station group owners now control 300 stations, up from 104 stations in 1995. Also, group owners can now purchase TV stations with a maximum service area cap of 39 per cent, up from the previous limit of 35 per cent (it should be noted that the limit was just 25 per cent in 1985). Further, with rules relaxed on cable ownership, 90 per cent of the top 50 cable companies are owned by parent companies that own broadcast networks.

On the other side of the Atlantic, there are no Europe-wide media ownership rules. Each EU member state has treated the issue separately, mostly in a reregulatory fashion (Noam, 2009: 24). The European Commission, triggered by the European Parliament, entered this area in the early 1990s by issuing a Green Paper (EC, 1992) with the objective of assessing whether extensive concentration could damage media pluralism. In the end, the Commission came to the conclusion that the protection of pluralism is a national concern and that intervention in national ownership rules could only be justified if the proper functioning of the internal market was at stake, but not in order to safeguard pluralism.

Combined with the reregulatory philosophy preoccupying the EC and the fact that the Commission has become sympathetic to the enlargement of European corporations in order to enable them to compete globally (see Iosifidis, 2005, 2010c), the absence of a Europe-wide mechanism to limit the concentration of media ownership has left a few large communications conglomerates unhindered to expand their activities across the continent. At the same time, in the UK the passing of the Communications Act 2003 freed up the communications industry far more than was expected, removing most of the ownership regulations that characterized British broadcasting, as it was thought that these deprived companies of the economies of scale and scope required to expand into foreign markets. So, should media ownership rules be maintained to protect pluralism and diversity?

Why is it difficult to maintain media ownership rules?

Ownership restrictions that are tied to vertically integrated sectors, which link programming production and dissemination to audiences, might not make sense if the same programming can be provided by firms that range across the current terrestrial and satellite broadcasting, cable and telecommunications sectors. Indeed, convergence has already revealed the inadequacy of EC initiatives to harmonize sectoral ownership regulation (Gibbons, 1998; Iosifidis, 1997). Increased pluralism, it is said, can be achieved through permitting the delivery of a greater range of services more closely targeted to individual needs and through lowering entry barriers so as to permit a greater number of actors to take part in the media.

However, diversity of sources does not always result in diversity of media content. As shown earlier, the model of external or numerical diversity, in which diversity of content is provided by separate media outlets, naturally favors the concentration of capital and ownership in the broadcasting business. The formation of large, vertically integrated and diversified units has led to a corporate structure in which shares are often widely dispersed, in which financial institutions and industrial corporations have significant holdings, and in which highly qualified managers make key decisions. In situations of dispersed share ownership, it is indeed very difficult to identify, first, who controls the firm in question and, second, the extent of the influence they can exert in the cultural and political domain. That is why it is difficult to sustain structural ownership rules.

The first issue – whether ownership can be equated with control – had led the EC to initiate a study in order to reach a definition of 'controller'. The study, carried out by The European Institute for the Media (EIM, 1994), identified five factors that can influence a firm's decision-making center: *direct links, indirect links, family connections, external financial or contractual relationships* and *unofficial agreements*. The study also identified five ways of wielding influence: *through ownership links (capital), through links with staff, through financial links (debts)* and *through contractual links (supplies, distribution).* The study concluded that, although ownership links are the most effective way of exerting influence in the market, the other three – financial, staff and contractual links – are also significant.

On the basis of these criteria it is possible, with respect to each player, to evaluate the extent to which they may exert an influence on the operation and eliminate political pluralism and cultural diversity. Although such a qualitative definition of media control seems both to be better adapted to the complexity of current ownership and control/dependency structures and to respond to various attempts to circumvent media ownership rules, it was not favored by the EC. Apparently the Commission was concerned that the criteria of wielding influence defined in the study were not clear enough to ensure the fair and impartial application of such a control mechanism throughout the EU.

The second issue – the identification of the most appropriate criterion for the measurement of levels of concentration and consequently media influence – has proven even more difficult to resolve. First, the number of independently owned media outlets in a given market is not a good indicator of the amount of independently produced programmes, particularly news and current affairs programmes, where political pluralism matters. Second, the definition of the relevant market in a multimedia context is not a straightforward task, and therefore the measurement of market shares is also problematic. The difficulty here is that the outcome is extremely sensitive to the specific way in which restrictions are formulated. In particular, the choice between restrictions on total audience reached, share of ownership in a channel, share of industry revenues, and so on, is crucial and leads to disparate results as to the level of concentration and the influence exerted. My earlier work (Iosifidis, 1997) showed that, even though the measurement of 'influence' is problematic, there is a clear linkage between economic power and political/cultural pluralism, particularly because economic power can affect the range of material offered.

The close relationship between economic power and pluralism indicates that criteria that are being used for the measurement of market power can also be used, at least in principle, for the measurement of media influence, and vice versa. Financial criteria, for instance – long established as a method for measuring market power – could also be adopted for measuring 'influence', that is, audience exposure to mass media. These, however, should be accompanied by audience figures, supposed to be more efficient for measuring pluralism in the marketplace for ideas. In the absence of a direct measure of influence, my work concluded that it is necessary to develop an approach combining the various sets of methods (numerical criteria, such as the number of channels controlled, economic criteria, such as company turnover and advertising/subscription income, and audience criteria, such as audience share and audience reach) and use it as a coherent policy to establish media firms' impact in the marketplace for ideas.

A less controversial solution: media ownership transparency

In this context, sector-specific regulation is gradually losing ground to general competition law that applies to all sectors. Given the above difficulties and complexities, this volume calls for increased transparency of media ownership. Transparency of media ownership presupposes that a great deal of information is made available to the relevant media regulator. Such information, extracted from a wide range of indicators, will assist the regulator to decide whether the influence of a particular company is a cause for concern. As Stolte and Smith (2010) noted, the availability of up-to-date and accurate data on media ownership lies at the very heart of any media pluralism regulation, as it would be impossible to take steps to address excessive media concentrations without the tools to identify them.

There is interest in media transparency on several levels in the EU. In the last few years, both the Council of Europe and the European Parliament have brought out recommendations regarding media transparency. The non-binding Council of Europe Recommendation on Media Pluralism and the Diversity if Media Content (CM/Rec (2007) 2) directly addressed transparency and ownership, whereas the non-binding Resolution of the European Parliament of 25 September 2008 (P6_TA(2008)0456) specifically encouraged the disclosure of details of the ownership of all media outlets to help achieve transparency relating to the aims and background of broadcasters and publishers. These recommendations have not been acted upon. Yet a regulatory initiative focussing solely on transparency would be much less controversial than earlier attempts by the EC to compile a Directive on media ownership (see EC, 1992). This is because member states would not be required to modify existing media ownership structures.

The legally binding AVMS Directive requires member states to ensure that audiovisual media service providers under their jurisdiction 'shall make easily, directly and permanently available to the recipients of a service at least the following information: a) the name of the media service provider; b) the geographical address at which the media service provider is established; c) the details of the media service provider, including his electronic mail address or website, which allow him to be contacted rapidly in a direct and efficient manner; d) where applicable, the competent regulatory or supervisory bodies' (Art. 3a). However, according to Stolte and Smith (2010), the transparency requirements in the Directive are not designed to defend the citizen's right to know who has provided news and information. Rather, they ensure that consumers have the information they need to exercise their right of reply or complain about material transmitted, for example. This provision is thus convenience rather than rights oriented.

The Electronic Commerce Directive (EC, 2000b), briefly described in Chapter 7, applies almost identical transparency requirements to commercial communications. The 1989 Council Regulation on the control of concentrations between undertakings as amended in 2004 (EEC, 1989) requires information relating to major shareholdings in large companies listed in regulated markets to be made publicly available. But this only applies to undertakings that are of a 'Community dimension', therefore leaving many companies outside its scope. In its Green Paper on the Interconnection of Business Registers (EC, 2009c), the EC highlighted the significance of access to information on firms that are active in various member states. As it stated, 'the current financial crisis highlighted once again the importance of transparency across the financial markets'. Nevertheless, many media enterprises are not likely to fulfil the requirements as not all issue public securities, or issue them on regulated markets – for example, PSBs and certain private companies, trusts and partnerships (see Stolte and Smith, 2010).

Ensuring transparency of ownership and control of media actors is a crucial regulatory role. This is often neglected but is the key to all other regulatory actions; it is of greater importance now than ever in the midst of a financial crisis (as it is acknowledged by the EC), but also given the increasing complexity of the alliances in media and communications. The most effective tool for regulation is information. If regulators have the power to collect information and make it public, potential problems relating to media concentration can eradicate many potential problems. All parties are well informed, and the market environment is at least a little closer to the ideal, perfectly competitive, market of economic theory, which assumes that all actors have perfect information. Information deficiencies can be diminished in the information society if supranational bodies (for example, the EU) and national independent regulators ensure than adequate information about the sector and the operators is made public.

A proactive approach to ownership

A relevant issue is that, to date, policy approaches to ownership have been essentially *means* rather than *ends* based: that is, taking as a starting point that pluralism is a 'good thing', policymakers promote it by putting in place a regulatory framework designed to prevent excessive concentration. Through the means of plural ownership, it is assumed that diverse ownership will be guaranteed. The emphasis has therefore been on restricting consolidation in order to sustain variety of owners or controllers. This is certainly a *reactive* approach to policy intervention in that it embraces preventive measures, rather than a *proactive* approach that establishes an enabling or empowering regime with clearly defined ends.

Burnett (2009) suggested that a more constructive policy approach, better attuned to the new media world and new economic realities, would start with a sophisticated analysis of the kinds of output regulators should seek to promote. Conventional approaches have focussed almost exclusively on the issue of diversity of voice and concentrated on the threat of a tiny cartel of media barons wielding excessive media influence. But while accepting that this concept of diversity is still relevant, Burnett points out that there are many indicators of diversity, among others: whether serious issues of relevance to people in their everyday lives are being addressed; to what extent the values of accuracy and integrity are being incorporated into everyday professional practice; whether specific local and regional issues are being adequately covered. These require a proactive approach to policy intervention (ibid.).

Conclusion

The last three chapters investigated the concept and process of convergence and presented the challenges that it poses to policymakers. Convergence has brought down the barriers that once divided the communications industry: barriers between sectors; barriers between applications; barriers between producers and users; and barriers between countries. New media have emerged and the pace of technological changes is rapid, which has implications for many areas of media regulation: access to spectrum, content regulation, ownership and control. Meanwhile, competing newspapers, TV channels and Internet networks are forming alliances to tackle a variety of technological, editorial and market-based opportunities and challenges, thereby raising levels of media market concentration. A change is also taking place in the consumption of media technologies as people are becoming less dependent on (and less loyal to) any single media type. The direction and speed of future convergence are unclear; what is clear is that the process of convergence presents a challenge for communications regulation.

The present chapter examined the current importance of traditional regulatory mechanisms and assessed the need for imposing a new regulatory framework in the age of digital convergence. The argument put forth was that market rights and market creation envisaged by governments, industrialists and international institutions, such as the European Commission, should go hand in hand with the defence of public interest rights and freedoms. A combination of economic regulation with certain elements of sectoral regulation is required in the communications sector in order for it to meet technological, economic/structural and social changes in the new era. In particular, emphasis should be placed on competition regulation to deal with key access points in the new environment, ensure open access for media companies and prevent anticompetitive corporate alliances.

The provision of social objectives, including the plurality of views and content, could be achieved through maintaining flexible content regulation (including self-regulation) and through promoting transparency of media ownership, which would give power to the regulator to collect detailed information and make it public. Meanwhile, international cooperation to tackle new threats to privacy and freedom of information brought about by the development of new technologies and the Internet should be encouraged. However, any new policy initiatives should rest on the principle that overregulation or inappropriate regulation of new on-line media and the Internet should be avoided.

Conclusion

A wide range of technological, political, economic and sociocultural processes has traditionally shaped media and communications systems and their policy and regulation at national level, attached to the territorial boundaries and distinct regulatory approaches depending on the political system. However, national media and communications systems have been forced to evolve owing mainly to the phenomena of globalization, reregulation and liberalization, which have brought to the fore the neoliberal philosophy of regulatory frameworks and the transnational dimension of media governance. Since the 1990s, scholars have been using the term 'neoliberalism' for global market-liberalism ('capitalism') and for free-trade policies. 'Neoliberalism', denoting free markets and global free trade, is often used interchangeably with globalization and assumes that social development should proceed according to the dictates of the global market, with minimum government interference (Croteau and Hoynes, 2006). The trends towards political, economic and cultural globalization, coupled with technological developments and the rise of transnational corporations have all influenced the emergence of a global media and communications system. Within this context of globalized, liberal media structures and processes involving state, nonstate and international policy actors, new media policy issues emerge and consideration should be given to fresh approaches to address the new issues and support their governance.

This volume covered key issues that emerge in the context of new media policies in the light of the emergent spaces for global media policy governance. A prime example of new structures is the convergence of the media and telecommunications sectors, which affects policies that apply to the two sectors and prompts calls for a converged regulatory framework. Technological convergence has become the object of the regulatory shifts at global level. Technological advances are systematically utilized to spread the principles of neoliberalism into all fields of the economy, including the media and cultural industries. In fact, the convergence of technologies that enable the dissemination of audiovisual material over the Web constitutes another step towards liberalization, as the new services can be classified as telecommunications, rather than broadcasting, thereby freeing them from strict regulation and making audiovisual services subject to general competition law. Technological advances like digitalization, and technological convergence, as well as that of companies, industries and markets, have called regulators to look beyond traditional media policies, which applied different rules to different sectors, and towards the spaces where traditionally distinct boundaries of policy and governance overlap.

In this context, there is a growing tendency to rely on competition law to deliver public services. Not only does the neoliberal paradigm assert that market mechanisms are generally sufficient and preferable to interventionist policies, but it also proposes that sector-specific regulation should be replaced by general competition (anti-trust) law. This argument is reinforced by the convergence of technologies, which calls for the elimination of strict sectoral rules and greater dependence on generic regulation applicable to all communications sectors. The regulatory agencies' shift away from public interest measures and normative principles towards more rigorous, yet narrow, economics-based assessments of market power is another reason for the emergence of competition policy as the preferred mechanism to tackle issues in media and communications at the expense of sector-specific structural and content regulation. However, this study has shown that while competition can in general terms prevent adverse economic impacts on markets and the formation of dominant positions, it falls short in relation to the defence of sociocultural values like political pluralism, cultural diversity and editorial independence.

The inadequacy of competition law to capture problems of media power in the political and cultural sphere can be seen if one considers the tendency towards concentration of media ownership and increasing cross-media ownership. The process of market integration and consolidation has been with us for quite some time as firms pursue trans-media synergy (the sharing of editorial, journalistic and news-gathering tasks, expertise and resources) using the ownership of publishing, film, video, electronics and broadcasting interests to benefit from economies of scale and scope (see Dyson and Humphreys, 1990: 18; Gibbons, 1999; Humphreys, 1996). This process of cross-media integration and synergy has given rise to the conditions of cross-promotion – that is, the promotion of one media service or product through another (Hardy, 2010: 179). But as media consolidation has gathered momentum in recent decades due to convergence, reregulation and the rise of the Internet, concerns have been raised about the preservation of media pluralism. This principle still applies in a digital converged era and should be safeguarded through transparency of media ownership, flexible content regulation, including self and/or co-regulation, and the preservation of public service broadcasting (PSB).

Media and communications policy has tended to analyze the public interest partly in terms of economics but primarily in terms of politics and culture because of the wider policy concerns of symbolic representation, national and civic identity, and media influence on public opinion. The means for preserving these principles have typically been sector-specific structural and content rules, rather than generic competition law, due to the special significance attached to the mass media in forming public opinion. The preservation of PSB has also been high on the agenda of European policy. The EU broadcasting system, with the UK as its frontrunner, has traditionally been preoccupied by public service ideals, and differs substantially from the American commercial model with its minimal regulation of broadcasters. In the USA, a strong tradition of freedom of the individual enshrined in the First Amendment to the US Constitution has acted against any form of government involvement in broadcasting matters and has instead encouraged the development of a free-market mechanism for the delivery of popular culture and commercial entertainment. As a result, public broadcasting in the USA functions as a 'market failure' project and has negligible impact on people.

But it is not a secret that lately PSB has been under attack across Europe. Contemporary European public policy is increasingly driven by economic and commercial logic. An inherent tension in the EU policy process has been evident as neoliberal values have come into collision with traditional PSB regimes. These divisions have been played out in the Competition Directorate's issuing of state aid restrictions on the distortion of markets by PSBs through their receipt of public subsidies (Wheeler, 2010). The EU's media policies have in some cases – technological convergence, harmonization of rules – led to more choice and more content for consumers as well as new forms of content in terms of production and of consumption, but there are public interest concerns over pluralism, diversity, media consolidation and the survival of the traditional mass media.

Another example of regulatory reform central to the theme of this book is the policies that operate simultaneously at national and global levels and the role of the nation-state in maintaining its power to regulate in a globalized world. The increased attention afforded to the globalization of communication, and in particular to the transnational flows resulting from the rapid advances of electronic media and ICT, has resulted in a new, post-national way of thinking in which national and supranational spaces are linked. The emergence of international and regional treaties like the WTO and the EU could further redraw the map of political space and sovereignty, decouple nation-states and challenge the continuity of one's identity. Media policy in a globalized world is informed by various players including the *state* (core executive), the *market* (private/business actors including the media) and *civil society* (voluntary and community sector actors). Nonstate actors like individuals, scientific networks, journalists and nongovernmental organizations (NGOs) also contribute greatly to the shaping of the agenda for global public policy. Within a universal communication system characterized by shared communicative and cultural/political practices, the nation-state does not disappear but it instead shows remarkable persistence and even a tendency to increase its power.

The state is indeed affected by the emergence of multinational corporations, NGOs and the trends towards liberalization and commercialization, but also affects the national and international scene. While this volume acknowledges external pressures stemming from regional and international fora, it nevertheless argues that the nation-state still has a considerable effect on the way media policies are negotiated and conducted. National governments maintain a good deal of autonomy to shape national policy agendas and influence arrangements in the international environment. The modern state retains a considerable degree of control over media flows within its territory, issues binding laws and uses legitimate force to ensure compliance. At European level, this is shown by the diversity of broadcasting policy styles and traditions that persist despite EU harmonization efforts. In this regard, the book conceptualizes media and communications policy as an intrinsically political process and a contested territory, which simultaneously involves national and supranational dynamics. Its approach has been to place laws and market regulation in their political and sociocultural context at global level, an approach that departs from narrow national considerations.

Regulation in the public interest in a world governed by the principles of free (but not even) flow of information is a key topic, closely related to the fundamental relationship between media policy and democracy and the role of the media in promoting cultural diversity. This publication has advocated a citizenship-centred approach for media policy development. To this effect it calls for contemporary media policies that would ensure the defence of traditional social values, including plurality of views and contents. Other issues of policy concern in a global context are access to media systems and communication rights, Internet governance, and the role of civil society in shaping global media policy. Privacy, freedom of expression, copyright protection and network neutrality have also emerged as hot topics in the current global networked era. Some of these objectives could be achieved through traditional mechanisms such as maintaining PSB and through the promotion of transparency of media ownership, while others could be guaranteed through flexible content regulation, including self-regulation and international cooperation. In any case, regulatory intervention should aim to facilitate market development, so any policy initiatives should rest on the principle that over-regulation or inappropriate regulation of new online media and the Internet should be avoided. This, however, does not mean that no rules should apply, as safeguarding the public interest in the new global epoch continues to be of paramount importance.

Media policy has always been – and perhaps will always continue to be – controversial, since it assumes state intervention, which limits freedom of expression and the right to communication. This publication has brought together theoretical analysis and empirical findings to make sense of the key contemporary debates and tensions in the rapidly shifting communications environment. It has taken an expansive approach to the media and communication platform addressed. It has tackled issues ranging from media ownership and content to public service media and Internet governance. Its intention has been to contribute to the understanding of the dynamics of media and communications policy at global level. The reader will judge whether this has been achieved.

Notes

Introduction

1. By nation states, I refer to the institutional set comprising the whole state. According to Castells (2010: 42), this includes national governments, the parliament, the political party system, the judiciary, and the state bureaucracy.
2. Media pluralism (or media diversity) is one of those topics that return again and again to the discussion table. The concept cannot simply be defined as 'more than one medium' but entails a range of factors, including media outlets, media owners and controllers, programme genres and formats, quality, choice, creativity, experimentation and innovation, the representation of various 'voices', editorial approaches, and platforms. To add to the complexity, Napoli (1999) noted that pluralism or diversity means very different things to different regulators, including diversity of programme *genre*, *viewpoint*, *ownership* and *source*. At the risk of oversimplifying, I would argue that *pluralism* refers to the wide availability of media outlets and *diversity* to a wide range of media content. However, the issue cannot be limited to defining the term, for there is a need to develop a model for sustaining this value in the digital era.
3. 'Reregulation' refers to the relaxation of strict rules for broadcasting and telecommunications, while 'deregulation' calls for the abandonment of such rules. I believe that the term reregulation reflects more accurately what has been happening in the communications industry in the last three decades or so as most national governments across the globe have relaxed rather than abolished the relevant rules and introduced 'light touch' regulatory frameworks.
4. These were the Independent Television Commission, Office of Telecommunications, Broadcasting Standards Council, Radio Authority and Radiocommunications Agency.
5. One of the main reasons for strictly regulating broadcasting has been technical: as governments in the past allocated a finite number of broadcast frequencies, they could regulate the licensees of those frequencies. However, most governments today have relaxed broadcasting regulation. This decrease in the degree of regulation is attributable in large part to the collapse of the spectrum-scarcity rationale. Advances in technology have made the number of frequencies now almost limitless.
6. While in the case of self-regulation, regulations are specified, administered and enforced by the regulated organization(s), in the case of co-regulation regulations are specified, administered and enforced by a combination of the state and the regulated organization(s). The nature of these mechanisms is different from statutory regulation, where regulations are specified, administered and enforced solely by the state (see Chapter Ten).
7. Curran and Seaton (2010: 377) argue that another social market experiment is the Swedish press subsidy system that keeps alive 'political papers' which would otherwise fold in free market conditions.
8. Among the sites to close include teen services *Switch* and *Blast* and community site *606*. The changes, which will see BBC Online's budget cut by £34 million,

are part of the BBC's cost-cutting measures aimed at making 20 per cent savings as a result of the latest licence fee settlement.

9. However, as this book is close to completion, significant developments are taking place including the closure of *News of the World*, one of the UK's most popular newspapers, as well as News Corporation's withdrawal of its bid for BSkyB because of concerns about media plurality.

10. EU policy is analyzed in Chapter Seven.

11. Citizenship is a widely used yet contested and 'slippery' concept, whose meaning largely depends on specific historical and political circumstances. While discussions on citizenship today take off from Marshall's classic 1950 study *Citizenship and Social Class*, which asserted that citizenship is equated to membership in a community, the idea is being challenged by the emergence of growing social and cultural pluralism and the fact that some members of a community may be excluded despite the existence of common rights (see Tsaliki, 2007: 163–4).

12. This mostly applies to Rupert Murdoch's News Corporation, which, although still barred from launching mainland channels, has been allowed to introduce a satellite TV service available in Hong Kong and in expensive hotels.

1 Media Policy in the Public Interest

1. Habermas is a member of the Frankfurt School, a leftish think tank generally associated with the Institute of Social Research at the University of Frankfurt, which from the mid-1920s attracted philosophers and social thinkers who developed 'critical theory' with the aim of applying philosophical ideas to social problems.

2. In economic terms, a 'public good' is a good or service whose consumption by an individual does not reduce its availability for consumption by the rest of the citizenry. This non-rivalry characteristic is accompanied by non-excludability in that no one can be excluded from consuming the good/service. Watching terrestrial free-to-air television and listening to the radio are examples of a public good in the media and communications terrain.

3. A social network can be described as a set of actors (individuals, organizations, families, neighborhoods, and so on) and the relations that hold the actors together (maintain ties) (Haythornthwaite, 2002). The study of social networks can be perceived as a disciplinary enquiry into the patterning of relations between social actors. The core aspect of the study of social networks is that network structure and position have important behavioral, perceptual and attitudinal implications for the individuals and the social system (Emirbayer, 1997).

4. Web 2.0 is a nascent movement towards a more interactive and collaborative Web as it provides a platform for online social participation in communities of interest.

2 Media Regulation in the Public Interest

1. The Blue Book was developed by the FCC in 1946 to evaluate the discrepancy between the programming 'promises' and the actual 'performance' of radio broadcasters. It required licensees to promote the discussion of public issues, serve minority interests and eliminate superfluous advertising. However, as commercial broadcasters were opposed to it, the Blue Book was rendered obsolete within just five years of its launch (The Museum of Broadcast Communications, no date).

2. As a policy, the Fairness Doctrine guaranteed diversity and the presentation of both sides of a controversial issue. Congress declared it part of the Communications Act of 1959 to safeguard the public interest and First Amendment freedoms. Its constitutionality was upheld by the Supreme Court in the case of Red Lion Broadcasting Co. v. FCC (1969), but it was repealed in the 1970s as broadcasters challenged its constitutionality by claiming that it promoted censorship instead of diversity (The Museum of Broadcast Communications, no date).

3. The term War on Terror was introduced in 2001 by then US President George W. Bush in response to the 11 September terrorist attacks in New York, to denote a global military, political, legal and ideological struggle against terrorist organizations (particularly al-Qaeda) and regimes that were accused of having a connection to them (particularly militant Islamists).

4. The historic justifications for establishing public service broadcasting monopolies have been well documented in a number of works including Garnham, 1989; Humphreys, 1996; Tracey, 1998; Iosifidis, 2007.

5. Many scholars argue that 'quality' is the defining feature of PSB (McQuail, 1992a; Ishikawa, 1996; Brands and de Bens, 2000). A widely accepted definition of quality programming is content that is distinctive, informative, socially relevant and accessible to all. It is, of course, difficult to measure in any quantitative and objective way how well the programmes screened by public channels meet these standards of quality. For this purpose the McKinsey & Company (1999) report measured the amount of time devoted to factual and cultural programmes, as well as to shows for children, and called this kind of programming 'distinctive'. The British media regulatory agency Ofcom (2004a) considered total spend by programme genre, spend per hour by genre and the level of first-run origination by genre in an evaluation of the quality of output, as they indicated the level of resources being spent on each genre. Whatever the definition of quality, most market reports and media analysts agree that quality does not automatically generate viewers.

6. The 'Amsterdam Protocol' (added to the European Treaty) provides, *inter alia*, that: 'The provisions of the Treaty establishing the European Community shall be without prejudice to the competence of Member States to provide for the funding of public service broadcasting insofar as such funding is granted to broadcasting organisations for the fulfilment of the public service remit as conferred, defined and organised by each Member State, and insofar as such funding does not affect trading conditions and competition in the Community to an extent which would be contrary to the common interest'.

7. Relevant markets are defined first in terms of geography and second in terms of products or services (the good in question). The definition of the marketplace can have an impact on what is perceived as its structure. The geographical dimension of market definition determines the scope of the market – that is, whether markets are defined as being local, regional, national or international. Besides being geographically defined, markets are also product- (or service-) defined. The products chosen must form part of a group with characteristics that separate them in an economically sensible way from all other products (Frazer, 1992: 14).

8. The Youth Justice and Criminal Evidence Act 1999 (c. 23) was drawn up and is being implemented in stages as a result of papers called 'Speaking up for Justice' and 'Action for Justice'.

9. Media plurality is conceptualized and operationalized as a policy rationale in various ways. However, in relation to media concentration, an operational definition

of media plurality has been developed around the axis of an external/internal dimension. The Council of Europe's Committee of Experts on media concentration and pluralism (MM-CM) conceived plurality as 'internal in nature, with a wide range of social, political and cultural values, opinions, information and interests finding expression within one media organization, or external in nature, through a number of such organizations, each expressing a particular point of view (CoE, 1994).

10. Royal Commission on the Press (1949) Report: Sir W.D. Ross (Chairman), Cmnd 7700, HMSO, London; Royal Commission on the Press (1962) Report: Lord Shawcross (Chairman), HMSO, London; Royal Commission on the Press (1977) Report: O.R. McGregor (Chairman), Cmnd 6810, HMSO, London. According to Hardy (2010: 164), each Royal Commission identified the growing influence of cross-media ownership on editorial, the influence of advertisers on the economics and editorial of the press, and the (more diffuse) pressures of commercialization. However, the PCC resisted introducing rules governing commercial influence.

11. Committee on Privacy and Related Matters (1990) Report: D. Calcutt (Chairman), HMSO, London.

12. The current Conservative–Liberal Democrat coalition government has a clear intention to downsize the BBC, as would do with cutting Ofcom down to size by removing its policymaking functions as part of its pledge a cut in the number of quangos (quasi-autonomous nongovernmental organizations) in a bid to save costs and create greater accountability (see Cameron's speech of 6 July 2009, available at http://www.brandrepublic.com/News/918047/Cameron-outlines-plot-cut-Ofcom-down-size, accessed 2 October 2009).

13. As Ted Koppel, an ABC News veteran, argues, cable and satellite networks give people 'what they want' instead of 'what they need to know' because it is the best way to secure advertising profits (see http://www.slate.com/id/2274927/, accessed 26 November 2010).

14. Empirical research is required to test the validity of these arguments, but this falls outside the scope of this book.

15. This paragraph builds upon a Newsletter from NORDICOM titled 'Summary and Analysis of Some Major Media Policy Issues in 2010'.

3 Media Policy and Regulation in the Public Interest: Looking Ahead

1. Webster (2006) provides the following five definitions of an information society: a) technological (based on the development of new technologies); b) economic (availability of new products and services); c) occupational (new jobs created in new media sectors); d) spatial (geographic proximity – information networks link locations and impact on the organization of time and space); and e) cultural (cultural proximity – round-the-clock TV programming, video technologies and satellite channels have led to an increase in cultural and social circulation).

2. There are signs that the FCC's policies with regard to media ownership (and beyond) might change under the chairmanship of Genachowski, but this remains to be seen in practice.

3. Setanta, the Irish pay-TV company that broke BskyB's monopoly on live English Premier League coverage in 2006, collapsed in 2009 due to its inability to pay £30 million to the Premier League. The rights to broadcast 46 live football matches in 2010–2011 were resold to American broadcaster ESPN.

4. Kangaroo was the working title for a proposed video-on-demand platform offering content from the commercial arm of the BBC (BBC Worldwide), ITV.com and Channel 4's catch-up service dubbed '4 on Demand', projected to launch in 2008 but rejected by the Competition Commission in 2009. The project was eventually bought by Arqiva (a telecommunications company that provides infrastructure and broadcast transmission facilities in the UK and Ireland) for about £8 million.

5. The Public Interest Test, inserted into the 2002 Enterprise Act by the 2003 Communications Act, was designed to protect media plurality when long-standing restrictions on media cross-ownership were removed. For cross-ownership transactions, there are currently three such public interest considerations: maintaining sufficient plurality; ensuring both high quality and a wide range of material in broadcasting; and commitment to the requirements relating to harm, offence and impartiality laid down in section 319 of the Communications Act (see Barnett, 2009).

6. The IAMCR (International Association of Media and Cultural Research) is mainly an academic organization, founded in Paris in 1957 and describing itself as the worldwide professional body in the field of media and communication research. As a former IAMCR president mentioned, the association's statutes highlight its ambition to provide a meeting place mainly for academics and to seek 'to improve media and communication research, policy and practice, especially from international and interdisciplinary perspectives' (Mansell, 2007: 284).

7. Melody is best known for his seminal work on telecommunications reform, but his writings on broadcasting have also been significant and remain inspiring for scholars in the field, as he analyzed the exchange of cultural products and services at international level through the lens of the regulatory concerns raised by the development of international television and European satellites.

4 Global Communication Paradigms

1. But key cultural globalization theorist Robertson (1995) also claimed that cultural globalization refers to the process by which the relations between the local and the global are being transformed: on the one hand, global media companies constantly adjust their production in order to meet the standards of local markets and the preferences of local consumers; on the other, local cultural corporations may reorganize to globally marketed phenomena. Robertson dubbed this process 'glocalization'.

2. The often cited 'CNN effect' in the last part of the previous century was taken as an indication of American domination of cultural products and cultural homogenization.

5 Globalization and the Nation-State

1. This chapter will touch only briefly on the influence of the EU on national policymaking, as the next chapter will look more closely at this and provide a number of cases to test the influence of supranational (notably EU) regulation on the formation of national media policy.

2. The world order of nation-states was conceived at the Treaty of Westphalia in 1648, which aimed to end religious wars and create sovereign nation-states – that is, states with a defined territory, a government and a permanent population.

3. The Act, effective from April 2000, applies to the online collection of personal information from children under 13 years of age by persons or entities under US jurisdiction.
4. The European Convention on Human Rights, an international treaty to protect human rights and fundamental freedoms in Europe, was drafted in 1950 by the Council of Europe and came into force in September 1953. All Council of Europe Member States (47 as of September 2010) have ratified the Convention.
5. Interoperability refers to the ability of diverse systems and organizations to work together (inter-operate). In the communications domain it mostly applies to information technology systems or services and telecommunications networks.
6. The difference between an authoritarian and a totalitarian regime is that in the case of the latter, citizens have merely accepted the official ideology and not internalized it, as it is the case with totalitarianism, which recognizes no limits to authority, and have permitted and even encouraged a degree of escapism (Mungiu-Pippidi, 1999).
7. Within Marxist literature *state capitalism* is basically a social system that combines capitalism (the economic system in which the means of production are privately owned) with ownership or control by state apparatus. In other words, state capitalism is a structure in which the productive forces are controlled by the state in a capitalist manner.
8. In 2010, China's state-owned firms controlled 6 per cent of the world's stock of foreign direct investment (FDI), which includes takeovers and greenfield investments. This reflects China's economic muscle at a time when most economies are in decline. However, it should be noted that in 1914 Britain owned 45 per cent of the world's FDI, while in 1967 America's share peaked at 60 per cent. Such comparative data and statistics show that China is certainly an emerging superpower – not merely inward-looking, but also using its vast resources abroad – but it may not for some time (if at all) reach the point of domination that Britain and America enjoyed in the past. Still, the current transactions may be problematic partly because of cultural differences and partly because of the role of the Chinese state (*The Economist*, 2010g: 85).

6　Supranational Bodies, Non-State Actors and Global Media Policy

1. Due to space limitations, other important organizations are not examined here. They include the multilateral agreement on investment OECD (Organization for Economic Cooperation and Development), the international clubs G8/G20, which govern global information structures, the World Bank, which addresses development issues, and NAFTA, the North American Free Trade Agreement signed by the governments of the USA, Canada and Mexico, creating a trilateral trade bloc in North America. The role of the European Union is investigated in the next chapter.
2. The ABT was implemented on 5 February 1998. It improves market access for telecommunications equipment suppliers, vendors and service providers by ensuring that all service suppliers seeking to take advantage of scheduled commitments have reasonable and nondiscriminatory access to and the use of basic telecommunications networks and services. Services covered by this agreement include voice telephony, data transmission, telex, telegraph, facsimile, private leased circuits (including the sale or lease of transmission capacity), fixed and mobile satellite systems and services, cellular telephony, mobile data services,

paging, and personal communications systems. Value-added services were not covered in this agreement, but they have been included in more recent telecommunications services negotiations.

3. The Doha negotiations are currently suspended, as trade talks between the six 'core' negotiators, USA, EU, Japan, Australia, India and Brazil, failed to make any headway in reconciling differences over agricultural trade liberalization. The USA wanted cuts in import tariffs for farm products, which were rejected by the EU, Japan and India, who asked for cuts in agricultural subsidies.

4. According to Freedman (2008: 207), Britain was not keen on the process, but it did not want to be the only one of the EU states to vote against the convention.

5. This part should be read in conjunction with Chapter Ten, which provides more detailed information and references.

6. UNESCO 21st General Conference Resolution on NWICO, Belgrade, Yugoslavia, 23 September 1980–20 October 1980. The conference noted, among other things, the increasing attention devoted to communication issues and stressed the need for a new international order in the fields of information and mass communication.

7. Intellectual property is divided into two categories: industrial property, which includes inventions (patents), trademarks, industrial designs and geographic indications of source; and copyright, which includes literary and artistic works such as novels, poems and plays, films, musical works, artistic works such as drawings, paintings, photographs and sculptures, and architectural designs. Rights related to copyright include those of performing artists in their performances, of producers of recordings, and of broadcasters in their radio and television programmes (see http://www.wipo.int/about-ip/en, accessed 4 June 2010).

7 Media and Communications Policy in the European Union

1. 'Spectrum scarcity' is the term given to the situation in which there are not enough wavelengths to match the number of channels that wish to broadcast (see http://www.mediadictionary.com/definition/spectrum-scarcity.html, accessed 2 December 2010). This situation has been abolished by the advent of digital broadcasting.

2. Case C-155/73, Giuseppe Sacchi; also Case C-52/79, Procureur du Roi v Marc J.V.C. Debauve et al.

3. The CoE's interventions of the 1960s–1990s in the media and cultural field have included:

- CoE (1967) Resolution 338 on Press Concentration, 26 January 1967.
- CoE (1970) Resolution 428 containing a declaration on communication media and human rights, Consultative Assembly, Document 2867, DH-MM (85)6.
- CoE (1972) Report on media concentration (draft resolution), presented by the Political Affairs Committee, by Bjork and Van Der Sanden, Consultative Assembly, Doc. 3178, 3 October 1972.
- CoE (1972) Opinion on press concentrations, presented by the Legal Affairs Committee, by Fanelli, Consultative Assembly, Document 3188, 12 October 1972.

- CoE (1974) Resolution 43 on press concentrations, Committee of Ministers, 16 December 1974, DH-MM (85)5.
- CoE (1975) Recommendation 747 on press concentrations, Consultative Assembly, Document 3536, 23 January 1975, DH-MM (85)6.
- CoE (1978) Recommendation 834 on threats to the freedom of the press and television, Parliamentary Assembly, Document 4090, 28 April 1978, DH-MM (85)6.
- CoE (1981) Recommendation 926 on questions raised by cable television and by direct satellite broadcasters, Document 4756, 02 October 1981, DH-MM (88)3.
- CoE (1986) 1st European Ministerial Conference on Mass Media Policy, Vienna, 9–10 December.
- CoE (1987) Recommendation 1067 on the cultural dimension of broadcasting in Europe, Document 5782, 8 October 1987, DH-MM (88)3.
- CoE (1988) 2nd European Ministerial Conference on Mass Media Policy, Stockholm, 23–4 November.
- CoE (1991) 'Which Way Forward For Europe's Media in the 1990s?', 3rd European Ministerial Conference on Mass Media Policy, MCM (91)8, Nicosia (Cyprus), 9–10 October.
- CoE (1994) Recommendation No. R (94)13 of the Committee of Ministers to member states on measures to promote media transparency, adopted on 22 November 1994, DH-MM (94)10.
- CoE (1994) 'The Media in a Democratic Society', 4th European Ministerial Conference on Mass Media Policy, MCM (94)5, Prague, 7–8 December.

A significant relevant Recommendation that the CoE passed in more recent years is the 2007 Recommendation on Media Pluralism and the Diversity of Media Content (CM/Rec. (2007). This document can be viewed as an update of previous Recommendations to enhance plurality and the transparency of media ownership, taking into account of the technological advances that have occurred since the 1990s.

4. During the 1980s/1990s the EP published several non-binding interventions asking the EC to take a more interventionist approach in media pluralism and concentration, including: Resolution on media takeovers and mergers, OJ C 68, 19 March 1990; Resolution on media concentration and diversity of opinions, OJ C 284, 2 November 1992; Resolution on the commission Green Paper 'Pluralism and media concentration in the internal market', OJ C 44, 14 February 1994; Resolution on concentration of the media and pluralism, OJ C 323, 21 November 1994; Resolution on pluralism and media concentration, OJ C 166, 3 July 1995. In 2008 the European Parliament issued yet another Resolution aimed at pluralism in all media to ensure diversity and the transparency of ownership (Final Document P6_TA(2008)0456), showing that in the digital era there is a continuing interest in fostering media pluralism.

5. It should be noted that this was a 'new style Green Paper' since it was not accompanied by a proposal for a Directive of the EC Council. Up to then, Green Papers used to present the Commission's point of view in combination with a proposal for a Directive. The Maastricht Treaty on European Union (OJ C 191, 29 July 1992, pp. 1–113), however, made the Commission more cautious since it restricted actions in areas where the Commission had not been given absolute competence – media policies is such an area (Van Loon, 1993: 5).

6. According to the study, other broadcasters (typically non-media players) tended to hold stakes as long-term investments, letting one majority shareholder control

the channel operations and programme content. Also, such rules tended to pro-mote partnerships between large media groups that would otherwise be compet-ing with each other.

7. A firm may play a gatekeeper role if it possesses a certain technology, know-how or technical standard that allows it to exert a significant degree of control in respect of the access to a given market.

8. The six cases were: MSG Media Service in 1994, Nordic Satellite Distribution in 1995, RTL/Veronica/Endemol (Case No IV/M.553 – RTL/Veronica/Endemol, OJ L 134/32, 5 June 1996), Deutsche Telekom/Beta Research in 1998, Bertelsmann/Kirch/Premiere in 1998 (MSG II), and WorldCom/Sprint in 2000. The proposal for a merger between AOL/Time Warner and EMI in 2000 was withdrawn after it became clear that the EC would prohibit it.

9. Unless otherwise indicated, this section builds upon the work of Soltesz, 2010.

10. The regulatory framework for electronic communications consists of five Directives:

- Directive 2002/19/EC – on access to, and the interconnection of, electronic communications networks and associated facilities (the Access Directive).
- Directive 2002/20/EC – on the authorization of electronic communications networks and services (the Authorization Directive).
- Directive 2002/21/EC – on a common regulatory framework for electronic communications networks and services (the Framework Directive).
- Directive 2002/22/EC – on universal service and users' rights relating to electronic communications networks and services (the Universal Service Directive).
- Directive 2002/58/EC – concerning the processing of personal data and the protection of privacy in the electronic communications sector (the Privacy Directive).

11. Unless otherwise indicated, this section builds upon my own earlier works: Iosifidis, 2006 and Iosifidis, 2011a.

12. Due to space limitations EU telecommunications policy has not been analyzed extensively in this chapter, but for an overview of the field see among others Chakravarthy and Sarikakis, 2006: 51–84.

8 The Convergence Phenomenon in Media and Communications

1. Electronic commerce or electronic business is the buying and selling of products and services using electronic means such as the Internet.

2. 'Quad-play' providers offer landline telephony, mobile telephony, television and broadband services in a single package. However, only a few firms have attempted to apply the concept of quad-play bundles to attract and keep customers, among them Virgin Media and France Telecom.

3. According to the UK regulator, Ofcom, the take-up of digital television services reached 92.7 per cent of UK households in the second quarter of 2010 (see http://www.digitalspy.co.uk/digitaltv/news/a280866/uk-digital-tv-penetration-reaches-927-percent.html, accessed 8 October 2010).

4. This does not mean that all vertical mergers have been successful, for AOL has now been split from Time Warner and in 2010 it published its first earnings report.

9 Regulatory Convergence

1. The Organization for Economic Cooperation and Development (OECD), which originated in 1948, is an international economic forum of 33 countries. This think tank provides a setting for comparing economic policy practices, seeks solutions to common problems, identifies good practices, and coordinates the domestic and international policies of its members.
2. Office of Communications Bill (HL) 2001/02. In an explanatory text it is stated that 'because it will be a complicated and time-consuming task to establish a new regulatory regime and because the Communications Bill will not attain Royal Assent before 2003, this Bill proposes to bring forward the establishment of an Office of Communications and to give it a preparatory function to ease the transition'.
3. This section is bound to include some issues already discussed (in Chapter Seven), although every effort is made here to narrow the discussion to matters relating to convergence.
4. The Green Paper presented three possible regulatory options:

   - The separate development of current regulatory structures in the IT, print, telecommunications and broadcasting industries.
   - The setting-up of separate, horizontal legislation to oversee new convergent services in conjunction with existing ones.
   - The development of a comprehensive, common, horizontal regulatory regime for all ICT services.

5. Since 1998, the EC has been successful in initiating liberalized legislation. Examples of this are the provision for liberalizing all telecommunications services and networks in January 1998 and the provision for liberalizing the local loop in December 2000. In spite of its success on the liberalization front, however, the EC has suffered drawbacks on the harmonization and implementation fronts. There may have been rapid development in competition, as illustrated by falling tariffs and the growing number of operators, but this has been uneven and the local EU telecommunications market is dominated by incumbent operators in most member states.

10 Guidelines for Regulatory Reform

1. This and the next two sections build upon a Newsletter from NORDICOM titled 'Summary and Analysis of Some Major Media Policy Issues in 2010'.
2. The 13 participating GPEN privacy enforcement authorities were:
   US Federal Trade Commission; Office of the Privacy Commissioner of Canada; Commission Nationale de l'Informatique et des Libertés (France); Office of the Privacy Commissioner, New Zealand; Israeli Law, Information and Technology Authority; Office of the Privacy Commissioner, Australia; Office of the Data Protection Commissioner, Ireland; Agencia Española de Protección de Datos (Spain); Information Commissioner's Office (United Kingdom); Garante Per La Protezione Dei Dati Personali (Italy); Dutch Data Protection Authority (the Netherlands); Federal Commissioner for Data Protection and Freedom of Information (Germany); Office of the Victorian Privacy Commissioner (Victoria, Australia).

3. These were Frank LaRue (UN Special Rapporteur on Freedom of Opinion and Expression), Miklos Haraszti (OSCE Representative on Freedom of the Media), Catalina Botero (OAS Special Rapporteur on Freedom of Expression) and Faith Pansy Tlakula (ACHPR Special Rapporteur on Freedom of Expression and Access to Information).

4. Unless otherwise indicated, this section builds upon a Newsletter from NORDICOM titled 'Summary and Analysis of Some Major Media Policy Issues in 2010' and an article in *The Economist* (2011).

Bibliography

Abramson, B. D. (2001) 'Media Policy after Regulation?', *International Journal of Cultural Studies* 4(3): 301–26.

Althusser, L. (1971) 'Ideology and the Ideological State Apparatus' pp. 121–76 in L. Althusser (ed.) *Lenin and Philosophy and Other Essays* (London: New Left Books).

Ampuja, M. (2004) 'Critical Media Research, Globalisation Theory and Commercialisation', *Javnost/The Public* 11(3): 59–76.

Ang, J. (1991) *Desperately Seeking the Audience* (London: Routledge).

Aronson, J. D. (2010) 'Book Review', *International Journal of Communication* 4: 584–8.

Aufderheide, P. (1992) 'Cable Television and the Public Interest', *Journal of Communication* 42(1): 52–65.

Aufderheide, P. (1999) *Communications Policy and the Public Interest* (New York: Guilford Press).

Australian Government (2000) 'Convergence Review', Department of Broadband, Communications and the Digital Economy, Australia.

Baer, W. S. (2010) 'Future Directions for US Public Service Media' pp. 258–72 in P. Iosifidis (ed.) *Reinventing Public Service Communication: European Broadcasters and Beyond* (Basingstoke, UK: Palgrave Macmillan).

Bagdikian, B. H. (2004) (7th ed.)*The New Media Monopoly* (Boston: Beacon Press).

Baldi, P. and U. Hasebrink (eds) (2007) *Broadcasters and Citizens in Europe: Trends in Media Accountability and Viewer Participation* (Bristol, UK: Intellect).

Baldwin, R. (2004) 'The New Punitive Regulation', *Modern Law Review* 67(3): 351–83.

Baldwin, R. and M. Cave (1999) *Understanding Regulation: Theory, Strategy and Practice* (Oxford: Oxford University Press).

Bardoel, J. (2007) 'Governing Media Arrangements in Europe' pp. 445–59 in G. Terzis (ed.) *European Media Governance: National and Regional Dimensions* (Bristol, UK: Intellect).

Barker, C. (2000) *Cultural Studies: Theory and Practice* (London: Sage).

Barnett, S. (2009) 'Journalism, Democracy and the Public Interest: Rethinking Media Pluralism for the Digital Age', Working Paper, September. Available at: http://reutersinstitute.politics.ox.ac.uk/fileadmin/documents/Publications/Journalism_ Democracy___Public_Interest_for_website.pdf (accessed 30 October 2010).

Barnett, S. and J. Seaton (2010a) 'Letter', *Financial Times* 23 October.

Barnett, S. and J. Seaton (2010b) 'Why the BBC Matters: Memo to the New Parliament about a Unique British Institution', *The Political Quarterly* 81(3): 327–32.

Bartle, I. and P. Vass (2007) Self-Regulation and the Regulatory State: A Survey of Policy and Practice Centre for the Study of Regulated Industries (CRI), Research Report 17 (University of Bath). Available at: http://www.bath.ac.uk/management/cri/pubpdf/Research_Reports/17_Bartle_Vass.pdf (accessed 22 September 2010).

Baughman, J. (1985) *Television's Guardians: The FCC and the Politics of Programming 1958–1967* (Knoxville, USA: University of Tennessee Press).

Bennett, T. (1992) 'Putting Policy into Cultural Studies' pp. 23–37 in L. Grossberg, C. Nelson and P. Treichler (eds) *Cultural Studies* (London: Routledge).

BIPE (2002) 'Digital Switchover in Broadcasting', Study for the European Commission, Directorate General Information Society 12 April (EU: Brussels).

Blachford, N. (2003) 'Television and Computer Convergence: Not When but If', *Genesi* 9, December. Available at: http://www.osnews.com/story/5359 (accessed 7 July 2010).

Blumler, J. G. (1992) *Television and the Public Interest: Vulnerable Values in West European Broadcasting* (London: Sage).

Boeder, P. (2005) 'Habermas' Heritage: The Future of the Public Sphere in the Network Society', *First Monday* 10(9), 5 September. Available at: http://firstmonday.org/ htbin/cgiwrap/bin/ojs/index.php/fm/article/view/1280/1200 (accessed 12 November 2009).

Bollier, D. (2007) 'The Rise of Collective Intelligence: Decentralized Co-creation of Value as a new Paradigm of Commerce and Culture', Report on the 16th annual Aspen Institute Roundtable on Information Technology (Washington DC: The Aspen Institute).

Booz-Allen & Hamilton (1992) 'Study on Pluralism and Concentration in Media – Economic Evaluation', Report to the Commission of the European Communities, DG III/F-5, 6 February (Brussels: European Commission).

Bourdieu, P. and J. D. Wacquant (1992) *An Invitation to Reflexive Sociology* (Chicago: University of Chicago Press).

Boyd-Barrett, O. (1977) 'Mass Communication in Cross-Cultural Contexts', *Mass Communication and Society* (Unit 5) (Milton Keynes: Open University Press).

Boyd-Barrett, O. (2010) 'Media Imperialism Reformulated' pp. 139–53 in D. K. Thussu (ed.) *International Communication: A Reader* (London: Routledge).

Braman, S. (2004) 'Where Has Media Policy Gone? Defining the Field in the Twenty-first Century', *Communication Law and Policy* 9(2): 152–82.

Braman, S. (2009) *Change of State: Information, Policy, and Power* (Cambridge, MA: MIT Press).

Brants, K. and E. de Bens (2000) 'The Status of TV Broadcasting in Europe' pp. 7–23 in J. Wieten, G. Murdock and P. Dahlgre (eds) *Television Across Europe: A Comparative Introduction* (London: Sage).

Breen, M. (2010) 'Digital Determinism: Culture Industries in the USA-Australia Free Trade Agreement', *New Media & Society* 12(4): 657–76.

Bremmer, I. (2010) *The End of the Free Market: Who Wins the War between States and Corporations?* (New York: Viking).

Brennan, T. J. (1989) 'The Fairness Doctrine as Public Policy', *Journal of Broadcasting* 33(4): 419–40.

Brown, D. H. and J. L. Blevins (2008) 'Can the FCC Still Ignore the Public? Interviews with Two Commissioners Who Listened', *Television & New Media* 9(6): 447–70.

Buckley, S., D. M. Kreszentia and T. Mendel (2008) *Broadcasting, Voice, and Accountability: A Public Interest Approach to Policy, Law, and Regulation* (The World Bank).

Burton, G. (2010) (2nd ed.) *Media and Society: Critical Perspectives* (New York: Open University Press).

Cariño, L. V. (no date) 'The Concept of Governance'. Available at: http://unpan1. un.org/intradoc/groups/public/documents/EROPA/Monograph-WorldCOG-Chap1.pdf (accessed 3 March 2010).

Casarosa, F. (2010) 'Media Policies and Regulatory Practices in a Selected Set of European Countries, the EU and the Council of Europe: The Case of the European Union and the Council of Europe', project funded by the Seventh Framework

Programme under the Socio-economic, Science and Humanities (Brussels: European Commission).

Castells, M. (1996) *The Rise of the Network Society: Information Age: Economy, Society, and Culture,* Vol. I (Oxford: Blackwell).

Castells, M. (2000) 'Toward a Sociology of the Network Society', *Contemporary Sociology* 29: 693–9.

Castells, M. (2007) 'Communication, Power and Counter-Power in the Network Society', *International Journal of Communication* 1: 238–66.

Castells, M. (2010) 'The New Public Sphere: Global Civil Society, Communication Networks, and Global Governance' pp. 36–47 in D. K. Thussu (ed.) *International Communication: A Reader* (London: Routledge).

Castells, M. and G. Cardoso (eds) (2006) *The Network Society: From Knowledge to Policy* (Washington DC: John Hopkins Center for Transatlantic Relations).

Castendyk, O., E. J. Dommering and A. Scheuer (2008) *European Media Law* (The Netherlands: Kluwer Law International BV).

Chakravarthy, P. and K. Sarikakis (2006) *Media Policy and Globalization* (New Delhi: Rawat Publication).

Chalaby, J. (2007) 'Beyond Nation-Centrism: Thinking International Communication from a Cosmopolitan Perspective', *Studies in Communication Sciences* 7(1): 61–83.

Clements, B. (1998) 'The Impact of Convergence on Regulatory Policy in Europe', *Telecommunications Policy* 22(3): 197–205.

CoE (Council of Europe) (1994) MM-CM, Council of Europe's Committee of Experts on Media Concentrations and Pluralism 'The Activity Report of the Committee of Experts on Media Concentrations and Pluralism', submitted to the 4th European Ministerial Conference on Mass Media Policy, Prague, 7–8 December 1994.

CoE (Council of Europe) (2000) Recommendation (2000)23 of the Committee of Ministers to member states on the independence and functions of regulatory authorities for the broadcasting sector, Adopted by the Committee of Ministers on 20 December 2000.

Coleman, J. S. (1988) 'Social Capital in the Creation of Human Capital', *The American Journal of Sociology* 94: S95–S120.

Coleman, J. S. (1999) 'Cutting Out the Middle Man: From Virtual Representation to Direct Deliberation', pp. 195–210 in B. N. Hague and B. D. Loader (eds) *Digital Democracy: Discourse and Decision-Making in the Information Age* (London: Routledge).

Coleman, J. S. and J. G. Blumer (2008) *The Internet and Democratic Citizenship: Theory, Practice and Policy* (Cambridge: Cambridge University Press).

Collins, R., N. Garnham and G. Locksley (1988) *The Economics of Television: The UK Case* (London: Sage).

Compaine, B. (2005) 'Global Media' pp. 97–101 in E. P. Bucy (ed.) *Living in the Information Age: A New Media Reader* (2nd ed.) (Belmont: Wadsworth Thomson).

Conti, G. (2009) *Googling Security: How Much Does Google Know About You?* (Boston: Addison-Wesley).

Corcoran, F. (2010) 'Civic Engagement and Elite Decision-Making in Europe: Reconfiguring Public Service News' pp. 76–87 in P. Iosifidis (ed.) *Reinventing Public Service Communication: European Broadcasters and Beyond* (Basingstoke, UK: Palgrave Macmillan).

Costanza-Chock, S. (2003) 'WSIS, the Neoliberal Agenda and Counterproposals from Civil Society', Working Paper, The Media Research Hub. Available at: http://mediaresearchhub.ssrc.org/wsis-the-neoliberal-agenda-and-counterproposals-from-civil-society/resource_view (accessed 1 June 2010).

Costanza-Chock, S. (2005) 'The Globalization of Media Policy' pp. 259–75 in R. McChesney, R. Newman and B. Scott (eds) *The Future of Media: Resistance and Reform in the 21st Century* (New York: Seven Stories Press).

Couldry, N. (2010) *Why Voice Matters: Culture and Politics After Neoliberalism* (London: Sage).

Croteau, D. and W. Hoynes (2006) *The Business of Media: Corporate Media and the Public Interest* (Thousand Oaks, CA: Pine Forge Press).

Cukier, K. N. (2008) 'The Future of Convergence & Regulation: Trends – and Errors – from the US and EU', Keidanren Kaikan Convergence Regulatory Symposium, 26 February, Tokyo, Japan.

Cunningham, S. (1992) *Framing Culture: Criticism and Policy in Australia* (Sydney: Allen & Unwin).

Curran, J. (1991a) 'Rethinking the Media As a Public Sphere' pp. 27–57 in P. Dahlgren and C. Sparks (eds) *Communication and Citizenship* (London: Routledge).

Curran, J. (1991b) 'Mass Media and Democracy: A Reappraisal' pp. 82–117 in J. Curran and M. Gurevitch (eds) *Mass Media and Society* (London: Arnold).

Curran, J. and J. Seaton (2010) (7th ed.) *Power without Responsibility: Press, Broadcasting and the Internet in Britain* .(London: Routledge).

Dadashzadeh, M. (ed.) (2002) *Information Technology Management in Developing Countries* (USA: IRM Press).

Dahlberg, L. (2007) 'Rethinking the Fragmentation of the Cyberpublic: From Consensus to Contestation', *New Media and Society* 9(5): 827–47.

Dahlgren, P. (1995) *Television and the Public Sphere* (London: Sage).

Dahlgren, P. (2005) 'The Internet, Public Spheres and Political Communication: Dispersion and Deliberation', *Political Communication* 22(2): 147–62.

Dahlgren, P. (2008) *Media and Political Engagement: Citizens, democracy and Communication* (New York: Cambridge University Press).

Davis, J. (1993) 'Media Ownership: Why the EC Proposals are Doomed to Fail', *Media Policy Review* 3(4): 6–9 (March/April).

DCMS (Departments of Culture, Media and Sport) and DTI (Department of Trade and Industry) (2000) *A New Future of Communications* Cm 5010 (London: TSO).

DCMS/DBERR (Departments of Culture, Media and Sport and Department for Business Enterprise and Regulatory Reform) (2009) *The Digital Britain White Paper*, 16 June (London: Crown Copyright).

De Sola Pool (1983) *Technologies of Freedom* (Cambridge: Belknap Press of Harvard University Press).

De Witte, B. (2006) 'Non-market Values in Internal Market Regulation' pp. 61–86 in N. N. Shuibhne (ed.) *Regulating the Internal Market* (Cheltenham: Edward Elgar).

Deuze, M. (2010) 'Convergence Culture in the Creative Industries' pp. 452–67 in D.K. Thussu (ed.) *International Communication: A Reader* (London: Routledge).

Dewey, J. (1983) [1927] *The Public and Its Problems* (Athens: Swallow Press).

Downs, A. (1962) 'The Public Interest: Its Meaning in a Democracy', *Social Research* 29(1): 1–36.

Drezner, D. W. (2001) 'Globalization and Policy Convergence', *The International Studies Review* 3(1): 53–78.

Dunbar, J. (2005) 'Who is Watching the Watchdog?' pp. 127–40 in R. W. McChesney, R. Newman and B. Scott (eds) *The Future of Media: Resistance and Reform in the 21st Century* (New York: Seven Stories Press).

Dutton, W. H. (2007) 'Through the Network (of Networks) – the Fifth Estate', Inaugural Lecture, University of Oxford, 15 October. Available at: http://people.oii.ox.ac.uk/

dutton/wp-content/uploads/2007/10/5th-estate-lecture-text.pdf (accessed 16 July 2010).

Dyson, K. and P. Humphreys (1988) 'The Context of New Media Policies in Western Europe' in K. Dyson and P. Humphreys with R. Negrine and J.P Simon (eds) *Broadcasting and New Media Policies in Western Europe* (London: Routledge).

Dyson, K. and P. Humphreys (eds) (1990) *The Political Economy of Communications Policies: International and European Dimensions* (London: Routledge).

EC (European Commission) (1992) *Green Paper, Pluralism and Media Concentration in the Internal Market, an Assessment of the Need for Community Action*, COM(92) 480 final (EU: Brussels).

EC (European Commission) (1993) *Growth, Competitiveness, and Employment – The Challenges and Ways Forward into the 21st Century*, COM (93) 700 Final (EU: Brussels).

EC (European Commission) (1994) Europe and the Global Information Society – Recommendations to the European Council, High-level Group on the Information Society – Bangemann Report (EU: Brussels).

EC (European Commission) (1995) Directive 95/46/EC of the European Parliament and of the Council of 24 October 1995 on the Protection of Individuals with Regard to the Processing of Personal Data and on the Free Movement of Such Data, Official Journal L 281, 23/11/1995 P. 0031 – 0050 (EU: Brussels).

EC (European Commission) (1997) *Green Paper on the Convergence of the Telecommunications, Media and Information technology Sectors, and the Implications for Regulation: Towards an Information Society Approach*, COM(97) 623 (EU: Brussels).

EC (European Commission) (1999a) *The 1999 Communications Review: Towards a New Framework for Electronic Communications Infrastructure and Associated Services*, COM (1999) 539, Commission Communication to the European Parliament, the Council, the Economic and Social Committee and the Committee of the Regions (EU: Brussels).

EC (European Commission) (1999b) *Report on the Value Added of an Independent European Regulatory Authority for Telecommunications*, September 1999 (EU: Brussels).

EC (European Commission) (1999c) *Results of the Public Consultation on the Convergence Green Paper*, COM (1999) 108, March 1999, Commission Communication to the European Parliament, the Council, the Economic and Social Committee and the Committee of the Regions (EU: Brussels).

EC (European Commission) (1999d) *Principles and Guidelines for the Community's Audiovisual Policy in the Digital Age*, COM (1999) 657, December 1999, Commission Communication to the European Parliament, the Council, the Economic and Social Committee and the Committee of the Regions (EU: Brussels).

EC (European Commission) (2000a) Presidency Conclusions 2000, Lisbon European Council, March 2000 (EU: Brussels).

EC (European Commission) (2000b) Directive 2000/31/EC on Certain Legal Aspects of Information Society Services, in Particular Electronic Commerce in the Internal Market, OJ L178/ I–16 (EU: Brussels).

EC (European Commission) (2001a) Presidency Conclusions 2001, Stockholm European Council, March 2001.

EC (European Commission) (2001b) Communication from the Commission on the Application of State Aid Rules on Public Service Broadcasters, 15 November, OJ 2001 C 320/5 (EU: Brussels).

EC (European Commission) (2003) Communication on Digital Switchover – Transition From Analogue to Digital Broadcasting, From Digital Switchover to Analogue Switch-off, COM(2003) 541 Final, 22 September (EU: Brussels).

EC (European Commission) (2005a) Communication on Accelerating the Transition from Analogue to Digital Broadcasting, COM(2005) 204 Final, 24 May (EU: Brussels).

EC (European Commission) (2005b) Commission Expects Most Broadcasting in the EU to be Digital by 2010, IP/05/595, 24 May (EU: Brussels).

EC (European Commission) (2006) Commission Decision of 22/III/2006 Relating to a Proceeding Pursuant to Article 81 of the EC Treaty (Case COMP/C-2/38.173 – Joint Selling of the Media Rights to the FA Premier League. Brussels 22/III/2006 C(2006)868 Final. Available at: http://ec.europa.eu/competition/antitrust/cases/decisions/38173/decision_en.pdf (accessed 20 January 2010).

EC (European Commission) (2007) Directive 2007/65/EC, AVMS Directive (EU: Brussels).

EC (European Commission) (2009a) Communication from the Commission on the Application of State Aid Rules to Public Service Broadcasting, (EU: Brussels).

EC (European Commission) (2009b) *Internet Governance: The Next Steps*, Communication from the Commission to the European Parliament and the Council (COM(2009) 277 Final, 18/6/2009 (EU: Brussels).

EC (European Commission) (2009c) Green Paper – The Interconnection of Business Registers, SEC(2009) 1492, COM(2009) 614 Final.

EC (European Commission) (2009d) Commission Staff Working Document on the External Dimension of Audiovisual Policy, SEC(2009) 1033 final 14/7/2009 (EU: Brussels).

ECJ (European Court of Justice) (2003) Judgment of the Court (Regulation (EEC) No. 1191/69 – Operation Of Urban, Suburban and Regional Scheduled Transport Services – Public Subsidies – Concept of State Aid – Compensation for Discharging Public Service Obligations (Luxemburg: ECJ).

The Economist (2006) 'Reshaping the BBC: Back on Top', 18 March, pp. 28–31.

The Economist (2010a) 'The Growth of the State: Leviathan Stirs Again', 23 January, pp. 22–24.

The Economist (2010b) 'The Net Generation, Unplugged', Technology Quarterly, 6 March, p. 10.

The Economist (2010c) 'New Media and the Election', 20 March, p. 33.

The Economist (2010d) 'The State and the Economy: Re-enter the Dragon', 5 June, pp. 94–5.

The Economist (2010e) 'The Emerging Online Giants', 10 July, pp. 65–6.

The Economist (2010f) 'Social Networks and Statehood: The Future is another Country', 24 July, pp. 54–5.

The Economist (2010g) 'Brussels Wants to Delve Deep into the Running of National Economies – It should beware of Digging too Far', 2 October, p. 52.

The Economist (2011) 'Network Neutrality: A Tangled Web', 1 January, pp. 8–9.

Edelman, M. (1985) *The Symbolic Uses of Politics* (University of Illinois Press).

EEC (European Economic Community) (1989) Council Regulation (EEC) No. 4064/89, as Amended by Council Regulation (EC) No. 139/2004, OJ L24/I-22), The Merger Regulation (EU: Brussels).

EIAA (European Interactive Advertising Association) (2006) 'Social Networking to Drive Next Wave of Internet Usage', Press Release, http://www.eiaa.net/news/eiaa-articles-details.asp?id=106&lang=1 (accessed 7 July 2010).

EIM (The European Institute for the Media) (1994) 'Media Concentration in Europe: Commercial Enterprise and the Public Interest', Media Monograph No. 16 (Dusseldorf, Germany: EIM).

Emerson, R. (1976) 'Social Exchange Theory', *Annual Review of Sociology* 2: 335–62.

Emirbayer, M. (1997) 'Manifesto for a Relational Sociology', *The American Journal of Sociology* 103(2): 281–317.

Enzensberger, H. M. (1970) 'Constituents of a Theory of the Media', *New Left Review* 64: 13–36.

EPC (European Publishers Council) (1998) Response to EC Convergence Green Paper COM(97)623. Available at: http://www.epceurope.org/issues/epc-response-to-green-paper-on-convergence-of-telecommunications-media-and-information-technology-sectors-april-1998.shtml (accessed 12 November 2010).

EU (European Union) (1997) *Treaty of Amsterdam Amending the Treaty on European Union, the Treaties Establishing the European Communities and Certain Related Acts – Protocol Annexed to the Treaty of the European Community – Protocol on the System of Public Broadcasting in the Member States*, Official Journal C 340, 10/11/1997 P. 0109 (EU: Brussels).

EU (European Union) (2007) Directive 2007/65/EC Amending Council Directive 89/552/EC on the Coordination of Certain Provisions Laid Down by Law, Regulation or Administrative Action in Member States Concerning the Pursuit of Television Broadcasting Activities, OJ L332/27, 18 December (EU: Brussels).

EU Treaty (2006) Treaty on European Union and of the Treaty Establishing the European Community, Official Journal of the European Union, C 321 E/1, 29 December (EU: Brussels).

Europe Economics (2002) 'Market Definition in the Media Sector – Economic Issues', Report for the European Commission (Brussels: DG Competition).

Evans, D. (2010) 'New Media' 7 July, Speech, by the Editor-in-Chief of CPI, Jevons Institute colloquium on New Media and Competition. Available at: https://www.competitionpolicyinternational.com/david-evans-on-the-new-media (accessed 24 July 2010).

FCC (Federal Communications Commission (2006) FCC Regulation of Broadcast Obscenity, Indecency, and Profanity, June. Available at: http://www.ucop.edu/irc/services/documents/indecencymemo.pdf (accessed 17 October 2010).

Feintuck, M. and M. Varney (2006) *Media Regulation, Public Interest and the Law* (Edinburgh: Edinburgh University Press).

Fejes, F. (1981) 'Media Imperialism: An Assessment', *Media Culture and Society* 3: 281–9.

Ferguson, M. (ed.) (1986) *New Communication Technologies and the Public Interest* (London: Sage).

Ferguson, M. (2002) 'The Mythology about Globalization' pp. 238–48 in D. McQuail (ed.) *McQuail's Reader in Mass Communication Theory* (London: Sage).

Fiske, J. (1987) *Television Culture* (London: Routledge).

Flew, T. (2007) *Understanding Global Media* (London: Palgrave Macmillan).

Forester, T. (ed.) (1985) *The Information Technology Revolution* (Oxford: Basil Blackwell).

Fowler, M. S. (1982) 'The Public's Interest', *Communication and the Law* 4: 51–8.

Fox Television Stations Inc. vs. FCC, 280 F.3d 1027. 2002.

Fraser, N. (2007) 'Transnationalizing the Public Sphere. On the Legitimacy and Efficacy of Public Opinion in a Post-Westphalian World', *Theory, Culture & Society* 24(4): 7–30.

Frazer, T. (1992) *Monopoly, Competition and the Law* (London: Harvester-Wheatsheaf).

Freedman, D. (2003) (2nd ed.) *The Television Policies of the Labour Party, 1951–2001* (London: Frank Cass).

Freedman, D. (2008) *The Politics of Media Policy* (Cambridge: Polity Press).

Freepress Action Fund (2008) '2009 Media & Tech Priorities: A Public Interest Agenda', 2 December. Available at: http://www.freepress.net/files/2009techpolicy.pdf (accessed 22 October 2009).

Frieden, R. (2008) 'Academic Research and Its Limited Impact on Telecommunications Policymaking', *International Journal of Communication* 2: 421–8.

Gamble, A. (2000) 'Policy Agendas in a Multi-Level Polity' pp. 290–307 in P. Dunleavy, R. Heffernan, P. Cowley and C. Hay (eds) *Developments in British Politics 6* (Basingstoke, UK: Palgrave Macmillan).

Garnham, N. (1986) 'The Media and the Public Sphere', *Intermedia* 14(1): 28–33.

Garnham, N. (1989) 'West Europe Broadcasting', *Media, Culture and Society* 11(1): 163–8.

Garnham, N. (1990) *Capitalism and Communication* (London: Sage).

Garnham, N. (1995) 'Political Economy and Cultural Studies: Reconciliation or Divorce?', *Critical Studies in Mass Communication* 12(1): 62–71.

Garnham, N. and G. Locksley (1991) 'The Economics of Broadcasting' pp. 8–22 in J.G. Blumler and T.J. Nossiter (eds) *Broadcasting Finance in Transition: A Comparative Handbook* (Oxford: Oxford University Press).

Geller, H. (1985) 'The Role of Future Regulation: Licensing, Spectrum Allocation, Content, Access, Common Carrier, and Rates' pp. 283–310 in E. Noam (ed.) *Video Media Competition: Regulation, Economics, and Technology* (New York: Columbia University Press).

Gellner, E. (1983) *Nations and Nationalism* (Oxford: Blackwell).

Genachowski, J. (2009) 'Preserving a Free and Open Internet: A Platform for Innovation, Opportunity, and Prosperity', Speech, The Brookings Institution, Washington DC, 21 September. Available at: http://www.openinternet.gov/read-speech.html (accessed 10 March 2010).

Gibbons, T. (1998) (2nd ed.) *Regulating the Media* (London: Sweet & Maxwell).

Gibbons, T. (1999) 'Concentrations of Ownership and Control in a Converging Media Industry' pp. 155–74. in C. Marsden and S. Verhulst (eds) *Convergence in European Digital TV Regulation* (London: Blackstone Press).

Gibbons, T. (2008) 'Globalization, Regulatory Competition and Audiovisual Regulation: The United Kingdom and Canada', Paper submitted to ECREA conference, Barcelona 25–8 November.

Giddens, A. (1990) *The Consequences of Modernity* (Stanford University Press).

Gilder, G. (1992) *Life after Television: The Coming Transformation of Media and American Life* (New York: W.W. Norton).

Golding, P. and G. Murdock (1991) 'Culture, Communications and Political Economy' pp. 15–31 in J. Curran and M. Gurevitch (eds) *Mass Media and Society* (London: Edward Arnold).

Graber, C. B. (2006) 'The New UNESCO Convention on Cultural Diversity: A Counterbalance to the WTO?', *Journal of International Economic Law* 9(3): 553–74.

Graham, A. (2000) 'Public Policy Issues for UK Broadcasting' pp. 93–108 in S. Barnett, V. Bottomley and M. Cave *E-Britannia: The Communications Revolution* (Luton: University of Luton Press).

Graham, A. and G. Davis (1997) *Broadcasting, Society and Policy in the Multimedia Age* (Luton, UK: University of Luton Press).

Graham, S. and S. Marvin (2001) *Splintering Urbanism: Network Infrastructure, Technological Motilities and the Urban Condition* (New York: Routledge).

Gray, C. (2000) 'A Hollow State?' pp. 283–99 in R. Pyper and L. Robins (eds) *United Kingdom Governance* (Basingstoke, UK: Palgrave Macmillan).

Grossberg, L. (1991) 'Strategies of Marxist Cultural Interpretation' pp. 126–59 in R. K. Avery and D. Eason (eds) *Critical Perspectives on Media and Society* (New York: Guilford Press).

Grossberg, L. (1996) 'Cultural Studies Vs. Political Economy: Is Anyone Else Bored with this Debate?', *Critical Studies in Mass Communication* 12(1): 72–81.

Habermas, J. (1989) [1962] *The Structural Transformation of the Public Sphere: An Inquiry into a Category of Bourgeois Society* (Cambridge: Polity Press).

Habermas, J. (1994) 'Citizenship and National Identity' pp. 20–35 in B. van Steenbergen (ed.) *The Condition of Citizenship* (London: Sage).

Hall, S. (1982) 'The Rediscovery of "Ideology": Return of the Repressed in Media Studies' pp. 56–90 in M. Gurevitch, T. Bennett, J. Curran and J. Woollacott (eds) *Culture, Society and the Media* (London: Methuen).

Hall, S. (1992) 'The West and the Rest: Discourse and Power' pp. 275–320 in S. Hall and B. Gieben (eds) *Formations of Modernity* (Cambridge: Polity Press).

Hallin, D. C. and P. Mancini (2004) *Comparing Media Systems: Three Models of Media and Politics* (Cambridge: Cambridge University Press).

Halper, S. (2010) *The Beijing Consensus: How China's Authoritarian Model Will Dominate the Twenty-First Century* (New York: Basic Books).

Halpern, D. (2005) *Social Capital* (Cambridge: Policy Press).

Hamelink, C. (1994) *The Politics of World Communication* (London: Sage).

Hamelink, C. (2000) *The Ethics of Cyberspace* (London: Sage).

Hamelink, C. and K. Nordenstreng (2007) 'Towards Democratic Media Governance', pp. 225–43 in E. de Bens (ed.) *Media between Culture and Commerce* (Bristol, UK: Intellect).

Hans-Bredow Institut and EMR (2006) 'Final Report: Study on Co-Regulatory Measures in the Media Sector', Study for the European Commission, 13 January. Available at: http://www.cnpl.lu/upload/292.pdf (accessed 14 July 2010).

Harcourt, A. (2004) *The European Union and the Regulation of Media Markets*, European Policy Studies (Manchester: Manchester University Press).

Harcourt, A. (2010) 'The Role of the European Institutions in National Media Regulation' pp. 116–32 in S. Papathanassopoulos and R. Negrine (eds) *Communications Policy: Theories and Issues* (Basingstoke, UK: Palgrave Macmillan).

Harding, J. (2000) 'An Overhaul? Yes, But…', *Financial Times*, 12 December: 2–3.

Hardy, J. (2010) *Cross-Media Promotion* (New York: Peter Lang).

Harrison, J. (2006) 'The Political-Economy of Blair's "New Regional Policy" ', *Geoforum* 37(6): 932–43.

Harvey, D. (2005) *A Brief History of Neoliberalism* (New York: Oxford University Press).

Harvey, S. (2006) 'Ofcom's First Year and Neo-liberalism's Blind Spot: Attacking the Culture of Production', *Screen* 47(1): 91–105.

Harvey, S. and C. Tongue (2006) 'Trading Cultural Commodities or Promoting Cultural Diversity? UNESCO's New Convention' pp. 221–30 in S. Harvey (ed.) *Trading Culture: Global Traffic and Local Cultures in Film and Television* (Eastleigh: John Libbey).

Haythornthwaite, C. (2002) 'Strong, Weak and Latent Ties and the Impact of New Media', *The Information Society* 18(5): 385–401.

Held, D., A. McGrew, D. Goldblatt and J. Perraton (1999) *Global Transformations: Politics, Economics and Culture* (Cambridge: Polity Press).

Held, V. (1970) *The Public Interest and Individual Interests* (New York: Basic Books).

Heller, M. (2008) 'Global and European Information Society' pp. 29–46 in P. Ludes (ed.) *Convergence and Fragmentation: Media Technology and the Information Society* (Bristol, UK: Intellect).

Hendon, W., D. Shaw, and N. Grant (1986) *Economics of Cultural Industries* (Association for Cultural Economics).

Hesmondhalgh, D. (2005) 'Media and Cultural Policy as Public Policy: The Case of the British Labour Government', *International Journal of Cultural Policy* 11(1): 95–109.

Herman, E. (1996) 'The Propaganda Model Revisited', *Monthly Review*, July. Available at: http://www.chomsky.info/onchomsky/199607--.htm (accessed 21 July 2011).

Herman, E. (2000) 'The Propaganda Model: A Retrospective', *Journalism Studies* 1(1): 101–12.

Herman, E. and N. Chomsky (1988) *Manufacturing Consent: The Political Economy of the Mass Media* (London: Vintage).

Hills, J. (1998) 'U.S. Rules OK? Telecommunications since the 1940s' pp. 99–121 in R. W. McChesney, E. M. Wood and J. B. Foster (eds) *Capitalism and the Information Age: The Political Economy of the Global Communications Revolution* (New York: Monthly Review Press).

Hills, J. and S. Papathanassopoulos (1991) *The Democracy Gap* (London: Greenwood).

Hilmes, M. (2004) 'Citizen versus Consumer: Rethinking Core Concepts', 3 December. Available at: http://flowtv.org/?p=664 (accessed 22 October 2009).

Hindman, M. (2008) *The Myth of Digital Democracy* (USA: Princeton University Press).

Hirst, P. and G. Thompson (1996) *Globalization in Question* (Cambridge: Polity Press).

Hjarvard, S. (2007) 'News in a Globalised Society', Seminar, University of Copenhagen, 5 October. Available at: http://www.authorstream.com/Presentation/Spencer-17072-News-Globalized-Society-Oslo-2-Globalization-Two-definitions-Three-roles-media-Change-in-a-as-Product-Training-Manuals-ppt-powerpoint (accessed 5 February 2010).

Hoffman-Riem, W. (1992) 'Trends in the Development of Broadcasting Law in Western Europe', *European Journal of Communication* 7(2): 147–71.

Hohendahl, P.U. (1979) 'Critical Theory, Public Sphere and Culture: Jurgen Habermas and his Critics', *New German Critique* 16: 89–118.

Hooper, R. (2005) 'Content Regulation in the Multiplatform Multichannel Digital Age', Seminar hosted by the Hong Kong Broadcasting Authority and the Telecommunications Authority, 29 August. Available at: http://www.ofcom.org.uk/media/speeches/2005/08/hk (accessed 6 July 2010).

Horwitz, R. B. (1989) *The Irony of Regulatory Reform: The Deregulation of American Telecommunications* (New York: Oxford University Press).

Horwitz, R. B. (1991) 'The First Amendment Meets Some New Technologies: Broadcasting, Common Carriers, and Free Speech in the 1990s', *Theory and Society* 20(1): 21–72.

Howell, K. E. (2004) *Europeanization, European Integration and Financial Services: Developing Theoretical Frameworks and Synthesizing Methodological Approaches* (Basingstoke, UK: Palgrave Macmillan).

Hoynes, W. (1994) *Public Television for Sale: Media, the Market, and the Public Sphere* (USA: Westview Press).

Humphreys, P. (1996) *Mass Media and Media Policy in Western Europe* (Manchester: Manchester University Press).

Humphreys, P. (2000) 'New Labour Policies for the Media and Arts' pp. 221–39 in D. Coates and P. Lawler (eds) *New Labour in Power* (Manchester: Manchester University Press).

Humphreys, P. (2007) 'Comment on Raboy's speech' University of Exeter, 30 March. Available at: http://www.exeter.ac.uk/research/networks/information/MarcRaboy-GlobalMediaRegulationintheInformationSociety.shtml (accessed 20 October 2010).

Humphreys, P. (2008) *Redefining Public Service Media: A Comparative Study of France, Germany and the UK,* Paper for the RIPE@2008 Conference, Mainz.

Humphreys, P. (2009) 'EU Audiovisual Policy, Cultural Diversity and the Future of Public Service Broadcasting' pp. 183–212 in J. Harrison and B. Wessels (eds) *Mediating Europe: New Media, Mass Communications and the European Public Sphere* (New York: Berghahn).

Hutchison, D. (1999) *Media Policy: An Introduction* (Oxford: Blackwell).

Hutchinson, D. (2007) 'The EU and the Press: Policy or Non-policy?' in K. Sarikakis (ed.) *Media and Cultural Policy in the European Union,* 24 European Media studies (Amsterdam: Rodopi B.V.).

Independent Study (2009) 'Indicators for Media Pluralism in the Member States – Towards a Risk-Based Approach', Prepared for the European Commission DG Information Society and Media by K.U. Leuven – ICRI, Jönköping International Business School – MMTC and Ernst & Young Consultancy, April Preliminary Final Report (Leuven, Belgium).

Iosifidis, P. (1996) 'Merger Control and Media Pluralism in the European Union', *Tolley's Communication Law* 1: 247–9.

Iosifidis, P. (1997) 'Methods of Measuring Media Concentration', *Media, Culture & Society* 19(3): 643–63.

Iosifidis, P. (1999) 'Diversity versus Concentration in the Deregulated Mass Media Domain', *Journalism & Mass Communication Quarterly* 76(1): 152–62.

Iosifidis, P. (2002) 'Digital Convergence: Challenges for European Regulation', *Javnost/The Public* 9(3): 27–48.

Iosifidis, P. (2005) 'The Application of EC Competition Policy to the Media Industry', *International Journal of Media Management* 7(3&4): 103–11.

Iosifidis, P. (2006) 'Digital Switchover in Europe', *International Communication Gazette* 68(3): 249–68.

Iosifidis, P. (2007) *Public Television in the Digital Era: Technological Challenges and New Strategies for Europe* (Basingstoke, UK: Palgrave Macmillan).

Iosifidis, P. (ed.) (2010a) *Reinventing Public Service Communication: European Broadcasters and Beyond* (Basingstoke, UK: Palgrave Macmillan).

Iosifidis, P. (2010b) 'Pluralism and Funding of Public Service Broadcasting across Europe' pp. 23–35 in P. Iosifidis (ed.) *Reinventing Public Service Communication: European Broadcasters and Beyond* (Basingstoke, UK: Palgrave Macmillan).

Iosifidis, P. (2010c) 'Pluralism and Concentration of Media Ownership: Measurement Issues', *Javnost/The Public* 17(3): 5–20.

Iosifidis, P. (2010d) 'Measuring Media Concentration for the Purposes of Ensuring Pluralism and Diversity' pp. 108–24 in P.Y. Badillo and J.B. Lesourd (eds) *The Media Industries and Their Markets: Quantitative Analyses* (Basingstoke, UK: Palgrave Macmillan).

Iosifidis, P. (2011a) 'Growing Pains? The Transition to Digital Television in Europe', *European Journal of Communication* 26(1): 1–15.

Iosifidis, P. (2011b) 'The Public Sphere, Social Networks and Public Service Media', *Information, Communication & Society* 14(5): 619–37.

Iosifidis, P., J. Steemers and M. Wheeler (2005) *European Television Industries* (London: British Film Institute).

Ishikawa, S. (1996) *Quality Assessment in Television* (Luton, UK: John Libbey Media).

ITU (International Telecommunications Union) (2007) 'Telecommunications Regulatory Database'.

IWS (Internet World Stats) (2010) 'United Kingdom: Internet Usage Stats and Market Report – Usage and Population Statistics'.

Jakubowicz, K. (2007) 'The Eastern European/Post Communist Media Model Countries: Introduction' pp. 303–13 in G. Terzis (ed.) *European Media Governance: National and Regional Dimensions* (Bristol, UK: Intellect).

Jakubowicz, K. (2010) 'PSB 3.0: Reinventing European PSB' pp. 9–22 in P. Iosifidis (ed.) *Reinventing Public Service Communication: European Broadcasters and Beyond* (Basingstoke, UK: Palgrave Macmillan).

Jenkins, H. (2006) *Convergence Culture: Where Old and New Media Collide* (New York: NY University Press).

Jensen, K. B. (ed.) (2002) *A Handbook of Media and Communication Research* (London: Routledge).

Johnson, N. (1987) 'Regulating American Style', *Intermedia* 15(4/5): 31–3.

Johnson, D. R., S. P. Crawford and J. G. Palfrey (2004) 'The Accountable Net: Peer Production of Internet Governance', *Virginia Journal of Law and Technology* 9(9) Available at: http://cyber.law.harvard.edu/Accountable%20Net-ITU.pdf (accessed 22 July 2011).

Just, N. (2009) 'Measuring Media Concentration and Diversity: New Approaches and Instruments in Europe and the United States', *Media Culture & Society* 31(1): 97–117.

Just, N. and M. Latzer (2000) 'EC Competition Policy and Market Power Control in the Mediamatics Era', *Telecommunications Policy* 24: 395–411.

Kahn, F. (1978) (3rd ed.) *Documents of American Broadcasting* (NJ, USA: Prentice-Hall, Englewood Cliffs).

Kaldor M. (2003) 'The Idea of Global Civil Society', *International Affairs Journal* 79(3): 583–93.

Kalimo, H. and C. Pauwels (2009) 'The Converging Media and Communications Environment' in C. Pauwels, K. Donders, H. Kalimo and B.V. Rompuy (eds) *Rethinking European Media and Communications Policy* (VUBPRESS: Institute for European Studies, Brussels University Press).

Kalven, H. (1967) 'Broadcasting, Public Policy and the First Amendment', *Journal of Law and Economics* 10: 15–30.

Katz, Y. (2005) *Media Policy for the 21st Century in the United States and Western Europe* (Cresskill, New Jersey: Hampton Press).

Keane, J. (2001) 'Global Civil Society?' pp. 23–47 in H. Anheier, M. Glasius and M. Kaldor (eds) *Global Civil Society* (Oxford: Oxford University Press).

Keen, A. (2007) *The Cult of the Amateur: How Today's Internet Is Killing Our Culture* (New York: Doubleday).

Kellner, D. (1990) *Television and the Crisis of Democracy* (USA: Westview Press).

Kellner, D. (1997) 'Intellectuals, the New Public Spheres, and Techno-politics'. Available at: http://www.gseis.ucla.edu/faculty/kellner/essays/intellectualsnewpublicspheres.pdf (accessed 14 November 2009).

Kellner, D. (no date) 'Habermas, the Public Sphere, and Democracy: A Critical Intervention'. Available at: http://www.davidtinapple.com/comaff/Habermas_Public_Sphere_Democracy.pdf (accessed 15 November 2009).

Keohanne, R. O. and J. S. Nye (1998) *Power and Interdependence in the Information Age* (New York, USA: Council of Foreign Relations).

Kerr, C. (1983) *The Future of Industrial Societies: Convergence or Continuing Diversity?* (Cambridge, Massachusetts: Harvard University Press).

Kevin, D., T. Ader, O.C. Fueg, E. Pertzinidou and M. Schoenthal (2004) 'The Information of the Citizen in the EU: Obligations for the Media and the Institutions Concerning the Citizen's Right to be Fully and Objectively Informed', Final Report for European Parliament (Dusseldorf: European Institute for the Media) Available at: http://www.pedz.uni-mannheim.de/daten/edz-ma/ep/04/pe358896-en.pdf (accessed 22 July 2011).

Koss, S. (1981 and 1984) *The Rise and Fall of the Political Press in Britain*, Vols 1 and 2 (London: Hamish Hamilton).

Krugman, D. and L. Reid (1980) 'The "Public Interest" as Defined by FCC Policy Makers', *Journal of Broadcasting* 24(3): 311–25.

Kumar, S. (2010) 'Google Earth and the Nation State: Sovereignty in the Age of New Media', *Global Media and Communication* 6(2): 154–76.

Latzer, M. (2009) 'Convergence Revisited: Toward a Modified Pattern of Communications Governance', *Convergence: The International Journal of Research into New Media Technologies* 15(4): 411–26.

Lerner, D. (1958) *The Passing of Traditional Society: Modernizing the Middle East* (New York: Free Press).

Lessig, L. (2006) *Code: Version 2.0* (New York: Basic Books).

Levi-Straus, C. (1958) *Structural Anthropology* (New York: Penguin).

Levy, D. (1999) *Europe's Digital Revolution: Broadcasting Regulation, the EU and the Nation State* (London: Routledge).

Levy, D. and R. K. Nielsen (2010) *The Changing Business of Journalism and Its Implications for Democracy* (University of Oxford: Reuters Institute).

Levy, D. L. and A. Prakash (2003) 'Bargains Old and New: Multinational Corporations in Global Governance', *Business and Politics* 5(2): 131–50.

Lewis, J. and T. Miller (eds) (2003) *Critical Cultural Policy Studies: A Reader* (Oxford: Blackwell).

Lewis, J., S. Inthorn and K. Wahl-Jorgensen (2005) *Citizens or Consumers? What the Media Tell Us about Political Participation* (Buckingham: Open University Press).

Livingstone, S., P. Lunt and L. Miller (2007) 'Citizens and Consumers: Discursive Debates During and after the Communications Act 2003', *Media, Culture & Society* 29(4): 613–38.

Lloyd, M. (2006) *Prologue to a Farce: Communication and Democracy in America* (Chicago: University of Illinois Press).

Lowe, G.F. and J. Bardoel (2007) 'From Public Service Broadcasting to Public Service Media: The Core Challenge' pp. 9–28 in G.F. Lowe and J. Bardoel (eds) *From Public Service Broadcasting to Public Service Media*, RIPE@2007 (Göteborg, Sweden: NORDICOM).

Lunt, P. and S. Livingston (2007) 'Regulating Markets in the Interest of Consumers? On the Changing Regime of Governance in the Financial Service and Communications Sectors', pp. 139–61 in M. Bevir and F. Trentmann (eds) *Governance, Citizens and Consumers: Agency and Resistance in Contemporary Politics* (Basingstoke, UK: Palgrave Macmillan).

Lury, C. (1994) 'Planning a Culture for the People?' pp. 138–52 in R. Keat, N. Whiteley and N. Abercombie (eds.) *The Authority of the Consumer* (London: Routledge).

Manning, S. (1999) *Journal of World-Systems Research*, Special Issue on Globalisation V (2). Available at: http://jwsr.ucr.edu/archive/vol5/number2/jwsr-v5n2.pdf (accessed 3 December 2009).

Mansell, R. (2007) 'The Problem of Internationalizing Media and Communication Research', *Global Media and Communication* 3: 283–8.

Marsden, C. T. (2000) *Regulating the Global Information Society* (New York: Routledge).

Marsden, C. T. (2004) 'Co-regulation in European Media and Internet Sectors', online paper. Available at: http://www.anglia.ac.uk/ruskin/en/home/faculties/fhsc/depart ments/primary_socialcare/regulation/christopher_marsden.Maincontent.0001. file.tmp/Coregulation%20in%20European%20Media%20and%20Internet%20 Sectors.pdf (accessed 20 October 2010).

Marsden, C. T. and S. Verhulst (eds.) *Convergence in European Digital TV Regulation* (London: Blackstone Press).

Marshall, T. H. (1992) [1950] *Citizenship and Social Class* (London: Pluto).

Martell, L. (eds) (2001) *Social Democracy: Global and National Perspectives* (Basingstoke, UK: Palgrave Macmillan)

Mattelart, A. (1979) *Multinational Corporations and the Control of Culture* (Atlantic Highlands: Humanities Press).

McChesney, R. W. (1999) 'The New Global Media: It's a Small World of Big Conglomerates', *The Nation*, 29 November (article adapted from McChesney's book *Rich Media, Poor Democracy*, The New Press, 1999). Available at: http://www.hart-ford-hwp.com/archives/29/053.html (accessed 15 December 2009).

McChesney, R. W. (2005) 'The New Global Media' pp. 92–6 in E. P. Bucy (ed.) *Living in the Information Age: A New Media Reader* (2nd ed.) (Belmont: Wadsworth Thomson).

McChesney, R. W. and D. Schiller (2003) 'The Political Economy of International Communications: Foundations for the Emerging Global Debate on Media Ownership and Regulation', Paper, No. 11, Technology Business and Society Programme (Geneva: United Nations Research Institute for Social Development).

McGuigan, J. (2004) *Rethinking Cultural Policy* (Maidenhead, UK: Open University Press).

McKinsey & Company (1999) 'Public Service Broadcasters Around the World', McKinsey Report for the BBC, January.

McLuhan, M. (1964) *Understanding Media* (New York: Mentor).

McLuhan, M. and B. R. Powers (1993) *The Global Village: Transformations in World Life and Media in the 21st Century* (USA: Oxford University Press).

McQuail, D. (1992a) *Media Performance: Mass Communication and the Public Interest* London: Sage).

McQuail, D. (1992b) 'The Netherlands: Safeguarding Freedom and Diversity Under Multichannel Conditions' pp. 96–111 in J. Blumler (ed.) *Television and the Public Interest* (London: Sage).

McQuail, D. (2000) 'Media Policy: Premature Obsequies?' pp. 19–34 in H. Tumber (ed.) *Media Power, Professionals and Policies* (London: Routledge).

McQuail, D. (2003) *Media Accountability and Freedom of Publication* (New York: Oxford University Press).

McQuail, D. (2007) 'Preface' pp. 7–21 in A.W. Meier and J. Trappel (eds) *Power, Performance and Politics: Media Policy in Europe* (Germany: Nomos).

McQuail, D. and K. Sinue (eds) (1986) *New Media Politics* (London: Sage).

McQuail D & K Sinue (1998) *Media Policy: Convergence, Concentration and Commerce* (London: Sage).

Meikle, G. and S. Young (2008) 'Beyond Broadcasting? TV for the Twenty-First Century', *Media International Australia* 126: 67–70.

Melody, W. H. (1990) 'Communication Policy in the Global Information Economy: Whither the Public Interest?' pp. 16–39 in M. Ferguson (ed.) *Public Communication: The New Imperatives* (London: Sage).

Michalis, M. (2007) *Governing European Communications* (Lanham, MD: Lexington).
Michalis, M. (2010) 'EU Broadcasting Governance and PSB: Between a Rock and a Hard Place' pp. 36–48 in P. Iosifidis (ed.) *Reinventing Public Service Communication: European Broadcasters and Beyond* (Basingstoke, UK: Palgrave Macmillan).
Mill, J. S. (1978) *On Liberty* (Indianapolis: Hackett Publishing Press).
MMC (Monopolies and Mergers Commission) (1999) British Sky Broadcasting Group plc and Manchester United PLC: A report on the proposed merger. Cm4305. TSO, London.
Moe, H. (2008) 'Dissemination and Dialogue in the Public Sphere: A Case for Public Service Media Online', *Media, Culture & Society* 30(3): 319–36.
Monti, M. (2001) 'Does EC Competition Policy Help or Hinder European Audiovisual and Telecoms Industries?', Speech (London: British Screen Advisory Council).
Moran, M. (2003) *The British Regulatory State: High-Modernism and Hyper-Innovation* (Oxford: Oxford University Press).
Morley, D. (1980) *The 'Nationwide' Audience* (London: British Film Institute).
Morley, D. (1992) *Television, Audiences, and Cultural Studies* (London: Routledge).
Morozov, E. (2010) *The Net Delusion: The Dark Side of Internet Freedom* (USA: Public Affairs).
Morris, N. and S. Waisbord (eds) (2001) *Media and Globalization: Why the State Matters* (New York: Rowman & Littlefield).
Mortensen, F. (1977) 'The Bourgeois Public Sphere: A Danish Mass Communications Research Project', pp. 293–354 in M. Berg (ed.) *Current Theories in Scandinavian Mass Communications Research* (Grenaa, Denmark: GMT).
Mosco, V. (1996) *The Political Economy of Communication* (London: Sage).
Mungiu-Pippidi, A. (1999) *State into Public: The Failed Reform of State TV in East Central Europe* (The Joan Shorenstein Centre on the Press, Politics and Public Policy, Working Paper Series).
Murdock, G. (1990) 'Redrawing the Map of the Communication Industries: Concentration and Ownership in the Era of Privatisation' pp. 1–15 in M. Ferguson (ed.) *Public Communication: The New Imperatives* (London: Sage).
Murdock, G. (2000) 'Digital Futures in the Age of Convergence' pp. 35–57 in J. Wieten, G. Murdock and P. Dahlgren (eds) *Television across Europe* (London: Sage).
Murdock, G. (2004) 'Building the Digital Commons: Public Broadcasting in the Age of the Internet', Spry Memorial Lecture, University of Montreal, 22 November. Available at: https://pantherfile.uwm.edu/type/www/116/Theory_OtherTexts/Theory/Murdock_BuildingDigitalCommons.pdf (accessed 14 March 2010).
Murdock, G. and P. Golding (2000) 'Culture, Communications and Political Economy' pp. 70–92 in J. Curran and M. Gurevitch (eds) *Mass Media and Society* (3rd ed.) (London: Edward Arnold).
Murru, M. F. (2009) 'New Media – New Public Spheres? An Analysis of Online Shared Spaces Becoming Public Agoras' pp.141–53 in N. Carpentier, P. Pruulmann-Vengerfeldt, R. Kilborn, T. Olsson, H. Nieminen, E. Sundin and K. Nordenstreng (eds) *Communicative Approaches to Politics and Ethics in Europe* (Estonia: Tartu University Press) Available at: http://www.researchingcommunication.eu/reco_book5.pdf (accessed 22 July 2011).
The Museum of Broadcast Communications (no date) 'Public Interest, Convenience and Necessity'. Available at http://www.museum.tv/archives/etv/P/htmlP/publicintere/publicintere.htm (accessed 19 October 2009).
Nae, G., C. Grigore and G. Grigore (2006) ' "NGO's" Engagement in International Public Policy Making'. Available at: http://www.idec.gr/iier/new/3rd%20Panhellenic%

20Conference/NAE-GRIGORE-%20NGOS%20ENGAGMENT%20IN%20 INTERNATIONAL%20PUBLIC%20POLICY.pdf (accessed 5 October 2010).

Napoli, P. M. (1999) 'Deconstructing the Diversity Principle', *Journal of Communication* 49(4): 7–34.

Napoli, P. M. (2001) *Foundations of Communications Policy: Principles and Process in the Regulation of Electronic Media* (Cresskill, NJ: Hampton Press).

Napoli, P. M. (2007) 'Media Policy: An Overview of the Field', Working Paper, January (The Donald McGannon Communication Research Center).

Napoli, P. M. (2009) 'Navigating Producer-Consumer Convergence: Media Policy Priorities in the Era of User Generated and Distributed Content', *Communications & Convergence Review* 1(1): 32–43.

Negrine, R. (ed.) (1988) *Satellite Broadcasting* (London: Routledge).

Negroponte, N. (1995) *Being Digital* (New York: Hodder & Stoughton).

Nieminen, H. (2009) 'Media in Crisis? Social, Economic and Epistemic Dimensions' pp. 31–43 in N. Carpentier, P. Pruulmann-Vengerfeldt, R. Kilborn, T. Olsson, H. Nieminen, E. Sundin and K. Nordenstreng (eds) *Communicative Approaches to Politics and Ethics in Europe* (Estonia: Tartu University Press).

Nissen, C. S. (2006) 'Public Service Media in the Information Society', Report prepared for the Council of Europe's Group of Specialists on Public Service Broadcasting in the Information Society (MC-S-PSB), February (Media Division, Directorate General of Human Rights, Council of Europe, 2006).

Noam, E.M. (ed.) (1985) *Video Media Competition: Regulation, Economics, and Technology* (New York: Columbia University Press).

Noam, E. M. (2009) *Media Ownership and Concentration in America* (Oxford University Press).

Noam, E. M. (2010) 'Overcoming the Three Digital Divides' pp. 48–55 in D. K. Thussu (ed.) (2010) *International Communication: A Reader* (London: Routledge).

Noam, E. M. and J. Waltermann (eds) (1998) *Public Television in America* (Gutersloh: Bertelsmann Foundation Publishers).

Nordenstreng, K. and M.D. Lanham (2001) 'Epilogue' p. 224 in N. Morris and S. Waisbord *Media and Globalization: Why the State Matters* (New York: Rowman & Littlefield).

OECD (Organization for Economic Cooperation and Development) (2000) 'Information Technology Outlook'.

OECD (Organization for Economic Cooperation and Development) (2003) 'The Implications of Convergence for Regulation of Electronic Communications', DSTI/ICCP/TISP(2003)5/Final, 12 July.

OECD (Organization for Economic Cooperation and Development) (2007) 'Policy Considerations for Audiovisual Content Distribution in a Multiplatform Environment', DSTI/ICCP/TISP(2006)3/Final, 12 January.

OECD (Organization for Economic Cooperation and Development) (2010a) 'News in the Internet Age: New Trends in News Publishing', OECD Publishing. Available at: http://dx.doi.org/10.1787/9789264088702-en (accessed 8 January 2011).

OECD (Organization for Economic Cooperation and Development) (2010b) 'Guidelines on the Protection of Privacy and Transborder Flows of Personal Data', OECD Publishing. Available at: http://www.oecd.org/document/18/0,3343,en_2649_34255_1815186_1_1_1_1,00.html (accessed 10 December 2010).

Ofcom (Office of Communications) (2004a) 'Public Consultation on Quality', April (London: Ofcom).

Ofcom (2004b) 'Review of Public Service Broadcasting', May (London: Ofcom).

Ofcom (Office of Communications) (2007) 'New News, Future News' (London: Ofcom).

Ofcom (Office of Communications) (2008) 'The International Communications Market' (London: Ofcom).

Ofcom (Office of Communications) (2009) 'Second Public Service Broadcasting Review, Putting Viewers First', 21 January, London: Ofcom. http://www.ofcom.org. uk/consult/condocs/psb2_phase2/statement (accessed 30 November 2009).

O'Keefe, R., J. Kernaghan and A. Rubenstein (1975) 'Group Cohesiveness: A Factor in the Adoption of Innovations among Scientific Work Groups', *Small Group Behaviour* 6(3): 282–92.

Olsen, J. P. (2002) 'The Many Faces of Europeanization', *Journal of Common Market Studies* 40(5): 921–52.

Ó Siochrú, S. (2004) 'Social Consequences of Globalization of the Media and Communication Sector: Some Strategic Considerations', Working Paper No. 36, May (Geneva: International Labour Office). Available at: http://www.ilo.int/wcmsp5/ groups/public/---dgreports/---integration/documents/publication/wcms_079108. pdf (accessed 14 June 2010).

Ó Siochrú, S. and B. Girard (2003) *Communicating in the Information Society* (Geneva: UNRISD).

Ó Siochrú, S., B. Girard and A. Mahan (2002) *Global Media Governance: A Beginner's Guide* (Lanham: Rowman & Littlefield).

Oswell, D. (2007) 'Media and Communications Regulation and Child Protection: An Overview of the Field' pp. 475–92 in K. Drotner and S. Livingstone (eds) *International Handbook of Children, Media and Culture* (London: Sage).

Owen, B.M., J. Beebe and W. Manning (1974) *Television Economics* (Lexington: Lexington Books).

Padovani, C. (2005) 'Debating Communication Imbalances from the MacBride Report to the World Summit on the Information Society: An Analysis of a Changing Discourse', *Global Media and Communication* 1(3): 316–38.

Papadakis, S. (no date) 'Technological Convergence: Opportunities and Challenges', http://www.itu.int/osg/spu/youngminds/2007/essays/PapadakisSteliosYM2007. pdf (accessed 5 July 2010).

Papathanassopoulos, S. (2002) *European Television in the Digital Age* (Oxford: Polity).

Papathanassopoulos, S. (2010) 'The "State" of "Public" Broadcasting in Greece' in P. Iosifidis (ed.) *Reinventing Public Service Communication: European Broadcasters and Beyond* Basingstoke: Palgrave Macmillan.

Papathanassopoulos, S. and R. Negrine (eds) (2010) *Communications Policy: Theories and Issues* (Basingstoke, UK: Palgrave Macmillan).

Pauwels, C., S. De Vinck and B. Van Rompuy (2007) 'Can State Aid in the Film Sector Stand the Proof of EU and WTO Liberalization Efforts?', *European Studies* 24: 23–43.

Pauwels, C., H. Kalimo, K. Donders and B. V. Rompuy (eds) (2009) *Rethinking European Media and Communications Policy* (VUBPRESS: Institute for European Studies, Brussels University Press).

The Peacock Report (1986) Report of the Committee on Financing the BBC, Chairman: Professor Alan Peacock, Cmnd. 9824, London.

Peet, R. (2007) *The Geography of Power* (London: Pluto Press).

Peston, R. (2009) 'What Future for Media and Journalism?' Speech at the Richard Dunn Memorial Lecture at the MediaGuardian Edinburgh International Television Festival, 29 August. Available at http://www.bbc.co.uk/blogs/thereporters/robertpeston/2009/08/ what_future_for_media_and_jour.html (accessed 3 October 2009).

PHR (Privacy and Human Rights) (2004) Report. Available at: http://www.privacyinter national.org/article.shtml?cmd%5B347%5D=x-347-542782 (accessed 27 May 2010).

Picard, R. G. (2007) 'Subsidies for Newspapers: Can the Nordic Model Remain Viable?' pp. 236–46 in Herbert von Halem Verlag, H. Bohrmann, E. Klaus and M. Machill (eds) *Media Industry, Journalism Culture and Communication Policies in Europe* (Köln: Halem).

Pickard, V. (2007) 'Neoliberal Visions and Revisions in Global Communications Policy from NWICO to WSIS', *Journal of Communication Inquiry* 31(2): 118–39.

Pool, de Sola (1983) *Technologies of Freedom* (Cambridge, MA: Harvard Press, Belknap Press).

Powell, M. (2003) Should Limits on Ownership Broadcast Change? USA Today, 21 January.

Pritchard, D. (no date) 'Media Ownership Policy in the United States: An Update', Department of Journalism and Mass Communication, Center for Canadian-American Policy Studies (USA: University of Wisconsin-Milwaukee). Available at: http://www.cem.ulaval.ca/pdf/PropEtatsUnis.pdf (accessed 24 September 2010).

Prometheus Radio Project vs. FCC, 373 F.3d 372. 2004.

Prosser, T. (2000) 'International Lessons in Law and Regulation' pp. 99–101 in T. Lees, S. Ralph and J. Langham (eds) *Is Regulation Still an Option in the Digital Universe? Current Debates in Broadcasting 9* (Luton, UK: University of Luton Press).

Puppis, M. (2008) 'National Media Regulation in the Era of Free Trade: The Role of Global Media Governance', *European Journal of Communication* 23(4): 405–24.

Puppis, M. (2009) 'Media Regulation in Small States', *International Communication Gazette* 71(1–2): 7–17.

Putnam, R. (1993) *Making Democracy Work: Civil Traditions in Modern Italy* (Princeton, NJ: Princeton University Press).

Raboy, M. (no date) Media Policy and the Public Interest. Available at http://lirne.net/resources/netknowledge/raboy.pdf (accessed 29 October 2009).

Raboy, M. (ed.) (2002) *Global Media Policy in the New Millennium* (Luton, UK: Luton University Press).

Raboy, M. (2004) 'The World Summit on the Information Society and its Legacy for Global Governance', *International Communication Gazette* 66(3–4): 225–32.

Raboy, M. (2007) 'Global Media Regulation in the Information Society', University of Exeter, 30 March. Available at: http://www.exeter.ac.uk/research/networks/information/MarcRaboy-GlobalMediaRegulationintheInformationSociety.shtml (accessed 20 October 2010).

Raboy, M., S. Proulx and P. Dahlgren (2003) 'The Dilemma of Social Demand: Shaping Media Policy in New Civic Contexts', *Gazette: The International Journal for Communication Studies* 65(4–5): 323–9.

Raboy, M. and N. Landry (2005) *Civil Society, Communication and Global Governance: Issues from the World Summit on the Information Society* (New York: Peter Lang).

Raboy, M. and C. Padovani (2010) 'Mapping Global Media Policy: Concepts, Frameworks, Methods', *Communication, Culture & Critique* 3(2): 150–9.

Red Lion Broadcasting Co. v. FCC (1969) 395 U.S. 367.

Rheingold, H. (1993) *The Virtual Community, Homesteading on the Electronic Frontier* (Massachusetts: Addison-Wesley).

Rhodes, R. A. W. (1994) 'The Hollowing Out of the State', *Political Quarterly* 65(2): 138–51.

Rhodes, R. A. W. (2007) 'Understanding Governance: Ten Years On', *Organization Studies* 28(8): 1243–64.

Richards, Ed (2010) 'The Complex Regulatory Environment in the Communications Sector', Speech to the UCL Jevons Institute for Competition Law and Economics

Annual Colloquium, 13 July. Available at: https://www.competitionpolicyinter national.com/the-complex-regulatory-environment-in-the-communications-sector (accessed 15 July 2010).

Richards, D. and M. Smith (2002) *Governance and Public Policy in the United Kingdom* (Oxford: Oxford University Press).

Richardson, J. (1994) 'Doing Less by Doing More: British Government 1979–1993', *West European Politics* 17(3): 179–97.

Rideout, V. (2003) *Continentalizing Canadian Telecommunications: The Politics of Regulatory Reform* (Montreal: McGill-Queens University Press).

Robertson, R. (1995) 'Glocalization: Time-Space and Homogeneity-Heterogeneity' pp. 23–44 in M. Featherstone, S. Lash and R. Robertson (eds) *Global Modernities* (London: Sage).

Robinson, J. and M. Brown (2009) 'A Chilled Wind', The Guardian, 31 August. Available at http://www.guardian.co.uk/media/2009/aug/31/james-murdoch-attacking-bbc-ofcom (accessed 1 October 2009).

Rutkus, D. S. (1982) *The Public Trustee Concept in Broadcast Regulation* (Washington DC: Congressional Research Series).

Sabbagh, D. (2010) 'He's a Media Giant Already but is Rupert Murdoch on Course to be Britain's Berlusconi?', *Financial Times*,12 October.

Samuelson, P. (1999) 'Five Challenges for Regulating the Global Information Society', Conference on Communications Regulation in the Global Information Society, University of Warwick, June. Available at: http://people.ischool.berkeley.edu/~pam/papers/5challenges_feb22_v2_final_.pdf (accessed 21 July 2010).

Schiller, H. I. (1969) *Mass Communication and American Empire* (Boston: Beacon).

Schiller, H. I. (1976) *Communication and Cultural Domination* (New York: IASP).

Schlesinger, P. (2000) 'The Nation and Communicative Space' pp. 99–115 in H. Tumber (ed.) *Media Power, Professionals and Policies* (London: Routledge).

Schlesinger, P. (2009a) 'The Politics of Media and Cultural Policy', Media@LSE Electronic Working Papers.

Schlesinger, P. (2009b) 'Cultural and Communications Policy and the Stateless Nation', *Catalan Journal of Communication and Cultural Studies* 1(1): 9–14. Available at: http://eprints.gla.ac.uk/8800/1/8800.pdf (accessed 18 May 2010).

Scholte, J. A. [2005](2000) *Globalization: A Critical Introduction* (Basingstoke, UK: Palgrave Macmillan).

Schramm, W. (1964) *Mass Media and National Development* (Paris: Stanford University Press and UNESCO).

Schramm, W. (1979) *Mass Media and National Development* (Honolulu, Hawaii, USA: East-West Communication Institute). Available at: http://unesdoc.unesco.org/images/0003/000370/037073eb.pdf (accessed 3 December 2009).

Seymore-Ure, C. (1991) *The British Press and Broadcasting Since 1945* (London: Basil Blackwell).

Shaw, M. (2000) 'Book Review: Globalization: A Critical Introduction', *Millennium: Journal of International Studies* 29(2): 534–6.

Shin, Dong-Hee (2005) 'Technology Convergence and Regulatory Challenge: A Case from Korean Digital Media Broadcasting', *Info* 7(3): 47–58.

Shing, K. and K. Chung (2011) 'An Empirical Analysis of Online Social Network Structure to Understand Citizen Engagement in Public Policy and Community Building', *International Journal of Electronic Governance*, special issue on '(Re) Creating Public Sphere, Civic Culture and Civic Engagement: Public Service Media vs. Online Social Networks' (Guest-editors P. Iosifidis and M. Meimaris).

Siebert, F.S., T. Peterson and W. Schramm (1963) *Four Theories of the Press* (University of Illinois Press).

Sills, P. (1968) 'Public Interest', pp. 170–4 in *International* Encyclopaedia *of the Social Sciences* (New York: Macmillan).

Silverstone, R. (2007) *Media and Morality: On the Rise of Mediapolis* (Cambridge: Polity Press).

Sims, M. (1999) 'From Aiming too High to Aiming too Low', *Intermedia* 27(3): 4–6.

Singh, J. P. (1999) *Leapfrogging Development? The Political Economy of Telecommunications Restructuring* (Albany, US: State University of New York Press).

Sinue, K. (1998) 'Is Broadcasting Policy Becoming Redundant?' pp. 18–26 in K. Brands, J. Hermes and L. van Zoonen (eds) *The Media in Question, Popular Cultures and Public Interests* (London: Sage).

Skelcher, C. (2000) 'Changing Images of the State: Overloaded, Hollowed-Out, Congested', *Public Policy and Administration* 15(3): 3–19.

Smith, A. (1977) 'Subsidies and the Press in Europe', *Political and Economic Planning* 43: 569.

Smith, A. (1989) 'The Public Interest', *Intermedia* 17(2): 10–24.

Smith, P. (2006) 'The Politics of UK Television Policy: The Making of Ofcom', *Media, Culture & Society* 28(6): 929–40.

Soltesz, U. (2010) 'Tighter State Aid Rules for Public TV Channels', *Journal of European Competition Law & Practice* 1(1): 32–6.

Sparks, C. (2007) *Globalization, Development and the Mass Media* (London: Sage).

Splichal, S. (2009) '"New" Media, "Old" Theories: Does the (National) Public Melt into the Air of Global Governance?', *European Journal of Communication* 24(4): 391–405.

Steinmetz, G. (1999) 'Culture and the State' pp. 1–49 in G. Steinmetz (ed.) *State Culture: State Formation after the Cultural Turn* (New York: Cornell University Press).

Stolte, Y. and R. C. Smith (2010) 'The European Union and Media Ownership Transparency: The Scope for Regulatory Intervention', Open Society Media Program (Edinburgh: Edinburgh Law School).

Strange, S. (1988) *States and Markets: An Introduction to International Political Economy* (London: Pinter).

Streeter, T. (1996) *Selling the Air: A Critique of the Policy of Commercial Broadcasting in the United States* (Chicago: University of Chicago Press).

Stucke, M. E. and A. P. Grunes (2008) 'Toward a Better Competition Policy for the Media: The Challenge of Developing Antitrust Policies that Support the Media Sector's Unique Role in Our Democracy', Available at: http://works.bepress.com/cgi/viewcontent.cgi?article=1003&context=maurice_stucke (accessed 10 July 2010).

Stumpel, M. (2009) 'The Habermasian Implications of the Twittershere'. Available at: http://marcstumpel.wordpress.com/2009/10/04/the-habermasian-implications-of-the-twittersphere (accessed 11 March 2010).

Sullivan, B. (2006) 'La Difference is Stark in EU, US Privacy Laws'. Available at: http://www.msnbc.msn.com/id/15221111 (accessed 22 July 2010).

Sunstein, C. R. (2007) *Republic.com 2.0* (Princeton, NJ: Princeton University Press).

Svennevig, M. and B. Towler (2000) 'Regulating the Future: The Users' Views' pp. 102–5 in T. Lees, S. Ralph and J. Langham (eds) *Is Regulation Still an Option in the Digital Universe? Current Debates in Broadcasting 9* (Luton, UK: University of Luton Press).

Tambini, D., L. Forgan, C. Hall and S. Verhulst (2001) *Communications Revolution and Reform* (London: Institute for Public Policy Research).

Tambini, D. and J. Cowling (2004) (eds) *From Public Service Broadcasting to Public Service Communications* (London: Institute for Public Policy Research).

Thinkbox (2010) '7 Killer Facts about TV Advertising'. Available at: http://www.thinkbox.tv/server/show/nav.1131#3 (accessed 8 July 2010).

Thatcher, M. (no date) 'Delegation to Independent Regulatory Agencies in Western Europe', Online paper. Available at: http://www.essex.ac.uk/ECPR/events/jointsesions/paperarchive/grenoble/ws20/thatcher.pdf (accessed 15 October 2010).

Thatcher, M. (2002) 'Regulation after Delegation: Independent Regulatory Agencies in Europe', *Journal of European Public Policy* 9(6): 954 – 72.

Thussu, D. K. (ed.) (2010) *International Communication: A Reader* (London: Routledge).

Timms, D. (2005) 'Media Policy Dominated by "Cosy Cartel" MediaGuardian. Available at: http://www.guardian.co.uk/media/2005/sep/20/politicsandthemedia.pressandpublishing (accessed 18 November 2009).

Tomlinson, J. (2002) 'The Discourse of Cultural Imperialism' pp. 223–37 in D. McQuail (ed.) *McQuail's Reader in Mass Communication Theory* (London: Sage).

Tracey, M. (1998) *The Decline and Fall of Public Service Broadcasting* (Oxford: Oxford University Press).

Trappel, J. (2010) 'Squeezed and Uneasy: PSM in Small States – Limited Media Governance in Austria and Switzerland' pp. 209–21 in P. Iosifidis (ed.) *Reinventing Public Service Communication: European Broadcasters and Beyond* (Basingstoke, UK: Palgrave Macmillan).

Tsaliki, L. (2007) 'The Construction of European Identity and Citizenship' pp. 157–82 in K. Sarikakis (ed.) *Media and Cultural Policy in the European Union* (Amsterdam and New York: Rodopi).

Tumber, H. (ed.) (2000) *Media Power, Professionals and Policies* (London: Routledge).

Tunstall, J. (ed.) (1970) *Media Sociology: A Reader* (London: Constable).

Tunstall, J. (1972) 'News Organisation Goals and Specialist Newsgathering Journalists' in D. McQuail (ed.) *Sociology of Mass Communications* (London: Penguin Books).

Tunstall, J. (1977) *The Media Are American* (New York: Columbia University Press).

Tunstall, J. (1991) 'A Media Industry Perspective' in J.A. Anderson (ed.) *Communication Yearbook* 14 (London: Sage).

Tunstall, J. (2007a) *The Media Were American: US Mass Media in Decline* (New York: Oxford University Press).

Tunstall, J. (2007b) 'The National Media System As the Lead Player', *Global Media and Communication* 3(3): 321–4.

Tunstall, J. (2010) 'The BBC and UK Public Service Broadcasting' pp. 145–57 in P. Iosifidis (ed.) *Reinventing Public Service Communication: European Broadcasters and Beyond* (Basingstoke, UK: Palgrave Macmillan).

UNDP (United Nations Development Programme) (1997) *Re-conceptualizing Convergence* – Discussion Paper 2 (New York: Management Development and Governance Division: Bureau for Policy and Program Support).

UNDP (United Nations Development Programme) (1999) *Human Development Report* (New York: Oxford University Press.

Van Guilenburg, J. and D. McQuail (2003) 'Media Policy Paradigm Shifts: Towards a New Communications Policy Paradigm', *European Journal of Communication* 18(2): 181–207.

Van Loon, A. (1993) 'Legal Analysis of the EC Commission's Green Paper on Pluralism and Media Concentration in the Internal Market – COM(92) Final, March, pp. 1–84 (Amsterdam: Institute for Information Law – IVIR).

Van Zoonen, L. (2005) *Entertaining the Citizen: When Politics and Popular Culture Converge* (Lanham, MD: Rowman & Littlefield).

Vick, D. W. (2001) 'Exporting the First Amendment to Cyberspace: The Internet and State Sovereignty' pp. 2–20 in N. Morris and S. Waisbord (eds) *Media and Globalization: Why the State Matters* (New York: Rowman & Littlefield).

Vick, D. W. (2006) 'Regulatory Convergence?', *Legal Studies* 26(1): 26–64.

Ward, D. (2006) 'Can the Market Provide? Public Service Media Market Failure and Public Goods' pp. 51–64 in C. Nissen (ed.) *Making a Difference: Public Service Broadcasting in the European Media Landscape* (Eastleigh: John Libbey Publishing).

WDR (World Dialogue on Regulation) (2002) 'Some Implications for Regulation of ICT and Media Convergence', Discussion Paper 202, 30 January (CTI: Technical University of Denmark).

Webster, F. (2006) (3rd ed.) *Theories of the Information Society* (London: Routledge).

WGIG (Working Group on Internet Governance) (2005) Report. Château de Bossey, June. Available at: http://www.wgig.org/docs/WGIGREPORT.pdf (accessed 3 November 2009).

Wheeler, M. (2004) 'Supranational Regulation: Television and the European Union', *European Journal of Communication* 19(3): 349–69.

Wheeler, M. (2010) 'The European Union's Competition Directorate: State Aids and Public Service Broadcasting', pp. 49–62 in P. Iosifidis (ed.) *Reinventing Public Service Communication: European Broadcasters and Beyond* (Basingstoke, UK: Palgrave Macmillan).

White, R.A. (1994) 'The "Public Sphere" as an Integrating Concept for Development Communication' pp. 249–65 in C. Hamelink and O. Linne (eds) *Mass Communication Research: On Problems and Policies* (Norwood, New Jersey: Ablex Publishing).

Wilhelm, A. G. (1999) 'Virtual Sounding Boards: How Deliberative Is Online Political Discussion?' pp. 154–78 in B. N. Hague and B. D. Loader (eds) *Digital Democracy: Discourse and Decision-Making in the Information Age* (London: Routledge).

Williams, R. (1962) *Communications* (Harmondsworth: Penguin).

Williams, R. (1980) *Problems in Materialism and Culture* (London: Verso).

Williams, R. (1984) 'State Culture and Beyond', pp. 3–5 in L. Apignanesi (ed.) *Culture and the State* (London: Institute of Contemporary Arts).

Wu, I. (2004) 'Canada, South Korea, Netherlands and Sweden: Regulatory Implications of the Convergence of Broadcasting, Telecommunications and Internet Services', *Telecommunications Policy* 28(1): 79–96.

Wunsch-Vincent, S. and G. Vickery (2007) 'Comparative Web: User-created Content', OECD, Working Party on the Information Society, DSTI/ICCP/IE(2006)7/Final, 12 April.

Yoo, C. S. (2009) 'The Convergence of Broadcasting and Telephony: Legal and Regulatory Implications', *Communications & Convergence Review* 1(1): 44–55.

Index